LETTERS FROM

LISELOTTE

LETTERS FROM
LISELOTTE

Elisabeth Charlotte, Princess Palatine

and Duchess of Orléans,

'Madame'

1652-1722

TRANSLATED AND EDITED BY

MARIA KROLL

LONDON
VICTOR GOLLANCZ LTD
1970

Printed in Great Britain by
The Camelot Press Ltd., London and Southampton

CONTENTS

LIST OF ILLUSTRATIONS

INTRODUCTION

Of the innumerable contemporary accounts of Louis XIV's long and golden reign, three still seem as alive today as on the day they were written. Their authors are Mme de Sévigné, the Duc de Saint-Simon and the King's sister-in-law, Liselotte of the Palatinate. Of the three, Mme de Sévigné, whose letters to her daughter date from the days of the Sun King's *gloire*, was much the most stylish writer; Saint-Simon, writing during the decline of the reign and the subsequent Regency, the most accomplished reporter; Liselotte—spontaneous, bawdy, outspoken, extremely biased, a compulsive letter-writer for over half a century—the most unexpected.

The scope of her letters is vast. Theatre news, a cure for pink eye, observations on the nature of man, fashion notes, descriptions of the royal palaces and their occupants, childhood reminiscences and weather reports: her mind races from subject to subject and her pen races as fast as her mind. Failure to adapt herself to her environment is what has made her famous, and given her letters their unique quality. Unlike Saint-Simon's memoirs, which were written by someone on the periphery jealously guarding this position, her letters are by a person very much on the inside, yet often wishing to escape.

Elisabeth Charlotte of the Palatinate, Duchess of Orléans, called Madame and remembered as Liselotte, was the second wife of Philippe I d'Orléans, known as Monsieur, the only brother of Louis XIV. Her father was Charles Louis, Elector of the Palatinate, and she was born at Heidelberg on 27 May 1652, four years after the Thirty Years' War had ended with the Peace of Westphalia. At the time of her birth the Palatinate still bore all the terrible marks of thirty years of fighting, looting and burning; but the Elector threw his considerable energies and less considerable resources into the rebuilding of his country, and was so successful that within ten years the economy was once more on a stable basis, and the famous university reopened.

Liselotte's early childhood was stormy, for her father's marriage to Charlotte, daughter of the hereditary Landgrave of Hesse-Cassel, had failed. He had already chosen a new partner, Luise von Degenfeld, and since the Electress refused to agree to a divorce he married Luise without this formality, citing by way of precedent various instances in the

Old Testament, and reviving the ancient title of Raugravine for his new wife.

From this curious ménage, and the inevitable appalling domestic scenes (for the Electress was a violent woman), Liselotte was removed in 1659 and sent to stay with her aunt Sophie, the future Duchess of Hanover. She was away from home for four years, and was very happy during this period. Sophie was enchanted with her niece, and Liselotte's devotion to her *herzlieben tante* was touchingly deep all her life.

Sophie's mother, and Liselotte's grandmother, was Elizabeth Stuart, the 'Winter Queen' of Bohemia, who for many years had been living in exile in The Hague. In 1659 Sophie took her niece there on a visit. Liselotte was a great success with her grandmother—a triumph indeed, since that lady had the reputation, when her own children were young, of having preferred her pets. 'As for Liselotte, she is very pretty and you may believe me since I am taken with her,' she wrote to her son the Elector, 'for you know I care not much for children but I never saw one I like so well as her. She is so good-natured and witty, all The Hague is in love with her. . . . There is already great acquaintance between the little Prince and her. . . . I can assure you I love her extremely well, as well as her aunt does but not so fond, for she is monstrous fond of her.'[1]

Everyone continued full of praise for Liselotte. A dancing-master was engaged: 'She does already dance the *Sarabande* with castanets as well as can be.' A French master came, and she was given a little dog as a reward for progress. Sophie said of her that she had the *esprit* of a girl of twenty, and her worldly wisdom was generally admired. When someone described to her in glowing colours the project of marrying her to the little Prince William (later William III of England), she remarked that Cinderella had also been promised many splendid things, but had nevertheless been obliged to live in the ashes.

The Dutch visit came to an end in the spring of 1660. The party returned to Hanover, Sophie to prepare for the birth of her eldest son, later to become George I of England, and Liselotte to resume the roaming about the countryside which she had always loved so much. Her aunt had christened her the '*Rauschenblatt-Knechtchen*', or little-knight-of-the-rustling-leaves, a nickname that Liselotte often fondly referred to long after she had become Madame and full of dignity. She always remembered her years in Hanover as the happiest time of her life.

By the time she returned to Heidelberg, her mother had gone back to Hesse-Cassel. There were occasional sad little notes to her daughter,

[1] *The letters of Elizabeth, Queen of Bohemia*, L. M. Baker

and heart-breaking letters to Liselotte's governess, imploring her for news 'to tell her whether the child was alive or dead'. But Liselotte soon settled down to live happily with her father, whom she adored, his wife the Raugravine, and their ever-increasing family. Her education was taken over by a new governess. Jungfer Uffeln, who had formerly occupied this post, and had accompanied her charge to Hanover, had stayed there to marry one of Sophia's gentlemen, Freiherr von Harling. Liselotte never forgot her, and remained eternally grateful to her for finding a happy balance between kindness and firmness. She wrote later: 'If only good Frau von Harling had stayed with me until I got married, I should have turned out much better.'

Liselotte's formal timetable included all the subjects essential for the education of an important princess: singing, dancing, needlework and French. The reading of good books of historical or high moral content was encouraged, other books were almost totally prohibited. The Elector's enthusiasm for his collection of coins and medals stimulated her interest in history and antiquity; his tolerant religious beliefs greatly influenced her own views—like him, she had no patience with bigotry; and his total devotion to his country made her love the Palatinate more than any other place on earth. She was a fond and obedient daughter.

The Elector's sister-in-law, Anna Gonzaga, known as '*La Palatine*', lived in France, where she was regarded as something of a political genius. In 1671 she wrote to say that Liselotte was being considered for the position of Madame, now vacant through the death of Philippe of Orléans' first wife Henrietta, sister of Charles II. The Elector was very interested, for Monsieur must have been far and away the best match in Europe.

Liselotte, who had been courted with varying degrees of enthusiasm by a number of suitors, amongst them the Crown Prince of Denmark, the King of Sweden and the Electoral Prince of Brandenburg, would have preferred to remain single, or at least to marry in Germany; but she was soon made to realize that her father regarded the marriage as *une affaire importante pour toute la maison*. The Elector knew that Louis XIV was preparing to go to war against the Dutch, and dreaded the consequences of another conflict so near home. By establishing a family connection, he hoped that his dangerous neighbour would become less menacing. He felt that he would not so much lose a daughter as gain a protector, and Liselotte obediently agreed that royal marriages were more often affairs of reason than of personal inclination. So the matter was settled.

It was left to the Elector, whose miserliness was well known, to decide what dowry his daughter should have, but Anna Gonzaga had something to say regarding the trousseau. 'It would be a disgrace to send the daughter of the Elector to the King of France with six shifts. A dozen, and this marriage may be made to serve the interests of the Elector.'

Liselotte's conversion to the Catholic faith, the only absolute condition laid down by France, was a delicate matter. As a leading Protestant prince, the Elector was obliged to tread carefully. He decided that he should not be informed of the event until it had taken place, and pretended to be unaware of the fact that she was receiving instruction in Heidelberg. In late October 1671, he took her as far as Strasbourg, where he kissed her goodbye and left her to be received into the Church before she went on her way to Metz, where the marriage took place by proxy. She never saw her father or the Palatinate again.

II

'I am wearied to death with the continuous repetition of the same thing over and over again,' writes Mme de Sévigné, 'especially the marriage of Monsieur. I have just written to the Abbé de Poincarré to entreat him not to fill my head with any more of it, nor of *La Palatine* who is gone to fetch home the Princess, nor of the Maréchal de Plessis who is going to Metz to marry her, nor of Monsieur going to Châlons to consummate his nuptials, nor of the King's going to Villers Cotterets; in a word, I tell him that I will not hear another syllable about the business until they have slept together again and again.'

Monsieur, although the father of two children by his first wife, had little use for women. When Henrietta had suddenly died, there had been talk of poison. Monsieur himself had been under suspicion, together with his two fiendish favourites, the Chevalier de Lorraine and the Marquis d'Effiat, by whom he was positively possessed until shortly before his death. It is only fair to say that Liselotte never believed for a moment that her husband had been involved in any murder-plot, though she was to reserve her judgement with regard to the other two, who were soon to make her own life miserable.

From his earliest youth, every feminine trait in Monsieur's nature had been carefully fostered. This was done to prevent him from becoming a dangerous rival to his brother, King from the age of four. Minds did not have to stretch far back to remember Louis XIII's younger brother, Gaston d'Orléans, the last Monsieur, endlessly intriguing and plotting for power. In the case of this Monsieur, any

possible recurrence of such danger had to be avoided at all cost. He
showed a talent for soldiering (it was said that he was less afraid of
gunpowder than of exposing his skin to the sun), and had some
success in the field. But when there was too much *'Vive le roi et Monsieur!'* he was kept at home, where he fussed over his clothes, gave
parties and stuffed himself with sweets between meals.

Liselotte has recorded her first impressions of Monsieur. 'Never,'
she writes, 'were two brothers more dissimilar than the King and
Monsieur', although, she adds, 'they were very fond of each other all
the same'. Unlike the King, who was ash-blond, tall, manly, and of an
extraordinarily noble appearance, Monsieur's looks, she said, were only
fairly noble. His hair was pitch-black, as were his eyebrows and
lashes; his eyes were large and brown. His nose was large, his mouth too
small, and filled with ugly teeth. His manners were more womanish
than manly. He liked gambling, entertaining, dancing, eating and
dressing-up—in short, he liked everything that ladies like. And, very
different from his brother, who thoroughly enjoyed his *galanteries*,
Monsieur looked on women exclusively as comrades, and seems never
to have been in love in his life.

La Grande Mademoiselle, the King's cousin, who met Liselotte at
the first of a series of presentation balls, remarked that the new Madame
looked well enough to her, but added that Monsieur did not think so,
and seemed surprised by her favourable opinion. In fact, he thought
his new wife completely hideous. It is true that when first he saw her
she had been eating pomegranates, which had stained her teeth, and
had been out in the November air without the protection of a mask.
Moreover, she was absurdly overdressed in pale blue silk. But even if
she had been less purple-toothed and red-complexioned, and more
suitably dressed for the season, it is doubtful whether Monsieur,
scented, rouged and beribboned, would have found much to admire in
this girl, the prototype of all the hoydens ever to gallop into an exquisite
tableau. Elegance, he saw, was sadly lacking, although that cannot have
mattered too much: he was elegant enough for both of them.

An early portrait shows Liselotte to be a fresh-faced, medium-sized
girl with wide, intelligent eyes. While it is obviously impossible to say
how far the painter bent the truth to flatter the sitter, it is equally
obvious that she was then a very far cry indeed from the formidable,
square old lady whose portrait Rigaud painted forty years or so later,
and of whom Saint-Simon wrote a little earlier, 'A lady of the Old
Régime, German to the last drop of her blood, with the figure of a
Swiss guard.' The standards of beauty of the time made no provision

for apple-cheeked, pleasant-looking girls, and Liselotte, accustomed to
family jokes about her 'badger-nose' and 'bear-cat-monkey face', had
grown up considering herself extremely plain and was the first to make
fun of her looks. She did not so much give up the struggle to present
a fashionable appearance at the French Court as refuse to enter it in
the first place.

She would not take her wardrobe or her hair seriously. Monsieur in
person offered to apply make-up to her face, but she found the experience unpleasant. Even after that wretched blue silk had been forgotten (La Grande Mademoiselle had charitably remarked that, as
there were such quantities of fur in Germany, she expected that silk had
been intended to lend a more Frenchified air), the Court was in a continuous titter about Liselotte's clothes. Soon she appeared only *en
grand habit*, the official Court dress worn for formal occasions, or in her
riding-clothes. She wore these garments as if they were a kind of
uniform, with the security such camouflage bestows. She had her
grand habit constructed in a special way. For quick and convenient
dressing and undressing all the many separate parts—stays, petticoats,
underskirts and the slit overskirt—were joined together by little tapes;
and as soon as Madame was laced up she was ready to face the world.
The only further instructions to her tailors were to keep her clothes
light in weight, and this, in the days of silver and gold trimmings and
jewelled embroidery which made fashionable women's clothes as
heavy as horses' trappings, was no mean request.

Liselotte's disregard for her appearance was matched by her other
tastes. Small talk bored her. She did not care for gambling, the greatest
indoor amusement of the day. She liked neither parties nor balls, and
came to detest dancing.

The Court wit who declared that Monsieur was the most foolish of
women and Madame the most foolish of men was mistaken if he
thought that she was a lesbian. She had some sharp things to say about
women in love with each other and all that she described as unnatural
practices. Natural practices seemed to hold no interest for her either:
the Princesse de Monaco, after various futile attempts to introduce a
little love-interest into her life, declared, bursting into tears of frustra-
tion, that Germans were colder than other people. It is true that in
childhood Liselotte had often longed to be a boy, and had preferred her
brother's toys to her own dolls. It is true that the Court was convinced
that she was in love with the King. The Princesse de Tarent (another of
her aunts, and Mme de Sévigné's neighbour in the country, who used
to drive over on purpose to read out the letters she received from

Madame), referring to this rumour, said, 'All the world except for Madame herself knows very well what is the matter with her.' She was probably right; but, whatever Liselotte's tendencies, they remained firmly repressed, and she herself unconscious of them. She was not in the least amorous; nor was there a trace of coquetry in her. Shortly after her household was set up, Mme de Sévigné wrote that she rather pitied the ladies of the entourage, owing to the boredom they had to endure in the name of virtue.

Mme de Sévigné, who wrote to her daughter that the King showed an assiduity in providing diversions for this Madame that he never did for her predecessor ('Not a night passes at St Germain without balls, plays or masquerades'), found Liselotte much better than she had expected, and was greatly surprised at her wit, 'not so much for the sprightliness of her humour as for her good sense, although when her physician was presented to her, she said she had no business to offer, that she had never been bled or purged in her life, and that it was her custom, if she was ill, to take a two league walk, which cured her at once'.

Liselotte's love of walking made a great bond between her and the King. He said, rather sadly, that of all the Court she was the only one who truly appreciated the beauties of Versailles. They went for long walks together, and after she had learned to ride she went out hunting with him whenever possible. She became a very good rider indeed, and when she was no longer able to accompany the hunt on horseback, she followed in her *calèche*.

The fact that the King was well disposed towards her made an enormous difference to her *entrée* into Court society. While she was in no way overawed by the splendour of her new surroundings, she was grateful for a helping hand, or rather a helpful nudge from an elbow to indicate when she was to rise and when to sit during the ceremonial presentations that marked her appearance at Court. These the King provided with unfailing kindness. When he took her to be introduced to the Queen he whispered cheeringly, 'Courage, Madame, she is more frightened of you than you of her.'

III

When Liselotte arrived in France, the gilded splendour of Versailles was still to come. Building had started in 1662, but so far the palace was only the scene of occasional, breath-takingly beautiful fêtes. Until 1682 the Louvre was Louis XIV's official residence, and when the Court was in town Monsieur and his household stayed at the Palais-Royal. Monsieur's out-of-town palace was the château of Saint Cloud.

Wherever the King was staying, his day scarcely varied. It began with the *Grand Lever*. This was a highly ceremonious occasion. While the greatest privileges, such as the handing of the royal shirt or the royal gloves, were reserved for members of the King's family, some fortunate courtier might find himself distinguished by an invitation to hold the royal candle, and there was fierce competition for such honours. It was the King's deliberate policy to stimulate and encourage this rivalry, for when the nobles spent their lives in plotting for small distinctions they had little time to spare for political intrigue. Even the seating arrangements were subject to stringent rules. *Fauteuils* (or armchairs) were reserved for upper royalties. Lower royalties sat on armless chairs, while *tabourets*—large, upholstered, lowish footstools—accommodated anyone with permission to sit in the presence of the great.

Under Louis' régime—and again as a matter of policy—the aristocrats were totally excluded from affairs of state. All the same, leaving their estates to look after themselves, they gathered round their King, sole dispenser of honours. Away from the Court there was nothing to hope for. 'Someone we see only rarely,' the King would say disdainfully of anyone who did not appear regularly.

Between his *Lever* and his *Coucher*, Louis crammed a very full day indeed. Long walks in his parks or hunting in his forests, Mass and *Salut* in his chapel, extended visits to mistresses, copious meals, fêtes, masques, ballets, theatricals, and, most important of all, long, regular, working hours with his Council.

Since France was at war for almost fifty years of the King's reign, and a state of emergency was therefore normal, Liselotte's letters mention the wars only *en passant*, unless loved ones, Palatine, Hanoverian or French, were involved, when she writes blow-by-blow accounts. In the ordinary way, princes and courtiers of military age departed for the battlefield each spring when the season for fighting came round again. The King, often accompanied by the ladies, would appear at the front when victories were imminent, but for the rest of the time the pleasures of Court life unrolled in undiminished tempo. Louis relished his *métier de roi*, and saw to it that those about him had ample opportunity to share his tastes.

Besides the King and his Queen, the immediate royal family included the Dauphin whom the Queen had managed to produce ten years previously. Marie-Thérèse's many failures to provide living heirs for the throne of France (she suffered frequent miscarriages and still-births, and other children had died in infancy) was blamed by the doctors on the King. He had, they said, made a habit of providing his wife, whose bed he shared every night regardless of how he had spent the earlier part of the evening, with 'only the dregs of a bottle that had previously been all but drained by others'. 'Others', at the time of Liselotte's arrival, were Louise de la Vallière and Athénaïs de Montespan, to whom Mme de Sévigné refers, respectively, as the Dew and the Torrent.

Louise de la Vallière, the Dew, was good and beautiful, and, according to Liselotte, she was 'the only one of the King's mistresses who loved him unselfishly and for himself alone'. She was soon to retire to a convent, where she became Sœur Louise Miséricorde. Her daughter, the only one of her children by the King to survive for any length of time, was the first of Louis XIV's children to be legitimized; she became the Princesse de Conti.

Mme de Montespan, the Torrent, ambitious and capricious, in Liselotte's opinion 'loved the King out of pure self-interest'. She became the official favourite only after Louise's departure, although—besides having a son by her own husband—she was already the mother of two children by the King, the Duc du Maine and a baby girl who was to die young. (She was later to bear the Comte de Toulouse; a daughter who became Mme la Duchesse; and Liselotte's future daughter-in-law, Mlle de Blois.) These children were being secretly brought up in Paris. Their governess was the widow Scarron, later to become the Marquise de Maintenon, Mme de Montespan's successor in the affection of the King and Liselotte's greatest enemy at Court.

There were also Monsieur's two daughters from his previous marriage: Marie-Louise, aged ten, and Anne-Marie, aged two. Liselotte—not yet twenty when she became Madame—enjoyed tearing around with the former and mothering the latter. She kept up a regular, affectionate correspondence with both, when in due course they left home, Marie-Louise to become Queen of Spain and Anne-Marie to marry the Duke of Savoy.

And then there was Monsieur himself. Liselotte, fully aware that she had failed to please him, wrote, 'No witchcraft at work there, considering how plain I am, but I shall live with him on such good terms that he will get accustomed to my ugly face and come to like me.' To her credit, she was soon able to write to her aunt that Monsieur was the best man in the world and 'we live very well together'.

The halcyon days of the marriage lasted none too long, and in view of the couple's incompatibility it is amazing that they ever dawned at all. Three children, of whom two survived, were born before Monsieur and Madame decided to sleep in separate rooms.

B

Monsieur, who dreaded boredom more than anything in the world, and found his wife's company the reverse of entertaining, was soon amusing himself with his unspeakable friends. They turned him against Liselotte with little difficulty, and she found herself left to her own devices. This did not affect her too much so long as she enjoyed the King's friendship; but when France invaded her native Palatinate the climate of their relationship changed. Mme de Maintenon's appearance on the scene, and her determination to 'reform' the King, estranged them still further. Liselotte grew troubled and bewildered. The persecution of the Protestants, for which she mistakenly held Mme de Maintenon responsible, enraged her and made her hate the favourite even more. The most dreadful blow of all was the marriage of her son to the King's bastard daughter by Mme de Montespan. That the descendants of this match were to include Philippe Egalité and Louis Philippe of France, as well as kings of Bulgaria and of the Belgians, would have been no comfort to her. The descendants of her daughter's more suitable match, among whom were Marie Antoinette, Napoleon's wife Marie Louise, Austrian emperors and the kings of Italy, would have pleased her more. 'Mousedroppings among the pepper', as she called *mésalliances*, were the chief aversion of her life.

She had the strongest possible ideas of right and wrong, and her rigidity on questions of propriety became a byword. Hypocrisy was wrong. So was vice, from sodomy to indulgence in tobacco. Adultery was, naturally, wrong, double adultery worse. Priests were usually wrong, and so were 'those other charlatans, the doctors and the lawyers'.

Mme de Maintenon was always wrong: indeed, she was what was mainly wrong with France.

IV

Monsieur's death in 1701 did little to change Liselotte's position at Versailles, except that it effected a temporary reconciliation with Mme de Maintenon, by then secretly married to the King (Marie-Thérèse had died in 1683). Louis grew friendlier again, but not for long, and Madame was as much of a misfit at Versailles as she had always been. Her staunch and steadfast Germanness has often been offered in explanation, but, if she remained a foreigner in the place where she spent her life, she was no exception. Louis' dead Queen had always been more Spanish than French, and her daughter-in-law, the Dauphine, was a Bavarian to her dying day. William of Orange did not change into an Englishman when he was crowned King of England; nor did Liselotte's cousin, George of Hanover, after his assumption of the

English throne. In an age when kingship, like soldiering, was regarded as a profession, notions of patriotism, as we understand the term today, were unlikely to exist.

So when Liselotte criticized, as she never stopped doing, French manners, French habits, French morals, food, fashions and society, she was criticizing not the French nation, of which she had no concept, but the Court at which she lived. And when she writes of Germany, where it seems that even the pancakes were superior owing to richer soil, richer grass, sleeker cows that gave richer milk for richer butter, she was thinking of her childhood, youth, home, relations, and a happy, carefree life. In remembering all she had lost she was far from unique: so many little princesses posted abroad to marry sent home horrific accounts of the procedures in their new palaces. But they were less talented letter-writers than Liselotte, and none has gone down in history as such a very square peg in such a round hole as she, odd-Madame-out, for all posterity.

Ironically enough, she failed to adapt herself to her new world not because she was so strangely unlike its inhabitants but because she was so very like, sharing with them their main preoccupation in life, the respect due to rank.

The Court rank of *Madame* was beyond discussion, and no one would have dreamt of encroaching on any privilege arising from it. Twice, for extended periods, it caused her to become first Lady of France, once in the period between the death of the Queen and the marriage of the King's grandson, and again after the death of her own granddaughter. Nevertheless, she wore that title lightly. What concerned her was the rank she had been born to. She prided herself on her own pure-blooded lineage, and considered an elector the equal of any king. The French habit of not taking foreign titles seriously, their disregard for her illustrious electoral descent, hurt her *amour propre* and poisoned all her relationships. Her own ancestry included Mary Queen of Scots, and through her Stuart blood she had a better claim on the English throne than her cousin George, until her conversion to Catholicism made her ineligible. That her own daughter-in-law, the bastard daughter of the King, clearly regarded herself as superior to her husband, Liselotte's own son and the King's legitimate nephew, infuriated her. She was quick to spot any sign of disrespect to electoral visitors from abroad, and in return did not trouble to hide her contempt for what she considered the questionable and sometimes recent nobility of the courtiers, whom she thought presumptuous and impertinent.

Fond of plain-speaking—'I never praise what is ill-done, I am, thank God, a little too sincere for that'—she made no bones about her views on this and many other subjects. Although she would have liked to please, she was quite disastrously unprepared to dissemble, and many people, nervous of her sharp tongue, avoided her for her own sake and not only because she was out of favour.

So her correspondence came to take the place of her social life. When others would gather for a dish of tea or coffee (both exotic beverages only recently introduced), Liselotte would instead take up her position at her writing-table, placed to face the window that she usually kept wide open. Her little dogs would be grouped about her, each in its appointed place, and, if one of them should jump up on the table and blot a passage, she would express the hope that her reader would still be able to decipher it and calmly write on.

Each day of the week was reserved for writing to a different person. Some people, including her aunt Sophie, were allocated two post-days. There were occasions when she wrote letters at an unearthly hour of the morning, dressed only in her shift because of the unbearable heat. On other days she wrote from her bed, and even then could hardly hold her pen because of the freezing cold. There were the times when she could barely see the paper through her tears, as when the series of dreadful deaths wiped out almost the whole succession to the throne of France; and again after the death of the King, whose parting words assured her that he had, after all, always been her friend.

Writing letters gave purpose to her existence and backbone to her life. Aware that all Court correspondence was carefully examined by the postmaster and his *cabinet noir*, she reserved her more indiscreet comments for letters that she could safely send by hand. Even so, some of her letters sent by the regular post were considered questionable by the censors. Every now and then copies of these reached the King, and Madame would be taken to task for what she had written. After the King's death the Regent sometimes received copies, but he did not take his mother's letters very seriously. In any case, she was utterly unpolitical. She had not the slightest intention of interfering in the government of France. She observed that the country, to its cost, had been ruled by old women for all too long. She was thinking of the dreaded Mme de Maintenon, now retired to a convent, where she died, of the measles, in 1719.

In the passing of time, death removed many of Liselotte's correspondents. She missed them less for the letters they sent her than as recipients of her own letters, and replaced them as best she could. A good acquisition was Caroline, Princess of Wales, who had made her first appearance in Liselotte's correspondence when she was Caroline of Ansbach, years ago. Liselotte had never met her, but her aunt Sophie had been fond of her, and she made a link with old times. This enabled Liselotte to live her life all over again in her letters. As she conjures up the past, her memory seems astonishing. We know that she could never be bothered to copy any but business letters, but there are no inconsistencies, only slight variations in detail, in the events which she describes again after a lapse of many years.

Some of the old sadnesses are forgotten, though. The loneliness and isolation of those earlier years is not recalled; only the happy memories survive. The past is bathed in the glow of the Sun King's personality, a golden age when a Court was still a Court and people understood the art of living.

In 1722 Liselotte prepared to set out to Rheims to attend Louis XV's coronation. Questioned about the wisdom of this undertaking, for she was seventy and suffered from dropsy, she replied that the difficulty of going to heaven was no greater from Rheims than from Paris. She survived the occasion and returned, having once again seen her daughter, who was married to the Duc de Lorraine, and met her Lorraine grandchildren for the first and last time. She died in the night of December 8th, 1722. She was laid to rest without pomp, as had been her wish, in Saint-Denis on December 10th. A contemporary diarist, Mathieu Marais, notes on that day, 'On perd une bonne princesse, c'est une chose rare.'

V

Madame's letters are well known in Germany, almost as well known in France, and very little known in England. Here, her claim to fame rests mainly on her contribution of footnotes to historical works dealing with her contemporaries and the events of her period.

The importance of her letters as a source of information has long been recognized. Schiller and Ranke used part of her correspondence in their works on eighteenth-century history, and her letters to the Abbé Dubois, her son's tutor, form part of the standard work on that statesman. But they are most often consulted on points of French Court life, etiquette and domestic detail. She is regarded as an accurate reporter of these matters, whereas in the case of her reports on, say, Mme de Maintenon, when she allows herself to be carried away by her strong feelings, her statements should be taken with a grain of salt.

The first packet of Liselotte's letters was discovered in the Brunswick archives in 1747. The more scandalous passages were speedily copied out, and subsequently published in a little book called *Anekdoten vom Französischen Hof*. These original *Anekdoten* were translated into garbled French and appeared in 1788. They were then retranslated into German and reissued in 1789. In the meantime, more and more of her letters were found in various German princely archives. These were gradually published, and around the end of the nineteenth century there appeared the first selections of letters made from all the published material, in French translation for publication in France and in the original German for publication in Germany. The first English translation, a limited luxury edition of the letters that had first appeared in 1789, was published in 1904 by the Grolier Society. The second and only other English version, translated and edited by Gertrude Scott Stevenson, came out in 1924. It was based on the French Jaeglé edition, and was a good deal more comprehensive than the previous collection.

The material for this present book is drawn from the collections of Madame's German correspondence. Many of the letters will be new to English readers; others cannot be given here, for Madame wrote so much that a choice had to be made. None of her French correspondence is included.[1] For one thing, all her most intimate letters were written to German correspondents, and only in German does she express herself in the vigorous way for which she came to be admired. Her style, which in part relies on her use of colloquialisms, poses a problem for the translator. To give a true equivalent it is impossible, here and there, to avoid anachronisms, words and phrases that have only entered the English language since Madame's time. Where, for instance, she observes that Peter the Great's son is ripe for the *'Abdecker'*, which from time immemorial has been the term for the man who slaughters horses, the only English translation that adequately conveys her vivid language is *'knackers'*, a word that according to the *Oxford English Dictionary* did not come into use until 1847; and therefore to the knackers Alexej must go.

The object of this book is to present Madame's life, as written by herself. This means that her personal ups and downs, her interests and idiosyncracies, are as much to the point as more momentous affairs and the great set pieces which are so often quoted. It has also governed the omissions. Many of the bawdy stories had to go. So did her reports of a number of events which, though fascinating in themselves and

[1] The example of Liselotte's handwriting facing p. 27 is taken from a letter written in French, for when she writes in German she uses German script, and for all the insight this gives into her character she might be writing in Arabic.

fully treated by her contemporaries, did not directly impinge on her life. And there are only a few of the ghost stories she took such pride in not believing but religiously passed on just the same.

Repetition has, so far as is possible, been avoided, although, in order that a true picture might emerge, many of her strongest sentiments have been allowed to recur. For the sake of continuity, there are no ' . . . ' marks where passages have been omitted from the letters.

The brief linking notes are intended to sketch in the historical background to the letters rather than give a complete picture of the situation.

To say that this collection has no pretensions to scholarship would in itself be pretentious. If, by its end, Madame emerges as a real person, rather than a historical personage, then some light will have been thrown on the woman of whom Leibniz, an admirer, said, '*Elle a des lumières.*'

Letters from Liselotte

Madame

J'espere que vostre majesté me
fera bien la grace D'estre persuadée
que personne ne prent plus
de part que moy a la joye
quelle resent De l'heureuse
naisance Du prince quelle
vient De mettre au monde,
je luy souhaitte, Madame
une parfaitte santé accompag-
née De toutte sorte de prosperité
Et vous prie De croire que
je suis veritablement
Madame

Vostre tres affectionnée
soeur et servante,
Elisabeth Charlotte

a St eloud ce 28
juin 1688.

Madame's letter of congratulation to Mary of Modena on the birth of her son.

LETTERS FROM LISELOTTE

Liselotte's aunt Sophie, with whom she had stayed in Hanover as a child, was one of her favourite correspondents. The granddaughter of James I of England, Sophie married Ernest Augustus of Brunswick-Lüneburg, later Elector of Hanover. The English Act of Settlement nominated her as the successor to the throne of England, but she died, at the age of eighty-four, two months before Queen Anne. Her son, the Elector George Louis, succeeded to the throne and later became George I. The letter below was written when Liselotte had been at the French court for almost three months.

SOPHIE

St Germain 5 February 1672 My dearest aunt will not receive my portrait yet—even the one for papa wasn't dry enough to send. I would, of course, a thousand times rather deliver them myself, or that you and uncle should come and collect them, but I hardly imagine that either is possible.

It isn't that I take longer walks than I did at home, or more of them, but people here are as lame as geese, and apart from the King and Mme de Chevreuse[1] I don't know anyone who can walk twenty paces without puffing and panting.

As for my crying, it's true that I wept all night long, from Strasbourg to Châlons. I couldn't hide my distress after we had said goodbye.

Another of Liselotte's faithful correspondents was her former governess, who, together with her husband, was a member of Sophie's entourage.

FRAU VON HARLING

Versailles 23 November 1672 Oh, my dear Frau von Harling, how peculiar it feels to your little knight-of-the-rustling-leaves not to be allowed to run and jump, or even ride in a carriage now and then, but to be carried everywhere in a sedan-chair! If only it could be done with soon, it might be a different matter; but it must go on for nine months.

[1] Jeanne Marie Colbert, Duchesse de Chevreuse, daughter of the King's first minister.

What a sad business! When this egg is hatched at last, I wish I could post it to you at Osnabrück. I know from my own experience that it would be well looked after. You understand this trade better than anyone in this country. Here, no infant is safe. The doctors have already helped five of the Queen's into the next world. The last one died three weeks ago, and three of Monsieur's have been despatched in the same way, as he says himself.

A propos of bringing up children: if you want to send me one—a page-boy, that is—you must do so soon. One of mine is joining the military to-morrow or the day after, but I'll keep the position open until I hear whether or not you would like me to have one of your relations.

The Harlings, availing themselves of the privilege, sent a nephew, Eberhard Ernst Franz, aged six. He rose to become captain of Madame's guard in 1715, and remained a member of her household until she died.

St Cloud 30 May 1673   Thank you for the trust you and M Harling have shown in sending me your little nephew. You may be sure that I shall do my best to look after him. He is a sweet child, and not only Monsieur and I but all the others adore him. He already waits at table just like the other pages, and he's beginning to speak and understand French. I have lodged him apart from the others, in a house where the mistress takes care of him, and sees that his hair is combed every day, his linen washed and his prayers said. I am having a little canopied bed made for him so that he can sleep by himself. He eats with my young ladies, and I hope lacks for nothing. His first office here was to wait at table on one of my prettiest young ladies, which didn't displease him, because as soon as the meal was over she gave him a kiss. He thought that such an agreeable custom should be encouraged, and once, when she forgot to kiss him, the little man planted himself in front of her and held out his cheek. She said he was so adorable that she couldn't refuse him. So, you see, he has already become a *galant* here in France.

Liselotte's first son, Alexandre-Louis d'Orléans, Duc de Valois, was born on 2 June 1673. She wrote soon afterwards to Frau von Harling that 'since I have always been like your own child, you will now feel that you have a new grandchild, a fine healthy boy'. A second son, Philippe II d'Orléans, Duc de Chartres, was born on 2 August, 1674.

SOPHIE

St Cloud 22 August 1674 If my wish could come true, your little princess[1] would marry M le Dauphin instead of my son; he is a better catch and their ages are just right. Perhaps you could produce another daughter for my boy? I wish to God our princess in Heidelberg[2] would begin to follow our good example. But first and foremost I wish that God may soon send them peace, because, if M de Turenne carries off any more cattle, broth will become expensive in the Palatinate.[3]

I am being called downstairs. The King, the Queen and the Dauphin have come to pay me a visit. They are passing through on their way from Paris, where Te Deums have been sung everywhere because of the battle M le Prince has won.[4] He has defeated the Prince of Orange's *arrière-garde*, and taken much booty and many prisoners. All that may be well and good, but frankly I should prefer a prosperous peace, and for the dear Palatinate and papa to be left alone.

St Germain 16 November 1674 I must just tell you that a horoscope which has been cast for my younger son shows that he will be pope, but I'm very much afraid he's more likely to be the Antichrist.

Versailles 22 August 1675 My two holy terrors are making such a rumpus that I can hardly hear myself think. The elder one has been a little quieter this last fortnight: he now has five new teeth, including the eyeteeth. He will be weaned in the autumn, but already he's fond of eating chunks of bread, which he clutches in his fist like a peasant. The younger one is beginning to walk now and tries to run and jump too; he's even stronger than his brother. But I think that is enough about the boys.

Next Monday we go to Fontainebleau—the King is taking me. I have never been there before. I hope we shall have a gay time. All the huntsmen and actors are coming too.

St Cloud 14 September 1675 I must admit that I enjoyed myself wonderfully well at Fontainebleau, though it was a pleasure dearly

----

[1] Sophie Charlotte, Sophie's only daughter, then six years old.

[2] Liselotte's childless sister-in-law, Wilhemine Ernestine of Denmark.

[3] The Maréchal de Turenne was leading his troops through the neutral Palatinate.

[4] The battle of Seneffe. Henri-Jules III, Prince de Condé, was at the head of the victorious troops.

paid for. I came back to find my elder son at death's door. I told Monsieur that if I were in charge I should send my children to Frau von Harling in Osnabrück, because then I could be sure that they would neither die nor be pampered as they are here, which quite drives me out of my mind.

Liselotte's elder boy died in March 1676. She felt 'as though her heart had been plucked from her body'. 'If the Almighty doesn't take very special care of the child I am carrying now,' she wrote to Frau von Harling, 'I shall have little hope of its life and well-being, for it cannot have remained unaffected by my distress.' Her last child, a daughter, was born on 13 September 1676.

FRAU VON HARLING
St Cloud 10 October 1676   I feel as well as can be, though this labour was much harder than the other two. Frankly, it has quite put me off, and left me without the least desire to produce the organ-pipe you talk about. It is such a strain. If they survived it might be a different story, but just to see them die as I did earlier this year—truly, there is no joy in it.

Chartres, whom I so often wish in your care, is now in perfect health, thank heaven, and so is his sister. She is as fat as a Michaelmas goose, and large for her age. They were christened last Monday. They are called after Monsieur and me—the boy Philippe and the girl Elisabeth Charlotte. Now there is another Liselotte in the world.

SOPHIE
St Germain 14 December 1676   I do beg your pardon for not writing for such an eternity. First of all I have been at Versailles, where I was kept busy the whole day long. We hunted all morning, got back at 3 o'clock in the afternoon, changed, went up to gamble until 7 o'clock, then to the play, which never ended before 10.30, then on to supper, and afterwards to the ball until 3 o'clock in the morning, and then we went to bed. So you see how much time I had for writing.

Since I've been back I meant to write every day, but there have been constant interruptions, not the least of them tiresome visitors whom I wished upon myself by falling off my horse. I must tell you the whole story.

We had caught a hare and flushed a magpie, and were ambling along. My habit was uncomfortable, for some reason, and I leant down to adjust it. At that moment a hare started up and everyone gave chase. My horse, seeing the others go, tried to follow, and gave a great lunge. I was half out of the saddle already, and this suddenly threw me sideways. Without taking my foot out of the stirrup I reached for the pommel to remount, but in getting hold of it lost the reins. I called to the rider in front of me to stop my horse, but he came at me with such a rush that my horse was frightened, turned, and bolted in the opposite direction. I held on tightly while the others were in sight, but when I couldn't see them any longer I let go and calmly dropped on to the grass. All this went off so well, thank heaven, that I didn't harm myself at all. You will admire the King, whom you liked so much for being such a comfort to me during my lying-in, even more in this affair: he was the first by my side, pale as death, and though I told him that I hadn't hurt myself or fallen on my head he insisted on examining it very carefully. At last he was satisfied, and himself took me back to my apartments, where he stayed with me for some time to make certain I wasn't dizzy. When he was quite reassured he left. I must say, he shows me greater favour every day. He talks to me whenever we meet, and sends for me each Saturday to join him at Mme de Montespan's for *Medianoche*.[1]

Consequently, I am now very much *à la mode*, and whatever I say or do, good or bad, is vastly admired by all the Court, to such an extent that when I put on my old sable wrap during the recent spell of cold weather everybody rushed to have one made to the same pattern.[2] It's the height of fashion now. It makes me laugh. The very people who now admire this style, and even wear it themselves, used to jeer at my sables, so that I didn't dare wear them. But that's how it goes here. If people think you're in favour you can do no wrong, but if they think the opposite you would be considered ridiculous even if you had come straight from heaven. I wish you could spend a few months here and see what manner of life we lead. I'm sure we should have some good laughs.

Versailles 4 November 1677 Every other day, and sometimes two or three days running, I hunt with the King. We hunt as much here as we do at Fontainebleau. The King has acquired a taste for stag-hunting, which I am very glad about. I follow as often as I can, and love hunting as much as His Majesty. It is a real delight for a knight-of-the rustling-

[1] The midnight meal taken after a fast-day.
[2] Liselotte's fur-piece came to be called 'la Palatine', and this is still the dictionary term for a certain kind of shoulder-wrap.

leaves like me, and there is not so much dressing up or putting on
rouge as for parties.

St Germain 24 November 1677   You say you are glad that Corneille's
plays are coming into fashion again, and I must tell you that they are
all being performed now, one after the other, even the very oldest, and
this is my greatest amusement in Paris. Poor Corneille is so happy
about it: he assures me that it has given him a new lease of life, and he
means to write one more before he dies. I wish I could have the
happiness of taking you to see it, but I fear the war will last longer than
Corneille's life.

Monsieur showed me a letter from the Prince of Orange today, with
news of his marriage, which took place last Sunday or the Sunday
before. I wish the King of England and the Duke of York would
persuade the new bridegroom to consider making peace. It seems to me
that if only one could see the beginnings of a peace, the rest would
surely follow.

> William of Orange had married his cousin, Mary of York, daughter
> of the future James II of England. France, at war with William and at
> pains to keep on friendly terms with England, viewed this match with
> misgivings.

St Germain 11 January 1678   As New Year's day is celebrated in
Germany today,[1] I hope it is not too late to wish you a happy, peaceful
and joyous New Year and a long, healthy life. For myself, I wish for
peace so that I may once again have the happiness of waiting on you.
It seems so strange that I haven't seen you once in the last six years.

There is a great deal of talk about the Prince of Orange's wedding,
and among other things it is said that he went to bed in woollen drawers
on his wedding night. When the King of England suggested that he
might care to take them off, he replied that since he and his wife would
have to live together for a long time she would have to get used to his
habits; he was accustomed to wearing his woollens, and had no intention of changing now. And instead of having supper with the English
royal family he went to eat in the town, and kept the King and the
bride, who had been put to bed in the bridal chamber, waiting until
after midnight. When the King asked him what had kept him so long,
he replied that he had been gambling after supper, threw himself into
a chair and had his valet undress him then and there. I am not surprised

[1] In Germany the Julian calendar was in use until 1700.

Madame with her children, Elisabeth Charlotte and Philippe before he was breeched,
School of Pierre Mignard.

Monsieur in armour, School of Pierre Mignard.

that the princess is struck dumb at such manners. It reminds me of the comedy of the husband of the shrewish Kate.

St Germain 1 July 1678 You are quite right in thinking that I am as German as ever. It is very true, and I expect I shall remain the same Liselotte as long as I live. Now I am going riding with the King. He really is a dear, good man and I do love him, but my aunt and uncle will always take precedence in my heart.

St Germain 24 July 1678 I have received all your letters safely, but even if they had fallen into the hands of a stranger no one would have thought you foolish: your reputation for intelligence is far too great. Also, people here are not all that prudish, but talk openly enough about all sorts of natural functions. I know a *galant*, whose name I must not mention, who always accompanies his mistress to her close-stool; when she has finished he takes the seat, while they chat to each other. And another couple of my acquaintance always announce when either of them needs purging. I have heard this with my own ears. How the French would laugh if Germans went on like that, but when they do it themselves it is considered perfectly polite.

FRAU VON HARLING
St Cloud 20 August 1678 Here is the promised little box that cages my bear-cat-monkey-face. Portrait-painters always want to make one prettier than one really is, so they have made me fatter than I am. It is not my fault if it isn't very like; in order to oblige you I sat still for a whole afternoon, which was not very amusing.

SOPHIE
Paris 14 November 1678 I am flattered that you say I am better-looking than the portrait which I sent to Frau von Harling. But you haven't seen me for seven years—perhaps you would think just the opposite now.

Here comes Monsieur from Versailles with the news that next April we are to travel to Flanders, from there to Lorraine, and from Lorraine to Alsace. I hope we shall also to go Strasbourg and see the Elector and my brother and his wife. Do take a little trip there, it would be such a splendid rendez-vous. I think that if it really happened I should die of happiness. You would then be able to see that we all do our hair like Mesdemoiselles de Valence et Montargis.[1] All Frenchwomen, except

[1] Recent visitors to Hanover.

those who don't bother about their looks at all, wear their hair like that. How you would laugh if you saw me with my *touffettes à la dinde*.

Paris 3 February 1679   They are so stinkingly conceited here, so haughty and so arrogant, it is quite beyond description. Monsieur imagines that there can be no comparison between himself and any Elector. I have tried to find out if you are to have a *fauteuil*, but no, it is not to be thought of. So I shall tell you my plan. You must come incognito to some town in Flanders and let me know where you are lodged. I shall then pretend to visit the house and lock myself up with you and my uncle, and be nothing but the old Liselotte, entirely at your service, as I always am and shall remain until death.

The rendez-vous in Flanders came to nothing, but Sophie visited Versailles for the wedding of Liselotte's elder stepdaughter, Marie-Louise, to the King of Spain. As she travelled incognito, there were no problems regarding seating or precedence.

Staying with the Orléans at St Cloud, she found her niece 'the most fortunate woman in the world, happy in the love of her family, the respect of all the Court and the friendship of the King'. Liselotte was delighted that the French royal family greatly took to her beloved aunt, especially Monsieur, who was very much impressed with the way in which she helped to arrange a ribbon on his wedding-hat that had been giving trouble. There was only one small contretemps: Sophie's parting gift from the King. Such gifts were bestowed on visiting foreigners as evidence of the royal French magnificence, but in this case Monsieur was so shocked at the sight of '*la petite boîte des vilains diamants*' that he took them straight back to his brother. They were promptly exchanged.

St Germain 1 November 1679   This is a good opportunity to send you the diamond studs from the King. Monsieur is inconsolable not to be able to show you in person how they should be worn on the dress or sleeves, but he has already conferred with Mme de Mecklenburg,[1] who is to send you a paper pattern. Then my uncle will ask you, I hope, what you want with that rubbish, a question I should often like to ask Monsieur if I dared.

[1] Duchesse de Mecklenburg-Schwerin, a visitor to the Court.

St Cloud 24 September 1680 My eyes are so sore from weeping that I can hardly see. But though I have the greatest difficulty in writing, I can't let our prince[1] go without a letter for you. Now that I have the chance to speak openly I can say that, while your loss may be as great as mine, you are more fortunate than I am because you don't have to live with the very people who are responsible for the Elector's death through the grief they caused him. You said in your last letter how pleased you were that I was near the King, whom I like so much. Well, I admit that I did love him very dearly and have always been happy to be with him, but that was before he started persecuting papa. I can assure you that since then I have found it very hard indeed, and shall do as long as I live. I wish to heaven I could accompany the prince; I would rather weep with you than look at all those smiling faces here, which only help, if it were possible, to increase my sorrow.

Liselotte's father had died in August, distracted to the end by the high-handed behaviour of the French commissioners who, as members of one of Louis' Reunion Chambers—set up after the Treaty of Nijmegen had been signed in 1678—were in the Palatinate to examine ancient charters with a view to French territorial claims.

Shortly before his death, the Elector had asked Liselotte to intercede with Louis on his behalf, but the King had only responded with his famous '*Je verrai*'. 'Nothing,' she wrote, 'was less cheering. A downright "*non*" was far better, as never in his life did he accord anything after "*Je verrai*".'

St Germain 11 December 1680 I am afraid that Papa died of grief and disappointment. If the great man and his ministers hadn't tormented him so much, he might still be with us, and I might even have seen him once again.

Monsieur advised the Queen to make a vow on account of her son's health, but I said he would do better to suggest to the King that if he were to make a vow of justice, return other people's property and not keep for himself what doesn't belong to him, his son's health might well improve.

FRAU VON HARLING

St Cloud 10 April 1681 I must just tell you that I have become quite a venerable mother now. My son is in coat and breeches, he looks very sweet. I wish you could see him, he has become much more human and

[1] George Louis of Hanover, Sophie's eldest son, who had been on a visit to France.

sensible than when *ma tante* was here. But my girl is the funniest child you could ever wish to see; she chatters without drawing breath and says anything that comes into her head. She is a real terror, I can't think what will become of her.

Fontainebleau 29 September 1681 It will be a long time before I shall be able to write again, as the King is setting off post-haste tomorrow to the occupation of Strasbourg. The Queen, Mme la Dauphine[1] and I are going to follow in short stages to Nancy, where we are to stay. Adieu, my dearest Frau von Harling. I must go and pack.

On September 30th Strasbourg had been occupied by French forces in peacetime. Normally, Liselotte enjoyed travelling with the King, but on this occasion she could not restrain her tears. It had been in Strasbourg that she had parted from her father, and now she was riding through the city in the royal carriage opposite the man she thought responsible for his death. But there was another reason for the deterioration of the relationship between Madame and her brother-in-law—the ascendancy of Mme de Maintenon.

Neither Liselotte nor her friend the Dauphine, of whose entourage Mme de Maintenon was now a member, had a good word to say for the new favourite, but in the King's eyes she could do no wrong. Mme de Maintenon was a lady of strong religious principles. Under her influence the King took his own religious observances much more seriously. People were expected to emulate him and there was strict censorship to see that they did. Soon the courtiers were outdoing each other in the profession of piety for which until then they had not been renowned. The atmosphere at Court changed, and with it Liselotte's easy friendship with her brother-in-law.

The various cliques—Liselotte calls them *cabales*—were quick to register coolness, and Monsieur's favourites d'Effiat and Lorraine began scheming against her for their own advancement. Far from being 'the happiest woman in the world' Madame felt miserable, lonely and often furiously angry.

SOPHIE
St Germain 19 February 1682 I follow my straight course in the name of God, and should have imagined that if I did no harm to anyone I should be left in peace. But then I find myself attacked on all sides, and that is so very galling that I lose what little patience I have. When there is no one I can trust or turn to for help, no one to advise me how to

[1] Marie Anne Christine Victoire of Bavaria, who had married the Dauphin in 1680.

extricate myself from this labyrinth, then I grow moody and bad-tempered. And when I am bad-tempered my spleen swells, when it is swollen it sends the vapours to my head, these make me sad, and when I am sad I fall ill. This is part of the reason for my recent sickness, but the cause of it all is not to be trusted to my pen, because I know for certain that my letters are opened and read. The post office do me the honour of re-sealing my letters very cleverly, but the good Mme la Dauphine's are often sent in an amazing state, quite torn at the top.

All that glisters is not gold, and for all their vaunted liberty even their *divertissements* are too stiff and constrained for words. Moreover, since I've been here I've got used to seeing so much villainy that if I ever found myself in a place where hypocrisy didn't reign supreme, and lies were not the order of the day, I should think I had found Paradise.

Versailles 21 July 1682   Once again I am as miserable as an old dog. I really think that last year the devil must have put on human shape to drive me out of my mind and teach me all that devilish and human cunning is capable of. In this I am now so perfectly instructed that my masters could quite safely leave me alone. Every day I hear innumerable calumnies with not a grain of truth in them, promises which are never kept, and polite expressions which conceal thoughts of a very different nature. And they ask everybody why I am sad when all the time they know in their conscience that they themselves are the daily and hourly cause.

In an hour's time I am going to hear an opera which is to be performed in the riding academy. Mme la Dauphine will soon play a different kind of tune; she is expecting the birth of her child any time now.[1] I have no such worries; for the last four years I have been left to live in complete chastity, which I can tell you at this safe opportunity.

RAUGRAVE CHARLES LOUIS VON DEGENFELD[2]
Versailles 23 August 1682   Now my enemies have persuaded Monsieur to send my poor Théobon[3] away from me. I really believe they will torment the life out of me in the end. She committed no crime except that of loving me.

---

[1] The Duc de Bourgogne was born on 6 August 1682.

[2] Liselotte's favourite stepbrother, known as Carllutz.

[3] Saint-Simon says of this lady-in-waiting, who was married to the Comte de Beuvron, that she was tactful and intelligent, and, apart from her temper and a passion for gambling, kindhearted and a good friend.

S O P H I E

Versailles 12 September 1682   I should a thousand times prefer to live in
a place ruled by evil fiends and ghosts, because God would allow them
no power over me. But these damned knight-phantoms of all too solid
flesh and bone are permitted every conceivable wickedness by the
King and Monsieur. And although the Chevalier has already corrupted
the great man's son and said the most dreadful things about him, he
seems far more prosperous than people who never leave the straight
and narrow path. May God make your wish come true, and let Lucifer
take him to his kingdom soon. But since he may be frightened to go
alone, I wish him a companion for the journey: the Marquis d'Effiat,
who I am sure already knows the way. To judge by his horrible vices
and villainies, he must already be one of Lucifer's subjects.

I am very fond of Mlle de Théobon, and should always have been
very sorry to lose her, but I should not have been so extremely upset if it
weren't for the following circumstances: for the last three months my
enemies have been spreading the rumour that I had a *galanterie* and that
Théobon was carrying my letters. Then they made Monsieur send
Théobon away quite suddenly, with orders never to see me or speak to
me again as long as she lived.

What the world will make of this, I leave to your imagination. And
think how painful it is for me to know myself innocent and yet have to
endure such shame! There is more, though I cannot trust it to the post.
But I shall send you the whole story by Wendt.[1]

The 5,000 word letter (Liselotte calls it a book) that reached Sophie
contained a minutely detailed account of that autumn's events.

The rumours of Madame's *galanterie*, which supposedly concerned the
Chevalier de Saint-Saens, were all pure invention on the part of Monsieur's favourites. When Liselotte had learned that they were petitioning
Monsieur to take action against her by dismissing her faithful lady-in-
waiting, she had appealed to the King. Louis had told her that he thought
it better not to interfere in his brother's domestic affairs, though he was
sorry she had been so unjustly accused.

Outraged, she repeatedly demanded to be allowed to retire to Maubuisson, a convent near Paris where her aunt Louise Hollandine—
sister of Charles Louis and Sophie—a Catholic convert, was abbess.
The King refused permission. 'You are Madame, and obliged to uphold

that position. You are my sister-in-law, and my friendship for you prevents me from allowing you to leave me for ever. You are my brother's wife, and I cannot permit the sort of scandal that would harm him in the eyes of the world.' 'You are my King,' Madame replied, 'and consequently my master. Since you wish me to suffer and be unhappy for the rest of my life, I shall have to face it and obey.' The King, protesting that he did not want her life to be a misery, promised that she and Monsieur would be reconciled and that his friends would injure her no further. Not that the King wished to mislead her: in all future differences between Monsieur and Madame, he would take Monsieur's part. In quarrels between her and other people, however, he would side with her. It only remained for her to give him the names of the people she disliked in her household, and to trust him to double poor Théobon's pension.

The scene of reconciliation took place that very evening. Both the King and Monsieur declared that they believed Madame to be entirely guiltless of any *galanterie*, all three embraced, and honour was satisfied.

Lorraine, d'Effiat and Elisabeth de Grancey (who was Lorraine's mistress though Monsieur's *maîtresse en titre*) remained fixtures in the Orléans household and soon redoubled their efforts to divide the couple.

News of Liselotte's difficulties soon travelled abroad. '*On dit que Madame dit hautement qu'elle sait bien qu'on l'empoisonera comme on a fait à feue Madame. Je lui écris fortement sur ce sujet; je vous prie de me seconder,*' Sophie wrote to Carllutz early in November.

Paris 24 November 1682 I can call God, the whole Court and all my people to witness that in all my sadness I have never let Monsieur hear one angry word, nor remonstrated with him, nor ever talked about him behind his back. I have kept my own council, taken care not to say anything to which he could object, and, however much he needled me, I remained as silent as a mouse. And how could I have blamed Monsieur for the death of his wife when no one is more convinced than I am that it was done without his knowledge?[1]

I don't know how people can say that we live a cat-and-dog life. We have been extremely careful to preserve appearances, and in any case there was no quarrelling. The King was our mediator, and he spoke to both of us about the affair, but so far as Monsieur and I were concerned we only talked of impersonal matters, as though nothing was going on.

---

[1] Henrietta's death has long since been attributed to natural causes. Recent research shows that she died of porphyria, a disease that ran in the English royal family and caused the death of Queen Anne and the 'madness' of George III.

WILHEMINE ERNESTINE[1] OF THE PALATINATE
Versailles 6 December 1682 There is only an hour left for writing, because tomorrow, after the King's Mass, I am to go hunting with him, and then it will be too late to write as it is once again *jour d'appartement*.

To understand what this is, you must know that the King is building a great gallery, which will lead from his apartments to those of the Queen. It is not quite ready, and the King has divided off the part that is finished and painted and made it into a drawing-room. Every Monday, Wednesday and Friday is *jour d'appartement*. All the gentlemen of the Court assemble in the King's antechamber, and the women meet in the Queen's rooms at 6 o'clock. Then everyone goes in procession to the drawing-room. Next to it there is a large room, where fiddles play for those who want to dance. Then comes the King's throne-room, with every kind of music, both played and sung. Next door in the bedchamber there are three card tables, one for the King, one for the Queen and one for Monsieur. Next comes a large room—it could be called a hall—with more than twenty tables covered in green velvet with golden fringes, where all sorts of games can be played. Then there is the great antechamber where the King's billiard table stands, and then a room with four long tables with refreshments, all kinds of things— fruit-tarts, sweetmeats, it looks just like the Christmas spread at home. Four more tables, just as long, are set out in the adjoining room, laden with decanters and glasses and every kind of wine and liqueur. People stand while they are eating and drinking in the last two rooms, and then go to the rooms with the tables and disperse to play. It is unbelievable how many games there are: *lansquenet*, backgammon, piquet, *reversi*, *ombre*, chess, *Trou Madame*, *Berlan*, *summa summarum*, everything you can think of. If the King or Queen comes into the room, nobody has to rise. Those who don't play, like myself and many others, wander from room to room, now to the music, now to the gamblers—you are allowed to go wherever you like. This goes on from six to ten, and is what is called *jour d'appartement*. If I could describe the splendour with which all these rooms are furnished, and the amount of silver there is everywhere, I should go on for ever. It really is worth seeing.

The Gallery, upon completion, became the magnificent Galerie des Glaces. Accounts of the splendid furnishings which Madame had not sufficient time to describe were published in the Comptes des Bâtiments.

---

[1] Liselotte's sister-in-law, who had become Electress Palatine in 1680, when Liselotte's brother Charles succeeded his father.

They were very sumptuous indeed. There were sixteen massive silver chandeliers, twenty-four crystal *lustres* and two great silver *lustres*, each with eight branches. There were silver benches and chairs, and silver tubs on silver bases for the orange trees that stood, four in a row, between each pair of windows. The curtains were of white damask embroidered in gold with the King's cipher. The tables and vases were of porphyry and alabaster. The *Mercure Galant* and visiting foreign princes spread the news of the royal magnificence at Versailles, and soon every prince, duke and elector in Europe endeavoured to model his own Court on the pattern of the sun-palace.

SOPHIE

Châlons 15 July 1683   I have seen no sign yet of M de Morangis, nor of the sausages he is to bring, but I thank you all the same. They will arrive most opportunely for my breakfast when hunting begins on our return to Versailles.

In the meantime we hear masses of amazing news. There is a rumour that M de Monmouth[1] conspired against his father and plotted to have him assassinated, also that the Turks are so close to Vienna that the Emperor, from his windows, watched the Tartars setting fire to the villages.[2] This makes me hope that all Christian kings, princes and nobles will make peace amongst themselves, unite to check the Turks, and thereby put an end to war forever.

St Cloud 1 August 1683   I am sure you will be shocked to hear of the sudden death of her Majesty the Queen. It has affected me greatly, for in all my troubles the Queen always showed me the greatest friendship in the world. So you will understand how sad I was to see her give up the ghost before my very eyes. She had a fever on Monday night and died at 3 o'clock on Friday afternoon, through the ignorance of the doctors, who killed her as surely as if they had pierced her heart with a dagger. She had an abscess under her left arm, which they drove inward by bleeding her, and finally, last Friday, they gave her an emetic, which made the abscess burst internally. She died quite quickly and peacefully. The King is terribly sad. He can't stay here, and leaves for Fontainebleau tomorrow, and so do we all.

[1] James, Duke of Monmouth, the natural son of ~~the future~~ Charles II *(ruled (1660-85))* and of Lucy Walters. Liselotte refers to the Ryehouse Plot.

[2] The siege of Vienna was to last for two months before the Turks were defeated. Many of Liselotte's relations, including her Raugrave half-brothers and her Hanoverian cousins, fought for the Emperor.

By tradition, the King could not remain in the presence of death, and usually boarded his coach before the last breath had been drawn.

Marie-Thérèse was only forty-five when she died. Forty years later, Madame was to write to her half-sister Luise, 'I remember that on the Tuesday before the Queen's death the King gave a fête for her by the fountain called *l'Ancelade*. We had the finest weather in the world, it was the end of July. When the Queen returned to her closet she said to her favourite, Mme de Visse, whom she called Philippa, "Philippa, I have never enjoyed any fête as much as this. I can truthfully say that every fête the King has ever given was a source of grief, but now I am completely happy." On Friday at 3 o'clock in the afternoon she was dead. You see, Luise, the danger of perfect contentment in this world!'

The Queen's grief at any of the previous fêtes was understandable, as the King tended to plan them as treats for whichever mistress he wished to celebrate, and none of the ladies, apart from Mme de Maintenon, had ever convinced him that he was heading straight for damnation unless he lived on better terms with his Queen. Madame says that the Queen imagined she owed the Maintenon the greatest debt of gratitude in the world, because she chased away Mme de Montespan. It was said that on her death-bed the Queen slipped a ring from her own hand on to Mme de Maintenon's finger to indicate her choice of successor. The King did in fact marry Mme de Maintenon shortly afterwards, but the marriage was never made public.

Fontainebleau 29 August 1683 My troubles stem more from Monsieur than from anyone else. His friends, my enemies to a man, have such an influence over him that he of all people dislikes me most. When others hate or harm me, there is always the possibility of paying them back, but in this case there is no revenge; whatever affects Monsieur must affect me too. When he is angry I have to bear with his ill-humour; when he is unhappy there is nothing he can do without hurting me too. Everything bad I share. Only in what is good do I have no part. When he receives money he spends it on his friends, my enemies; when he is in favour he uses this condition to torment me.

If only I had some occupation, it might cheer me up a little, but my enemies have taken good care to prevent this. I am not allowed to talk to anyone. If I so much as ask the time, Monsieur suspects me of sending messages and wants to know what was said. You can imagine how that affects the respect my household has for me. If I say two words to my children, they are cross-examined for half-an-hour afterwards.

Fontainebleau 29 September 1683 My daughter is a real knight-of-the-rustling-leaves. She won't do her lessons—only her jaw is busy, for she chats and laughs all day long. She has all sorts of amusing ideas that would make you laugh. I must be careful not to be too familiar with her, for I am the only person in the world whom she respects. When Monsieur tries to scold her, she laughs in his face. She deceives her governess from morning till night. I don't know what's to become of the girl, she is so terribly wild. I wish she and her brother could exchange temperaments. He is intelligent too, but calm and dignified, just as a girl ought to be, whereas she is as rough as a boy. I think it must be in the nature of all Liselottes to be so wayward in childhood, and I hope that in time a little lead will find its way into the quicksilver, and that she will grow less impulsive, just as I have since I've been in France.

We hear that the King of Poland[1] found so many cases of gold in the Grand Vizier's tent that his personal booty amounts to 8 millions. A good case of ducats wouldn't hurt our Raugrave either.

Versailles 3 September 1684 There was to have been a great fête at Marly; the King had planned to give presents to all the ladies. Soon there was so much talk about it that every lady of any quality wanted to be present, and round about the time that we were to set off for Marly such quantities of ladies arrived that one hardly knew which way to turn. Some of them had even called on the tradespeople to find out what had been bought and how much it had all cost. The King was extremely annoyed when he heard of it. He said that people seemed to have such exaggerated ideas of the magnificence of his presents that they were bound to appear insignificant by comparison. He cancelled the party, made us gamble for the brocades and ribbons as well as the fans, and kept the precious stones for himself.

Versailles 11 May 1685 Today the King sent his confessor to mine, to ask him to reprimand me on three counts. First: I was too free in my speech, and had told the Dauphin that even if I were to see him stark naked from the soles of his feet upward I shouldn't be tempted by him, nor by anyone else. Secondly: I allowed my ladies to have *galants*. And thirdly: I had laughed with the Princesse de Conti about hers. These three things had annoyed the King so much that if I hadn't been his sister-in-law he would have had me banished from the Court. I admitted that the report of my conversation with the Dauphin was quite accurate, and added that I had never thought it a crime not to feel temptation. As for plain speaking, and what I might have said about

[1] John Sobieski, who fought for the Emperor in the defence of Vienna.

crapping and pissing, it was more the King's fault than mine, as I had heard him say hundreds of times that within the family one could talk about anything at all. He should have told me if he had changed his mind; it was the easiest thing in the world to correct.

On the second point, my ladies and their lovers: I never meddled in the affairs of my household, and shouldn't begin with the thing hardest to put to rights. But I knew such conduct to be not without precedent, and quite usual at any Court. As long as they did not prejudice their honour, I didn't think they did themselves or me any harm.

As for the third point, concerning his daughter: I was not her governess to stop her from having lovers if she wanted them, and could hardly be expected to weep when she told me of her adventures. But Mme la Duchesse could be my witness: I never interfere, and I felt very hurt at being treated so badly by the King, as though I had committed some frightful crime.

I must say, I am furious that the King should treat me like a chamber-maid. That may be perfectly suitable for his Maintenon, who was born to it, but not for me.

Liselotte's brother, the Elector Charles, died without heirs in 1685. The Electorate went to a different branch of the family, and the Rau-graves were left homeless and penniless. Louis claimed what he regarded as the Orléans inheritance on Liselotte's behalf: without consulting her— she thought he still regarded her as a Huguenot at heart—he sent her father's and her brother's wills, both of which he disputed, to the Pope in Rome for arbitration. Monsieur himself sent in a few claims on his own account, but Liselotte, when she heard of this, predicted that she would be dead and rotted in her grave before anything was settled.

St Cloud 5 May 1686   I pity the Raugrave children from the bottom of my heart. I wish with all my soul that I could help them, though I don't know how to set about it. I don't understand business matters at all. If the inheritance question depended on me alone, I should soon know what to do. But I'm told that I have no rights at all, and that Monsieur, as *maître de la communauté*, is its sole lord and master, and can use it as he pleases. To my mind this is absurd.

St Cloud 18 May 1686   I can't imagine why Brosseau[1] should think

---

[1] The Hanoverian political agent in Paris.

there was any magnificent funiture at Heidelberg. Except for the two tapestries, the Julius Caesar and the Feast of Bacchus, there can't be much. The last time I saw my mother,[1] she told me that it was a shame to see how badly my brother's house was appointed; there was scarcely a bed or a chair in the whole castle.

Versailles 4 June 1686 I'm not surprised that the Germans find it strange to see only Monsieur involved in the affair of the inheritance, but then they don't know that French marriage contracts lay down that everything due to a wife in her husband's lifetime belongs to both of them, which makes the husband lord and master of her fortune.

St Cloud 4 July 1686 My son is better-looking than his little sister. He doesn't lack intelligence, and, while he is less lively than she is, he is much more sensible. He enjoys copying grown-ups, and the ceremony of the Order was very much to his taste.[2] He certainly fancied himself making his *révérence*. It all went off with great solemnity. He doesn't in the least resemble me as far as love for ceremonies is concerned, but he assures all the world that he is less fond of them than Monsieur.

Versailles 11 August 1686 Our King is not well, it may turn out to be the four-day fever.[3] God help us if it does, for it will make him a hundred times crosser still. He imagines that he is being devout because he no longer sleeps with young women, but his piety consists of nothing but being ill-tempered and employing spies everywhere, who falsely accuse everyone, flatter his brother's favourites and pester everybody. The old hag, the Maintenon, amuses herself by ruling over the royal family. She makes the King hate every member of it except Monsieur. In order to make the latter live on good terms with her, and do whatever she wants, she praises him in front of the King. On the other hand, the old woman fears that people might really believe she likes Monsieur, so as soon as he is mentioned she calls him every horrible name she can think of.

[1] The Dowager Electress had died in March 1686. Liselotte had seen her mother during the royal visits to Alsace.

[2] The Duc de Chartres was now twelve, old enough to attend Court functions, and to receive the St. Esprit.

[3] The King was suffering from an anal fistula, which was operated on by Fagon, his chief doctor, in November. The attempt to keep this a secret had evidently been successful.

The Dauphine is very unhappy. She does her best to please the King, but the old hag sees to it that she is constantly tormented, and she spends her life in boredom and eternal pregnancy. The Dauphin cares about nothing in the world. He finds his pleasures where he can, and is becoming more and more debauched. So is Monsieur, whose only aim in life is to render me ill-service with the King, to insult me whenever he can, to recommend his protégés to the King and to bring them into favour. But he never dreams of trying to further his children's fortunes.

St Cloud 10 October 1686   I had better not tell you what I think of people who are so sure of their salvation that they calmly commit any act of wickedness in this earthly world, because on this point people here are extraordinarily sensitive. I got myself into trouble the other day, when I said that nowadays the devout seemed to be more hypocritical than pious and sought to torment and plague their neighbours instead of correcting their own faults. They rushed to Mme de Maintenon and told her that this was what I had said about her, when all the time I had only spoken *en général*.

Liselotte is referring to the growing persecution of the Protestants. The increasingly restrictive application of the Edict of Nantes, which had guaranteed their freedom, had led to a massive exodus from the country. When the King had formally revoked it in 1685, those who had remained in France were subjected to quite unbelievable atrocities in the name of '*un roi, une loi, une foi*'.
    Liselotte wrote, 'The old whore and Père Lachaise [Louis' confessor] convinced the King that all the sins he had committed with Mme de Montespan would be forgiven if he banished the Protestants, and therein lay the road to heaven. This the poor King firmly believed, and that is how the persecution of the Protestants began.'

Versailles 3 January 1687   In my next letter I shall be able to report on the christening of all three of M le Dauphin's princes,[1] which is to take place next Monday. I am to hold the Duc de Bourgogne with the King. A great many diamonds are being prepared for our adornment, but with my cold I shall probably look like a shat-on carrot (by your leave, by your leave).

[1] The Ducs de Bourgogne, d'Anjou and de Berry. While baptisms were performed soon after birth, christenings were separate ceremonies, often taking place years later.

St Cloud 13 May 1687   You ask if it is true that the King has married Mme de Maintenon, but I really cannot say. Few people doubt it, although I find it hard to believe so long as there has been no official announcement. And when I see what marriages here are usually like, I feel that if they were married their love would hardly be as strong as it is. But perhaps secrecy adds a spice not enjoyed by people in official wedlock.

Versailles 10 June 1687   It doesn't surprise me to hear that you are wearing coiffures of ribbon—everyone here does, from little girls to old ladies of eighty, the difference being that young people wear bright colours and old ones dark shades or black. The reason I don't wear them is that I can't bear anything on my head during the day, and at night I find the rustling of the ribbons too noisy; I should never get any sleep, so I have given this fashion a miss. Neither have I adopted the mode of wearing my hair scraped off the face and whitening my ears. I can't stand having my ears uncovered.

These ribbon-coiffures, *les fontanges*, are supposed to have taken their name from the Duchesse de Fontanges, at one time the King's mistress. She had been one of Madame's ladies ('a stupid little thing but as lovely as an angel'), who once tied up her hair with a ribbon when it had come loose while she was out hunting. She died, aged twenty, in 1681, but *les fontanges* survived her by thirty years. The name was first applied to a knot of ribbon, and later to the tall wired constructions worn to the front of the head.

St Cloud 1 October 1687   The Court is becoming so tedious, it is hardly to be endured. The King thinks he is being pious when he arranges for everyone to be eternally bored and pestered. I cannot describe how his son's wife is tormented by the old hags who surround her.

It is a miserable thing when people may no longer follow their own common sense but have to conform to the whims of whores and self-interested priests.

Versailles 13 December 1687   I thank the Lord that Carllutz and all our other good friends are safe and covered with glory.[1] Everything about this war sounds so perfectly poetic: I half expect Carllutz's letters to me to be in verse, now he has been up Mount Parnassus and

[1] The Raugraves and the Hanoverian princes were, in Liselotte's words, 'wiping the floor with the poor Turks'.

Helicon. Perhaps Athens will turn him into a perfect philosopher. As Count Königsmarck[1] is lodged in the palace of Achilles, I expect Carllutz is staying in Theseus's. If he found any of Medea's old books there, he could learn from them how to travel in the air, and I should have hopes of seeing him here on a flying visit and hearing him tell of the wonders he has seen.

Versailles 26 January 1688   The descriptions of the devoutness at Court are exaggerated; certainly diamond crosses are being worn, but for the purpose of adornment rather than piety. No one at Court wears a fichu. The coiffures grow taller and taller every day. The King told us at dinner today that a fellow by the name of Allart, who used to do people's hair here, has dressed all the ladies of London so tall that they can't get into their sedan-chairs, and have been obliged to have them heightened in order to follow the French fashion.

St Cloud 14 April 1688   Frau von Harling and her husband have asked me to send them their nephew, and I don't want to miss this safe opportunity to open my heart and tell you my troubles, which I could not entrust to the ordinary post.

I must confess to my dearest aunt that for some time I have been very low, though I try to show it as little as possible. I have been told, in confidence, the real reason why the King is treating the Chevalier de Lorraine and the Marquis d'Effiat so kindly. It is because they have undertaken to persuade Monsieur to petition the King to arrange marriages between his Montespan children and mine: my daughter's with the crippled Duc du Maine and my son's with Mlle de Blois. Even if the Duc du Maine were a proper prince and not a child born of double adultery, I shouldn't want him for a son-in-law, nor his sister for a daughter-in-law. He is hideously ugly, lame and full of bad qualities, his character is vile and he is as mean as the devil.

His sister's disposition may be better, but she is too sickly and her eyes are so bleary that she is bound to go blind in the end. Worst of all, they are both, as I said, bastards of a double adultery, and the children of the most evil and desperate woman on earth.

The Maintenon quite sides with the Montespan in the affair, because she has brought up both these bastards and loves the limping lad as though he were her own child.

Worst of all, I can't say a word of any of this to Monsieur because of his charming habit of carrying everything, much exaggerated, to the

[1] Carl von Königsmarck, brother of the famous Philip.

Madame's father, the Elector Charles Louis, by Anselm von Hulle.

Left: Madame's brother, the Elector Charles. Engraving by U. Kraus showing Heidelberg Castle before its destruction.
Below: Heidelberg Castle in ruins. Engraving by C. Willmore after the drawing of C. Stanfield.

King, and getting me into a hundred scrapes. I am in the greatest distress and hardly know where to turn. And I can't stop tormenting myself; every time I see those bastards my blood boils.

D'Effiat is said to have the promise of a dukedom and the Chevalier of a large sum of money. In the meantime they are raised to the skies with a hundred kindnesses, whereas I am treated very badly indeed. It seems a positive favour that I am allowed to live at all.

Now that I have lost all my family, who could be closer to me in the world than you and my poor children? To see them sacrificed to the *grandeur* of my enemies is worse than anything else. Perhaps I shall be exiled over this, for if Monsieur discusses it with me I shall certainly tell him my opinion, which he will then repeat to the King in his usual manner, as well as to his favourites, who will twist it to their own advantage when they pass it on. And should the King himself astonish me by mentioning this affair, I would tell him quite frankly that I am opposed to it, and that is certain to make him angry, however respectfully I may put it. I haven't been able to discover whether or not the King has married his Maintenon. A number of people say she is his wife, and that the Archbishop of Paris united them in the presence of the King's confessor and the Maintenon's brother. Others say no, it isn't true; it is quite impossible to get to the bottom of it. What is very sure is that he never felt such a passion for any mistress as he does for this one. To see them together is something to marvel at, for not a quarter-of-an-hour passes without his whispering into her ear or talking to her in secret, though he has already spent the entire day with her.

Paris 24 May 1688 I hardly know whether to send you my condolences or my congratulations on the occasion of the death of the Elector of Brandenburg.[1] I am aware that you knew him and that he was a close kinsman of yours, but I can't believe you are inconsolable to know that your daughter is now an Electress. So I shall offer you my compliments like the Comte de Gramont: *Vous me pouvez croire.* He finds this a fitting compliment for any occasion.

Fontainebleau 8 October 1688 On Saturday we went boar-hunting with the King. At the time I was very anxious about my daughter. We had just received news that she was ill again. I had begged Monsieur four times to let me go to Paris to help look after the poor child, but he didn't want me to, and all because of the *cabale*. The Grancey, who always

[1] The Great Elector was succeeded by his son Frederick, who had married Sophie Charlotte.

D

interferes in everything, wanted me to employ a doctor whom I refused to accept on her recommendation. But so that Monsieur may appoint him after all, they have summoned him to my daughter. And now, when my doctor says white the other one says black, and the poor child suffers accordingly. If I were in Paris I should find out which treatment would do her the most good and follow it quite impartially, and this is precisely why they have persuaded Monsieur not to let me go. Now I am forced to see my only daughter sacrificed to the interests of the *cabale*. I couldn't contain myself, and said a few words on the subject to Monsieur, who was highly offended, and now I can do nothing but recommend my poor child to the Almighty.

It is only too true that my children respect no one but me. Monsieur never takes the trouble to speak to them; their tutor and governess are the silliest, most stupid people in the world, and the children, who are, thank heaven, quite intelligent, can't help laughing at them. It falls to me to tell them what they may or may not do. Consequently they respect me, yet they love me too because they are quite sensible enough to see that what I say is for their own good. I seldom scold them, but when it is necessary I really let them have it, and this makes all the more impression. If they follow my advice they won't go far wrong, in spite of all the bad examples they constantly have before their eyes, poor children. But this is a text best passed over in silence.

The wrangles about the Orléans inheritance had continued over the last three years and, ostensibly to protect Liselotte's interests, French troops were sent into the Palatinate in the autumn of 1688. There, under General Mélac, they embarked on the systematic destruction of that country, as part of Louvois' plan to safeguard France from the east.

During this 'Orléans campaign', prelude to the War of the League of Augsburg, Heidelberg Castle was destroyed. It was never rebuilt. Sophie wrote, 'Only the great tun has remained intact. There the Elector can now play at being Diogenes.'

Fontainebleau 10 November 1688 Every day I have to listen to their plans for the bombardment of Mannheim, which the Elector, my father, rebuilt with such care. It makes my heart bleed. And then they are highly offended. During the ten days that I was ill in Paris the King didn't once send to ask after me, and when I wrote he didn't even reply. As I was curious to know what lay behind this, I had discreet enquiries made on my return here, and learned that the King was angry with me because of a conversation I had had with the Duc de Montausier. I'll tell you how it went: M de Montausier came up to me at Mme la Dauphine's and said, 'Madame, M le Dauphin is your champion; he is going to conquer your lands and properties for you.' At first I said nothing, but when he went on, 'You seem to be taking this very coolly', I answered, 'Monsieur, that is true. You are speaking of the matter I least want to hear, which is that my name is being used for the ruin of my homeland. Far from being pleased, I am very angry. I am not skilled in the art of dissembling, but I am well able to keep silent, and if I am not to speak my mind it would be better not to make me speak at all.' Apparently this offended the old man. He passed it on to others, who repeated it to the King, who has taken it in very bad part.

Versailles 20 March 1689   I had scarcely begun to recover from the shock of poor Carllutz's death[1] when the horrible, wretched sufferings of the poor Palatinate began. What distresses me most is that the poor people are plunged into their utter misery in my name. And when I weep they think it *fort mauvais*, but if they were to kill me for it I couldn't stop grieving over being, so to speak, the cause of my country's ruin, and seeing all my father's work and trouble undone at one blow. Indeed, I am so filled with horror at all the destruction there that every night, as I fall asleep, I seem to find myself in Mannheim or Heidelberg gazing at all the devastation. Then I wake with a start, and can't get to sleep again for at least two hours. I can't get out of my mind what it used to be like in my day, what has become of it, what indeed has become of me, and this makes me weep bitterly.

Versailles 14 April 1689   Although I wish the present Palatine Elector[2] no ill, I am not grieving on his account. What hurts me most is that the poor Palatines were so deceived in my name. The poor, guileless people, prompted by their affection for the late Elector my father, thought that the best thing they could do was to submit with a good grace. They believed that they would then become my subjects, and live more prosperously under me than under their present Elector because I have the blood of their former rulers in my veins. And now they find themselves not only disappointed in their hopes, wretchedly repaid for their loyalty, but plunged into infinite misery and despair. I simply cannot stomach it. The very people who are the cause of my

[1] Carllutz had died of a fever at the siege of Negroponte. He was thirty.
[2] Prince William of Pfalz-Neuburg, who had succeeded Liselotte's brother. The Pfalz-Neuburgs were Catholics.

country's ruin torment and persecute me to such a degree that not a single day passes without some new unpleasantness. And these are the people with whom I must spend the rest of my life. If only they said what they wanted, I expect one could act accordingly, but they say nothing and everything one does is wrong.

There is another thing that I've noticed. Whenever the King fears that Monsieur might be angry with him, as for instance when the bastards[1] are given great governorships and he nothing, when he is about to refuse a request, or when, as at present, the King keeps Monsieur sitting at home without entrusting him with a single command, then the King flatters Lorraine and all Monsieur's other favourites, and he, loving them and hating me, is content and asks for nothing more.

Here is a little *dictum* that I heard today. It will amuse you more than my lamentations. *Le prince d'Orange gouverne tout/ le cardinal de Fürstenberg brouille tout/ le roi de France demande tout/ le pape refuse tout/ l'Allemagne s'oppose à tout/ les Jesuites se mêlent de tout./ Si Dieu ne met ordre à tout/ le diable emportera tout.*

We are told here that the women of a small county in Ireland have revolted against King James and taken up arms for the Prince of Orange. It must be for the honour and glory alone, for no one can say he has any kindness for their sex—he is believed to have very different inclinations.

James II, deposed in 1688, had settled in France, and his daughter Mary and the Prince of Orange had ascended the English throne. England was now at war with France, together with the other members of the League of Augsburg.

Three months after his arrival at St Germain—'where he had been received by Louis like a brother'—James set off for Ireland hoping to regain his kingdom. It was the first of many unsuccessful expeditions, for all the French King's loading him with ships, frigates, troops, officers, services of plate, plain and gilt, and Louis' own arms for his person.

Liselotte, after taking her leave of James II on the eve of his departure, writes to Sophie that, though one really could not help feeling sorry for him, since he seemed goodness itself, it was impossible to be surprised at his fate. The Queen, on the other hand, seemed intelligent, and Liselotte liked her extremely.

[1] The Duc du Maine and the Comte de Toulouse, the King's sons by Mme de Montespan.

St Cloud 20 May 1689 When you suggest that Monsieur is the best man in the world, it is hardly fitting for me to disagree with you; only admit that you haven't seen enough of him to be able to judge, and that I know more about it. Indeed, I know him so perfectly by heart that perhaps I know only too well what to expect. I see that he has quite made up his mind to appoint the Marquis d'Effiat as my son's governor. The Marquis is my greatest enemy and is bound to set my son against me, just as Monsieur has done up to now. As for my daughter, I fear that this miserable war will prevent her from getting the electoral Prince. I can't give up hope, though. It would be such a comfort to think that my lamented father's grandchild ruled in the Palatinate, and that she would marry no limping bastard.

I fear that our Raugrave children must be in despair at losing all they have, and if I had any money I would most willingly send them some, but you can't imagine my poverty. I only have 100 pistoles a month, I can never give less than one pistole for anything, and within a week everything is spent on flowers, fruit and postage. When the King gives me any money, and he never does except for the New Year, I have to use it to pay off my old debts. Monsieur never gives me a single penny. If I want to buy the least trifle I have to borrow, so it is quite impossible for me to give presents.

St Cloud 5 June 1689 By now I should be used to knowing that my poor mother-country is in flames. I have heard of nothing else for so long, but every time I learn of another place being burnt down I hear it with pain and sorrow.

Monsieur recently told me something I hadn't heard before, which annoyed me extremely. It seems that the King collected money from the Palatinate in my name, and now the poor people must think that I have profited from their misery as well as being the cause of it all. It grieves me bitterly. I wish to God I had been given all the money that has been extracted from the Palatinate to do as I liked with: the poor Raugrave children and the poor Palatines would certainly be the better off for it. But the truth is that I haven't seen a single penny.

I have talked to M Rebenac[1] about the Queen of Spain's death. It is only too true, she was poisoned with raw oysters.[2] Our Mme la Dauphine, though apparently not poisoned, is growing more and more tottery every day, and I'm frightened to death that she won't last much

[1] The French envoy to Spain.
[2] The Queen of Spain, Liselotte's step-daughter, had died on February 12th.

longer. In the beginning the doctors, trying to please several old women
who shall be nameless but you can guess who, said that Mme la
Dauphine was a hypochondriac and only imagined she was ill. So
they let the disease take such a hold that I fear there is little to be done
now. Now that she is entirely bedridden they have to admit she is ill,
but they are very ignorant and only know of purging, blood-letting
and emetics, none of which are of any use to poor Mme la Dauphine.

Versailles 26 August 1689   You know that my enemies have put it into
Monsieur's head to make his first equerry, d'Effiat, my son's governor.[1]
Since all France knows as well as I do that this man is the most immoral
and depraved fellow in the world, I have asked Monsieur to select
someone else.

My reason is that it doesn't seem compatible with my son's honour
to be regarded as d'Effiat's mistress, for there is no greater sodomite in
the whole of France. It's a poor début for a young prince to start off in
life with the greatest debauchee in the world. Monsieur admitted that
d'Effiat had been depraved and fond of boys, but said that he had cured
himself of his vices long since. I said that only a few years ago a good-
looking German who was staying here had excused himself from
coming to see me as often as he would have liked because d'Effiat
pestered him whenever he set foot in the Palais-Royal. So he can't have
changed as long ago as his friends claim. And even supposing that he
hadn't practised his vices for a few years, I don't consider it is necessary
to use one's only son to test whether or not the Herr equerry has
renounced boys. I said that Monsieur was, of course, the lord and master
of his house, and at liberty to put my son in the hands of whomever he
pleased, but that I couldn't approve of d'Effiat as long as I lived, and I
should make this fact known.

Liselotte thought it most ominous that Mme de Maintenon was in favour
of the appointment and had, apparently, persuaded the King to agree to
it. She pointed out to Monsieur that Mme de Maintenon could ask for
nothing better than to see the Duc de Chartres ruined so that her old
charge, the Duc du Maine, might surpass him in virtue, but Monsieur
remained adamant. Then d'Effiat himself changed his mind, and Monsieur sent word to Madame that, if d'Effiat was now not appointed, it
was not because of her, but because he had declined the position.
Liselotte took some satisfaction in answering that, by paying her this
compliment, he had spared her the trouble of thanking him, but that

[1] The post was vacant through the death of the Duc de la Vieuville.

she was so overjoyed that she had difficulty in restraining herself from thanking not only Monsieur but d'Effiat himself. But even then the matter was not finally settled.

St Cloud 21 September 1689 Now for the continuation of this story. I have spoken to the King. His Majesty said it was pure invention that he wanted d'Effiat to be his nephew's governor; on the contrary, he had spent all last year trying to dissuade Monsieur from his choice. Whereupon I humbly begged his Majesty to find an honest man for my son and propose him to Monsieur, which he promised to do. Since then all has been quiet. I have found out that the King is keeping his word, and there is reason to hope that my son will soon have a new preceptor. God grant that we may be given an honest man.

The King appointed the Marquis d'Arcy. Philippe's real education, however, was conducted by his tutor, who was, and remained, the Abbé Dubois. He was to rise to the position of premier minister in Philippe's regency. Liselotte liked him well enough at first, but later blamed him for all her son's shortcomings and debauches.

St Cloud 30 October 1689 Yesterday I was told something which moved me so much that it made me cry. I heard that the poor people of Mannheim have returned to their ruined town. They have moved into their cellars, and live there as though they were in their old homes. They even hold their daily market just as if the town were still standing. And whenever a Frenchman comes to Heidelberg, the poor citizens crowd round him to ask after me. Then they begin to talk of His Grace, my late father the Elector, and of my late brother, and they weep bitterly. They have no love for the present Elector.

Versailles 8 February 1690 I am afraid we shan't have the Dauphine with us much longer. They are killing her with the distress they cause her, and do their best to put me in a similar state. But I am a harder nut to crack than Mme la Dauphine, and the old hags will lose a good many teeth before they polish me off. In order to drive them frantic, I take the greatest care of my health. The old Drab[1] is at least fifteen, if not twenty, years older than I am, and I think that if I am patient, and look after myself, I shall have the pleasure of seeing her depart to the next world before me.

[1] Mme Maintenon.

Versailles 12 June 1690 I wept for six solid hours at the funeral of poor Mme la Dauphine, and couldn't see out of my eyes for two days afterwards. I was sad enough already over the loss of the Dauphine, of whom I had been so fond, but when in addition I saw our arms all over the coffin, and the black hangings,[1] my thoughts went to the Elector my father, my mother, my brother, everyone dear to me whom I have lost, and I thought I should burst with crying. On the Wednesday after the dreadful ceremony we returned to Marly, where we stayed till Saturday. There, by rights, my grief should have evaporated, because life went on just as usual. All the rooms were full of gamblers, there was hunting in the afternoons and music in the evenings, but to tell the truth it made me sadder than ever. I was quite overcome by grief when I saw how quickly the dead were forgotten.

If only God had given me a nature as unfeeling as the Great Man's and his brother's! Nothing makes them sad. Truly, it is astonishing to see how hard these people are. If it were strength of character it might be acceptable, perhaps even admirable, but it is not that at all. They shriek while the spectacle of death is before their eyes, but as soon as they are outside the door they are all smiles, and don't give it another thought.

Versailles 30 July 1690 As the King of England was making his way back to St Germain in his carriage, he was met by one of his footmen a hundred yards outside the palace gates with the news from Ireland.[2] He said that Marshal Schomberg had fallen in battle, and the Prince of Orange[3] had died of his wounds. Since then we have heard that the reports of the poor Marshal's death are quite true, but the Prince is only slightly wounded.

However, the pleasure that the news of his death gave the *canaille* is quite impossible to describe. Two officers have already been detailed to put an end to the rioting, but in vain. For forty-eight hours the people celebrated furiously, and did nothing but feast and get drunk. Anybody who happened to pass was forced to join in. They lit bonfires, they threw fireworks, they put on fancy dress, and some of them staged a mock funeral, inviting passers-by to the Prince of Orange's burial. Others made a dummy out of straw and wax, named it the Prince of

[1] Liselotte and the late Dauphine shared the colours of the House of Wittelsbach.

[2] The Battle of the Boyne, in which William defeated James's supporters, had been fought on July 11th.

[3] This was King William III. In France William and Mary were not yet recognized and were stoutly referred to by their old titles.

Orange and shot at it all night long. The Franciscans lit a great bonfire in front of their monastery and sang and danced round it in a circle. If I were to tell you all the foolery that took place in Paris, I should have to write a book. But what is so strange is that our King's authority, absolute though it is, couldn't put a stop to it, for to say it was folly was to endanger your life.

St Cloud 20 August 1690 You will see that the new popular songs aren't precisely eulogies of our poor King of England. But they prove that, while people here love this King and hate the Prince of Orange, they admire the latter more than the former.

Last Thursday we had the poor King and Queen here. She was very serious but he was quite cheerful. I don't know what to make of the people who praise his intelligence so highly, I see little sign of it.[1] The more I see of this King, the more excuses I find for the Prince and the more admirable I think he is. Perhaps you will think that 'old love never grows stale',[2] but I certainly prefer an intelligence such as his to the other's handsome face.

St Cloud 23 August 1690 Although the great man has won many battles, he is still very cross. The old hags frighten him with the fires of hell in order to keep him for themselves and prevent him from looking at anyone younger, and such enforced piety goes entirely against his nature. It just makes him bad-tempered, and those who have nothing to do with it must pay.

Fontainebleau 20 October 1690 Now that I know King James better, I like him very much. Really, he is the best prince in the world. You can't help feeling sorry for him, his sighs are quite heart-rending. He took me on one side and cross-examined me about his daughter. Was it really true that she had been so grieved by his misfortune that she refused to dance at The Hague when the Electress of Brandenburg was there? Had she truly written to you that she was glad he had not lost his life in Ireland? I assured him that it was all very true, and this assurance seemed to give the unhappy King a little comfort.

[1] After a visit to the English Royals at Saint Germain Liselotte writes, 'I found the King stupider than ever, the Queen, on the other hand, the reverse.'

[2] Liselotte is, of course, referring to her meeting with William when she visited her grandmother at The Hague, where the possibility of a match between them had been discussed. Further negotiations had taken place in 1666. Neither of the young people had been averse to the plan, but Liselotte's father had let the matter slide as William's future was far from certain.

Liselotte further tells Sophie that she informed James of Mary's unhappiness at knowing that her father and her husband were on opposite
sides. He replied that her words might indicate that she loved him, but
her actions proved the contrary. Liselotte stood up for Mary, her
goddaughter. The King heard her out in silence—and since, says Liselotte, he was none too quick in his repartees, he often did well to remain
silent.

Versailles 2 February 1691 Thank you for your New Year wishes.
We are getting more and more devout every day. There is a rumour—I
don't know if it's true—that the King's old Drab has ordered all the
ladies who use rouge not to do so any longer. She has been spared the
trouble of paying me that compliment. This is what piety consists of here.

Paris 29 March 1691 The widower[1] is an original. I don't think his
equal in callousness exists anywhere. God knows whom my daughter
will marry, but I don't think they have the least intention of helping
him to find a new wife. I would much rather my daughter remained
Mademoiselle all her life than see her married unsuitably. She is growing enormously, and is almost as tall as I am. Her figure is not too bad
and her skin is lovely, but her features are plain. She has an ugly nose, a
large mouth, colourless eyes and a flat face, as you will see from her
portrait.

St Cloud 30 June 1691 The urchins of the *Holzmarkt* in Hanover must
be just like the *galopins* here. These grubby little fellows know everything, even the best-kept secrets. This was how we learned that the
King was going to besiege Mons. Whenever I hear any news I ask, 'Is
that what the street-urchins say?' If the answer is 'Yes', then I know it's
true, but if it's 'No' I have my doubts, however likely it may sound.
   As long as the old whore is alive, things will go badly with me at
Court. She detests me, and the more civilly I behave towards her the
worse it gets; so I am never one of the chosen few who are permitted to
watch the play at St Cyr,[2] which, to tell you the truth, I should vastly
prefer to the monotonous wail of the *Salut*.

   [1] The Dauphin.
   [2] St Cyr was the convent-school founded by Mme de Maintenon, with the help of
the King, for the education of three hundred daughters of impoverished noblemen.
Liselotte once heard the King remark that the standard of education was so high there
that he wished his own daughters might have had the benefit of it. The play referred
to was Racine's *Athalie*, which was specially commissioned for St Cyr by Mme de
Maintenon, following the success of *Esther* three years earlier.

Versailles 22 July 1691 Taking the waters doesn't seem to have done M de Louvois much good, but no one knows whether it was the mineral or the plain sort that did it. The doctors and surgeons who opened him up testified that he died of a dreadful poison. He was perfectly well and then, little more than a quarter-of-an-hour later, he was dead. I talked to him half-an-hour before his death. He looked so well and his colour was so healthy that I told him the waters of Forges[1] must have agreed with him. He politely offered to see me back to my apartments, but I wouldn't allow it as the King was expecting him. If I had let him come he would have died here, and that would have been a ghastly sight. Since he had to die, I could wish it had happened three years ago, and the poor Palatinate would have been the better for it.

> Louvois, Louis' minister of war, died suddenly after drinking a glass of water during a Council meeting which was being held in the apartments of his enemy, Mme de Maintenon. Any untimely death, however natural the cause, immediately attracted widespread speculation about poisoning. There had been the recent case of the Queen of Spain, whose death had been variously ascribed to a cup of chocolate (by Mme La Fayette), eel-pie (by Dangeau) and oysters, raw, by Liselotte. Queen Christine of Sweden was thought to have been poisoned in Rome. 'Really,' writes Liselotte, 'this fashion of poisoning is becoming too widespread. The poor Infanta of Portugal met her end in the same way.'

St Cloud 23 August 1691 If M de Louvois really was poisoned, I don't believe it was his sons' doing, however wicked they may be. I'm inclined to think that one of the doctors did it to please the old woman, who was furious when Louvois discussed her very freely with the King on the journey to Mons. The King doesn't seem to be particularly affected by Louvois' death. I haven't seen him so cheerful for a long time as he was a very few days afterwards.

I wish I could wait on you here just once before I die. I'm sure you would admire the new park; it's full of avenues and fountains, and we have the loveliest view in the world. Monsieur has levelled a hill behind the house, and made a parterre and an orangerie on the same level as his closet on one side and the gallery on the other. Frankly, I prefer our gardens to those at Versailles; they may be less magnificent, but they're closer at hand and have more shade.

St Cloud 1 November 1691 How can you say that to have the best

---

[1] A watering place in Normandy.

nature in the world is a fault? If that's a fault, what is virtue? It is not that we are tired of our good King James—only of his suffering.

Paris 27 December 1691 I can't imagine who could have told the Elector of Brandenburg that diamond aigrettes are worn on the hats here. Nobody, young or old, wears an aigrette, and I've never seen anyone wear one except a dancer from the Opéra. I can assure you that not a soul wears an aigrette on his hat, so I can't possibly send a pattern. But if the Elector wishes to wear diamonds on his hat, these are worn a great deal. Diamond buckles are fastened to the feather in front, and large diamonds, set in an *agrafe*, hold up the brim.

Versailles 10 January 1692 I can scarcely see out of my eyes, for I have been foolish enough to cry all night, but I can't let this Friday's post go without telling you of the horrible thing that happened yesterday. Monsieur came at about half-past three and said, 'Madame, I have a message for you from the King which will not please you overmuch. What he tells you is this: He, my son and I have agreed to the marriage of Mlle de Blois and my son, and you won't be such a fool as to oppose it. He is expecting your answer tonight.' You can imagine how this upset and troubled me. But I remembered the letter that you sent me through Harling after I first told you about this matter, when you said that if they were determined on the marriage I should have to submit; and when the King sent for me shortly after ten o'clock that night and asked me what I had to say, I answered, 'When your Majesty and Monsieur command me, what can I do but obey?'

The blow had fallen. D'Effiat and Lorraine had convinced Monsieur that his son would enjoy untold advantages by becoming the King's son-in-law, while the Abbé Dubois had worked on his seventeen-year-old charge. Liselotte found herself presented with a *fait accompli*, which so infuriated her that she resoundingly slapped her son's face in front of all the Court. Later that evening Saint-Simon observed her at the *appartement* pacing up and down the gallery, handkerchief in hand, looking like Ceres after the rape of Proserpine.

At dinner that night the three Orléans ate very little, even the gourmand Monsieur. Liselotte brusquely refused all the dishes that the King offered her with exquisite politeness. After the meal the King's bow to her was especially low, but he raised his eyes only to see her depart through the door, towards which she had manoeuvred herself by a pirouette. She never got over the horror of having a 'mouse-dropping' for a daughter-in-law, but she did, of course, have to come to terms with the inevitable.

Versailles 21 February 1692 You were misinformed when you were told that I behaved childishly at the wedding. I am, alas, no longer of an age for childish behaviour. I don't think I could be criticized for my conduct then. I put on the best possible face and affected a satisfaction which, frankly, I was far from feeling.

As for my daughter-in-law, I shall have no difficulty in getting on with her. We shan't spend enough time together to get on each other's nerves. Our ages are so very different that I can leave the task of keeping her amused to my daughter: as for me, saying *bonjour* and *bonsoir* in the mornings and evenings is soon done. As for my son's prospects, I only hope they will be as brilliant as you have been told.

Paris 5 March 1692 Thank God, the Duc du Maine's marriage is settled[1] and that weight is off my mind. I think the King's old drab must have heard what the people of Paris were saying, and it must have frightened her off. They said quite openly that it was a shame for the King to give his bastard daughter to a rightful prince of the line, but as my son would bestow his rank on his wife they would, reluctantly, let it pass. But should the old hag dare to give my daughter to the Duc du Maine they would throttle him before the wedding, and the old woman, whom they still call his governess, would be far from safe. As soon as she heard this, the other marriage was announced.

Versailles 12 April 1692 People talk of nothing but the King's journey to Flanders. All the ladies are going except for me; Monsieur vastly prefers the company of 2,000 pistoles to mine, and who can blame him? They are infinitely more use to him. Time was when I should have been annoyed to know that they were leaving me behind on my own to save money, but now I don't care, and it's all the same to me whether I'm here or in Flanders. My desire to be with those who make up our Court has completely disappeared.

St Cloud 31 May 1692 I almost begin to be afraid for my boy, for I hear that King William is on the march to Namur. My son is in M de Luxembourg's army, which is to attack it.

I hope the siege won't last too long. Already the town is in a state of

---

[1] The Duc du Maine married a daughter of the Prince de Condé.

panic. Over fifty ladies of quality, with their maids and children, have arrived on foot at the King's camp. They have been made prisoners of war and put in a convent. Either their opinion of the French soldiers was very high, or they were more afraid for their lives than for their honour and their jewels, for the poor ladies had all their diamonds with them. They were taken prisoner by soldiers out for loot. When they promised thalers all round they were taken, complete with bags and baggage, to the King's encampment, and not a penny was taken or a diamond touched.

Paris 28 June 1692 They say that the old *Rumpumpel*[1] is very bad-tempered in the town where her sweetheart has installed her. I hope it will make her ill. It is a sad thing for her not to have seen him for a whole month. I believe the joy will be great on both sides when the siege of Namur is over and they can be together again.

Although the great man and the whore lodge under the same roof when they are travelling, they don't sleep in the same room, and everything is conducted with much mystery, from which you see that he hasn't yet officially acknowledged her as his wife. But that doesn't prevent him from locking himself up with her and keeping the entire Court, the women as well as the men, waiting outside the door.

Paris 3 July 1692 We heard on Thursday that the citadel of Namur was won. On that day, when I was driving to the Arsenal to see some pretty Indian things in a little house there, my ladies called from the carriage to some of the tradespeople that Namur was taken. The *canaille*, imagining that I was driving about expressly to announce this news, crowded round my coach and cried, 'Vive le roi et Madame!'

St Cloud 7 August 1692 I must tell you of the dreadful fright I had last Monday night. Thank God, all ended happily. At midnight, when I was undressed and ready for bed, I suddenly heard Monsieur's voice in my antechamber. I knew he had gone to bed in his own rooms, and realized immediately that something had happened. I jumped out of bed and rushed to Monsieur to see what it was. He was holding an open letter in his hand and said, 'Don't be alarmed, Madame, your son is wounded, but only slightly. There has been a great battle in Flanders,[2]

---

[1] Mme de Maintenon. The word may have been derived from the French *ripopée*, the term for the useless solids left in the grape-press when all the liquid has been extracted.

[2] The Battle of Steenkirk.

the King's infantry has beaten that of the Prince of Orange, but there are no details yet.' You can imagine how frightened I was. I stayed on my balcony until three o'clock in the morning on the look-out for a courier from my son. Messengers arrived every half-hour. One brought news of the Marquis de Belfont's death, another reported that M de Luxembourg[1] had been mortally wounded. His mother, who happened to be staying here, and his mother-in-law, Mme de Ventadour, who loves him like her own son, began to weep. As their rooms were below mine, I could hear them crying. As well as feeling sorry for them, I thought how I might be getting similar news of my own son at any moment, and spent the whole night dreading it. I didn't hear any more until after dinner on the following day. M de Labertière, who used to be my son's under-governor, arrived and told us that my son had been hit twice.[2] The first shot had torn the shoulders of his coat without, thank God, touching him, the second shot hit him in the arm. He extracted the bullet himself, and as soon as he had been bandaged he returned to the fighting and stayed until it was all over.

I have been as polite as possible to the old Rumpumpel, who came to call on me, and whenever I see her I shall be as courteous as I can. But more than that is impossible. I simply cannot bring myself to wait in her antechamber as the others do, and never shall unless expressly commanded to do so by Monsieur or the King.

As for my son's wife, I can't complain about her, but I shall never grow fond of her as long as I live. She is the most disagreeable person in the world, with her crooked figure and her ugly face, though she considers herself a raving beauty and is forever fussing about her appearance and covering herself with *mouches*.

When I see all this and consider that she is nothing but a mouse-dropping, I confess that I often find it hard to endure and have some difficulty in not showing it.

St Cloud 14 August 1692 I am trying to find out how old the great man's whore is. Some people who think they are in the know say she is fifty-six, others make her sixty, but, alas, no older. Recently, when she was ill and frightened of dying, although she was in no danger at all, she had prayers for her recovery said in all the churches. But she was not

[1] This was a false report. The Duc de Luxembourg did not die until 1695.
[2] Going to the wars with their charges must have been an occupational risk for the tutors of important young persons. Dubois also accompanied Chartres on many of his campaigns.

mentioned by name, only as a person of quality important to the state, of which I am not so convinced.

Versailles 7 December 1692 Monsieur's new apartments are certainly very fine. In the closet at the end he has hung three pictures that are no strangers to you: they all came from Heidelberg. There is the death of the Virgin surrounded by the Apostles, the painting of Samson and the Philistines, and the picture of Prometheus with the vultures feeding off his liver. They are framed in gilt between the windows, and all the gilt, the mirrors and the pictures look very well together. There are five crystal chandeliers. When the candles are lit in the evening, everything looks very brilliant and beautiful. Monsieur uses this room for gambling. I wish you were here to see it—I shouldn't be in such a hurry to get back to my own apartments then.

Versailles 1 January 1693 I can't resist telling you of a splendid conversation I had with Monsieur. I hope it will amuse you as much as it did my two children. There were just the four of us in my apartments after supper: Monsieur, me, my son and my daughter. Monsieur, who didn't consider us fine enough company to trouble himself by talking, after a long silence let off a great long fart (by your leave, by your leave). He turned to me and said, 'What was that, Madame?' I turned my behind in his direction, let off in the same tone and said, 'That, Monsieur'. My son said, 'If it comes to that, I can do as well as Monsieur and Madame', and let off a good one, too. Then we all laughed and left the room. These are, as you see, princely conversations, and should anyone still be sufficiently inquisitive to open my letters to you, I offer the first one who does so this incense for the New Year.

Versailles 18 January 1693 I'm glad that our cracking conversation made you laugh. My son has so much wind that he can produce any kind of note, which is why he now plays the flute. I think that if he held it against his behind instead of his mouth, it would sound equally musical.

Paris 28 March 1693 There is one remedy for a bloodshot eye which can never do any damage: it is to melt some sugar-candy in a little white rosewater. When that is put into the eye, it will clear up in a few days.

The great man doesn't seem to care in the least about losing his teeth. It was his own fault, he had them all pulled out one after the other. Now he is the first to joke about having no teeth.

Versailles 28 June 1693 I don't know what took the King to Flanders, still less what brought him back, but that he has come back now I know very well indeed. He is much friendlier to me than he was before he went, though I can't think why. Mme de Chartres, Mme la Duchesse and the Princesse de Conti have all returned pregnant from their journey, so the King can't say it was a fruitless expedition.

Monsieur is bored to death at Vitry. As he was in his youth so is he now, and this winter alone he bought 200,000 guilders' worth of commissions in the guards-regiment for the young men who have amused him. For this no expense is spared, and that is the worst of it, otherwise I should hardly care.

Colombe 23 August 1693 War is an ugly thing. Those who are praised today may be taken off by a musket-ball to-morrow. I feel very frightened; the two armies are so close that I'm afraid they'll engage any time now. I hope you are right when you say that no harm comes to those whom God protects, but He hasn't sent me any promissory notes or letters to say that He will look after my son or anyone else dear to me, and I can't help worrying. I do thank you for your concern about my son. He has led five charges of the cavalry of which he is the general. He was in the thick of the firing for two hours, it's a wonder he is still alive. If my son, at his age, didn't go to war every year, he would be utterly despised, and no one here would look at him.

Fontainebleau 10 October 1693 The old whore is a false and wicked old devil, and it isn't my fault that she hates me so bitterly. I have done all I can to get into her good books. She is making the King cruel, which is quite contrary to his nature. In the past, he used to seem put out when his soldiers were looting, but now he admits, quite openly, that he himself orders the pillaging and sacking. She has made him so tyrannical and hard-hearted that he has no pity left.

Versailles 26 November 1693 My smallpox[1] left their mark but didn't alter my appearance, much to everyone's surprise. The older I grow the uglier I expect I shall be, but my humour and character can never change. The reason they hate me here is that they think I don't approve of their influence on the great man. Since I am well known for being

[1] Liselotte had contracted this disease during her early years in France.

outspoken, and the only person capable of making him see the great wrong he is doing himself through being overfond, I have to be kept well away from him.

FRAU VON HARLING

Versailles 16 December 1693   To-morrow or the day after I expect to be a grandmother. My son's wife is about to go into labour. When I write to *ma tante* to-morrow, my dear Frau von Harling may be able to learn if she has produced a 'he' or a 'she'. It's all the same to me, frankly I find it impossible to take an interest either way.

SOPHIE

Paris 28 March 1694   There can be no uglier, redder hands than mine in the whole world. 'Kiss your hand' must have come up as a compliment since I left Germany; it was hardly ever used in my day.[1] The report about me from Berlin is wrong. I have never worn a *manteau* in my life. I didn't wear black velvet at the ball, but the black cloth dress I wear every day. I wasn't dressed up at all, and never wear topazes. Monsieur no longer owns any; he gave the *parure* he used to have to the Queen of Spain.

Versailles 30 May 1694   If peace doesn't come soon it will go miserably here. Already conditions are indescribable, and not to be believed unless one sees them for oneself. I really think all that scorching and burning must have brought us bad luck, and that is why it is impossible to profit from all the battles that have been won and the cities that have been conquered. You hit the nail on the head when you compare the state of things here to cancer.

Dogs are the best people I have come across in France. I never have less than four about me.

Liselotte was surrounded by pets, including flocks of canaries and some parrots. 'I don't find that parrots smell, and I have any dogs' messes cleared away at once.' Her dogs were usually little French spaniels. They were with her all day, and slept on her bed at night. 'But,' she sadly observed, 'while a nice little dog can be a distraction, it can never be a comfort.'

[1] However, Monsieur often said, '*Je vous baise les mains*', chiefly when he had something disagreeable to add.

Versailles 6 June 1694 A little while ago I learnt that I have been reported to M le Reynie[1] by my coachman, who alleged that I held the state in contempt, wrote to Germany about everything I heard, and was planning to make my escape. I asked Wendt to tackle him and find out why he had done such a thing. He said that his confessor had ordered him to do it, for there was a feeling that I was still a Huguenot. Immediately afterwards the fellow ran away.

Versailles 16 December 1694 *Salut*, sermon and Mass may have their point so far as the next world is concerned, but for this one they are bitterly dreary. If by experiencing little joy and great tribulation one earns the right to go to heaven, my earnings should be enough to make me a great saint.

If the rumours are to be believed, our tedium will become greater still, because we hear that all operas and plays are to be abolished. The Sorbonne has instructions to take the matter in hand. What seems so astonishing to me is that they concentrate on such innocent things while all the vices are in full swing. No one says a single word against poisoning, violence and that horrible sodomy; all the clergy preach against the poor theatre, which does nobody any harm, and where vice is punished and virtue rewarded. It makes me furious.

Versailles 19 December 1694 I see that you like wearing heavy clothes as little as I do. When I order anything new I always ask for it to be kept light. There is no pleasure in walking when one is heavily dressed. You could afford to wear heavy clothes more easily than I can because you are slim, but I, with my large hips and (by your leave) larger behind, have enough of a job to carry myself about. Velvet trimmed with gold must be very heavy. I wear my velvet plain, but then they will give one trimmed underskirts, which often weigh far too much.

Paris 23 December 1694 Thank the Lord, the theatre is to stay. This greatly annoys the great man's old hag, as she was responsible for the proposed ban. But the clergy may shout against it from their pulpits as much as they like; as long as there are plays, I shall continue to go to see them. When there was a sermon against the theatre a fortnight ago and the preacher said that it inflamed the passions, the King turned to me and remarked, 'He doesn't mean me—I don't go to the theatre any longer. He means all of you who love it and do.' I said, 'I may enjoy the theatre, but M d'Agen isn't referring to me—he is speaking of the

[1] Nicolas Gabriel de la Reynie, minister of police.

people whose passions are aroused there, and I only go to be entertained. That is no sin.' The King was as quiet as a mouse, then.

> The Archbishop of Paris had warned that closing the theatre would drive the young people of Paris to more obnoxious vices. But since the clergy 'continued to denounce the theatre so violently,' says Liselotte, 'there are fewer actors to be found than ever. The poor devils expect to be sent packing from one moment to the next, and won't apply themselves to their trade, except for those in the King's troupe.'

Versailles 16 January 1695 I can't spend two hours in Paris without getting a headache and a scratchy feeling in my throat that makes me cough. Nor do I get much sleep, for the kitchens are right under my rooms. And then I can't hunt there, or enjoy the plays. To begin with, you have to drive out to get to the theatre, and, having arrived, you can't enjoy the performance because the stage is full of spectators who stand pêle-mêle with the actors. It's very annoying.

Then there is nothing more boring than the evenings in Paris. Monsieur plays *lansquenet* at a big table. I'm not allowed to watch, or show myself anywhere near the game, as he is superstitious and feels that the sight of me would bring him bad luck. Nevertheless, he insists on my being in the room, and I have the job of amusing all the old women who don't play.

Here, on the other hand, I am nice and comfortable. If the weather permits, I hunt; if there is a play, I only have to go down a few steps and there I am in the auditorium. There are no spectators on the stage, I see the play *dans son lustre*, and it doesn't cost me anything. If there is an *appartement* I listen to the music, and don't have to talk to old ladies afterwards as I do in Paris.

Versailles 6 February 1695 Two days ago I heard of another mean, spiteful thing the old whore has done. Two years ago the Dauphin wanted to marry my daughter, and mentioned this to the old Kunkunkel. She made no objection, for fear that, if she did, he would be more likely to tell the King of his intentions: instead she sent for the Princesse de Conti and her confidante Mlle de Choin.[1] She ordered them both not to give the Dauphin a minute's peace until he promised to dismiss any such idea entirely from his mind. The two of them gave him no rest for two whole months, until he gave them his promise. And he has

---

[1] Marie Emilie Jolie de Choin, the Dauphin's mistress.

kept it, too. So you see how much I am in debt to this old witch. She not only bribed my son to marry badly, she also ruined my daughter's chances. I really have no reason to spare her feelings, and if she should open this letter she will find nothing in it but the truth, and I don't care anyway, she can do nothing worse than she has done already, and I hope that for this she will go to hell, and be conducted there by the Father, the Son and the Holy Ghost.

Versailles 13 February 1695 You would never believe how vulgar and ill-mannered the French have become in the course of the last twelve or thirteen years. You won't find two young people of quality who know how to be polite in word or deed. There are two reasons for this: the piety prevailing at Court, and the excesses amongst the men. For one thing, it is no longer seemly for men and women to be seen speaking together; for another, men no longer wish to please anyone but each other, and the more debauched and impertinent they are, the more they are admired.

It may be a great honour to sit next to the King in church, but I would gladly relinquish it because His Majesty won't let me sleep. As soon as I doze off he nudges me with his elbow and wakes me up again, so that I am neither wholly asleep nor wholly awake. It gives me a headache.

> The next letter is addressed to the Raugravine Luise von Degenfeld, the eldest of Liselotte's half-sisters. She was a pious spinster, given to good works and fond of sermons, but this did nothing to diminish the affection between the two women. Liselotte regularly corresponded with her, covering much the same ground as when she wrote to Sophie. After the Electress's death Luise became the chief recipient of Liselotte's letters.

LUISE
Paris 14 May 1695 Dancing must be out of fashion everywhere. Here at parties people do nothing but play *lansquenet*, that is the game chiefly *en vogue* at the moment. Even the young people don't dance any more. I do neither the one nor the other. I am much too old to dance, and I don't gamble for two very good reasons: I haven't the money, and I don't enjoy it. The stakes are enormously high, and people behave like lunatics when they play. One will bawl, another bang the table so that the room shakes, a third blaspheme to make your hair stand on end—in short, they are like desperate madmen, it is frightening just to look at them.

Lenor[1] is here with me, and we talk about old times all day long. It is difficult to enjoy the fine weather here in town. I drive out whenever I can, and have been staghunting twice. You may think I am too old to hunt; if so, you are quite right. But I much prefer being ridiculous to being ill, and there is nothing better for the pain in my spleen than really hard exercise.

SOPHIE

Paris 15 May 1695   There is more shade in the gardens now; the trees have shot up since you were here, and it is very pleasant.[2] But it is impossible to enjoy walking here, there are always so many people about. You can't take a step without being watched from a hundred windows.

If it is true that one can become a virgin again after years and years of sleeping alone, I must certainly be one now, for it is seventeen years since Monsieur and I have slept together. But I wouldn't like to fall into the hands of the Tartars to have the point proved.[3]

St Cloud 15 September 1695   What happened at St Cyr was much worse and rather funnier: some of the young ladies there had fallen in love with one another; they were caught committing all sorts of indecencies. Mme de Maintenon is supposed to have cried her eyes out. She had all the relics put on display to drive out the devils of lechery. Also, she sent for a priest to preach against lewdness, but he talked about such hideous things that none of the modest ladies could bear to listen; they all left the church, but the culprits were overcome by uncontrollable fits of the giggles.

Fontainebleau 12 October 1695   King William is spoken of in quite a different tone now. Everywhere you hear remarks like, 'A great man, as great a king as he deserves to be', and so on. You are right when you say that the successful ones get all the admiration.

You made me laugh by what you said about the *château de derrière*. It is true that people here think of King William as belonging to that brotherhood, but they say he is less taken up with it now.

[1] Leonore von Rathsamshausen, a childhood friend and a popular, regular visitor at Court.
[2] The gardens of the Palais-Royal.
[3] A reference to reports from the Turkish wars, where the Tartars were said to rape old women in preference to young ones.

William III had captured the citadel of Namur in September—the success to which Liselotte refers.

His wife, Queen Mary, had died in March of that year. James II showed no signs of grief at his daughter's death, and particularly requested that no mourning should be worn by the French Court. This was considered very petty of him, and Liselotte could not understand how any man could so completely forget his own child. William, on the other hand, showed a depth of grief which amazed her, considering the rumours about where his inclinations lay.

LUISE

Versailles 11 December 1695 We don't dress our hair so very high now, still high but not so high as before. The headdresses are now worn bent forward and not straight up as they used to be. It isn't true that a tax has been put on the coiffures, someone must have invented that tale as a joke.

Liselotte finds this fashion rather inconvenient, for as soon as two women stand close to each other their headdresses catch and they can't disentangle themselves without calling a third person to their aid. She and her daughter keep getting entangled, and have many a good laugh before they are set free again. In 1716 she tells Caroline of Wales that the King had hated exaggerated headdresses, and how annoyed he was when he talked himself hoarse saying the coiffures were too high, and in spite of his royal authority no one showed the least inclination to humour him. But then some nonentity arrived from England, a woman no one had ever heard of (Saint-Simon says it was the Duchess of Shrewsbury), who wore her hair dressed quite flat, and overnight all the French princesses went from one extreme to the other.

SOPHIE

Versailles 26 February 1696 If you were a Catholic and obliged to go to church, you would find it the most tedious thing in the world, for there is never the slightest variation. You never hear anything sung but the vowels, only a-a-a-a-e-e-e-e-o-o-o-o-i-i-i-i, it drives one out of one's mind from sheer impatience. Eating after the midnight Mass is a Catholic custom, but when I've been to three Masses, lasting from ten o'clock in the evening until one o'clock in the morning, I'm so tired from kneeling that I would rather go to bed than eat. The ladies here think they need to get drunk in order to enjoy themselves.

Marly 7 March 1696   King James went to Calais the day before yesterday to embark for England with an army. What will come of this,
time alone will tell.

Mme de Klenck[1] came to say goodbye to me yesterday. She is leaving
to-morrow, or Saturday at the latest. This gives me a chance to tell my
dearest *tante* how things here are going. I will start with Monsieur. He
has only one interest: his young men, with whom he spends entire
nights eating and drinking. He gives them incredible amounts of
money, no expense is too great for them. In the meantime, the children
and I hardly have the barest necessities. When I need shifts or sheets, I
have to beg for them for a year and a day, while he gives ten thousand
thalers to La Carte[2] to buy linen in Flanders. As he realizes that I know
quite well where all the money is going, he is afraid that I may tell the
King, who might then send the boys away. Whatever I may say or do
to make him understand that I don't care what kind of life he leads, he
refuses to believe me, and every day he gets me into fresh trouble with
the King. Whenever there is an unpleasant rumour Monsieur tells the
King that it comes from me, and kindly adds a few lies. He himself
often admits saying all these nasty things about me. He's forever setting
my own children against me. So that my son shan't notice how little
is done for him, Monsieur encourages him in his debauches, in spite of
the fact that this makes the King angry. When I advise my son to behave himself in order to please the King, Monsieur just laughs and
takes my son off to Paris, where they lead such a life that it is a scandal.
My son's tendencies are good, and something could be made of him if
only Monsieur didn't corrupt him.

Thank heaven, he doesn't involve my daughter in any debauches.
In fact, the girl hasn't the slightest tendency toward *galanterie*. Monsieur,
however, won't let me take charge of her and surrounds her with such
riffraff that it is a miracle she hasn't gone to the bad. He talks her into
such a hatred of everything German that, since I am a German, she can
hardly bear to be in my company.

My son's wife is a beastly creature, drunk as drunk three or four
times a week. She has no affection for me. When we are together
anywhere I can't get a word out of her. It is all the Maintenon's fault.

For the rest, the King prefers all his bastard-daughters to me. Every
evening I have to watch Mme de Chartres disappear into the King's
closet, while the door is shut in front of my nose. I have told Monsieur
what I think of it, but he is well pleased with this state of affairs.

[1] The wife of the Hanoverian Chancellor.
[2] One of the young men for whom Monsieur had bought a commission.

Monsieur had all the silver from the Palatinate melted down and sold. The money has been given to his young men. New ones appear every day. If, God forbid, Monsieur were to die today I should, from to-morrow, be dependent on the King's charity for my daily bread. Monsieur openly declares, without making any attempt to keep it from my daughter or me, that he has no time to lose now that he is getting old. He intends to use his means without stint to amuse himself to the end, and those who survive him will have to look out for themselves. He says that he is more interested in himself than in his children or me.

Liselotte was particularly sad that her daughter had been given such an aversion for everything German, because it was still her dearest wish to see her marry into Germany. 'It is torture to me. As soon as you mention it to her, she bursts into tears.' In order that young Liselotte's likeness, at least, should be seen in Germany, Madame had commissioned a painter who had just finished a portrait of Monsieur. But when she sent for her daughter's picture the messenger returned empty-handed. He reported that the artist refused to start work: he hadn't yet been paid for painting Monsieur, and suspected that Madame wouldn't pay him either.

LUISE
Versailles 13 March 1696 My daughter, thank heaven, is in perfect health again, but she hasn't grown much fatter. She really has no need to grow any more, she is quite tall enough already, half a head taller than I am and not badly made. Between ourselves her face isn't bad, either. But my son is small, not good-looking, but not too bad so far as his figure goes.

I have now found another painter, and hope to send you, in time, the three portraits. The man who refused to do the painting was no more impertinent than any other Frenchman; impertinence is the height of fashion here.

SOPHIE
Marly 16 May 1696 When I return to St Cloud, I shall drink your health in Kräuterwein,[1] though at St Cloud we don't get drunk, we leave that to the mouse-droppings.

To my mind, the biggest proof of friendship is to let people live in peace. It is a great mistake to imagine that it is possible to possess another person's heart forever. I admit that it would be agreeable, but

[1] A white wine cup with herbs.

it cannot be. It would be idle to pretend that it could. What is very possible, though, is not to plague one's wife, not to slander her, not to make her disliked by all the world, not constantly to give her proof of one's inner aversion even when outwardly one puts a good face on it, and not always to make her do without even the barest necessities while giving to others in abundance, even using her own property for the purpose.

It is difficult to conceive how ignorant the great man is in matters of religion. In other subjects he is far from simple. It all comes from the fact that he has never read a word about religion, nor has he ever read the Bible, and now he believes whatever they choose to put into his head. When he had an irreligious mistress he wasn't pious either, but then he fell in love with one who talks of nothing but penitence, and he believes every word she says. Even when she is at odds with his confessor, he prefers her opinion to his. He never takes the trouble to find out for himself what is right and what is wrong.

The sausages will not, I fear, arrive as safely as the inkwell; they are far more tempting. I fear that they may be eaten by the *douane*. I should be sorry, for I'd rather eat them myself to your good health.

St Cloud 20 May 1696   I confess that I lose all patience when I hear our great man praised in church for the persecution of the Protestants. I can't bear to hear praised what is ill-done. On this point I have nothing to reproach myself with, I never praise what is not admirable.

Port Royal 15 July 1696   I hope there will soon be a general peace and my daughter may marry the Duc de Lorraine. As far as I can see, she will be happier with him than with the Roman king,[1] and I would say amen to the match.

Versailles 8 November 1696   I must tell you a little about the future Duchesse de Bourgogne,[2] who at last arrived at Fontainebleau on Monday. The King, Monseigneur, Monsieur and my son welcomed her at Montargis. I awaited her arrival in her apartments in Fontainebleau. When she arrived I really thought I should die of laughter: there was such a crush that poor Mme de Nemours and the Maréchale de la Motte were pushed the whole length of the room, so that they came at us backwards and finally fell on to Mme de Maintenon. If I hadn't

[1] The future Emperor Joseph I.
[2] Marie-Adelaide, Princess of Savoy, was Madame's step-grandchild. At the time of her arrival in Paris to marry the King's grandson she was eleven.

held her arm they would all have collapsed on top of one another like a pack of cards.

The princess is not exactly tall for her age. She has a nice little figure like a doll, lovely blonde hair and masses of it, black eyes and eyebrows; long, beautiful lashes, smooth skin, not very white; a little nose, neither pretty nor plain, a large mouth with thick lips: in short, the true Austrian mouth and chin. She moves well, her face has a pleasant expression and she is graceful in everything she does. She is serious for her age and astonishingly diplomatic. She makes little fuss of her grandfather, hardly looks at my son or me, but as soon as she sees Mme de Maintenon she smiles and goes up to her with open arms. You see how clever she is already.

Everyone is becoming a child again. The day before yesterday we were all playing blind man's buff with her—the Princesse de Harcourt, Mme Portchartain, M le Dauphin, Monsieur, the Prince and Princesse de Conti, Mme de Ventadour, two more of my ladies and me. Yesterday we played 'How do you like the company?' I wasn't at all sorry to tear about a little.

Paris 22 November 1696   The King can think of nothing but this child, and can't bear to be parted from her; he even sent for her while he was in Council. The girl is as artful as if she were thirty years old. There is an envoy here from her Court, her mother's first *écuyer*, whom she must know very well indeed. But she pretends she doesn't, hardly looks at him, and never speaks to him for fear the King might take offence and think she is still attached to her old country. I can't admire that, I think her good nature should prevent her from suppressing her feelings, and she ought not to be ashamed of loving her parents and her country. People who don't love those who brought them into the world are hardly likely to love strangers.

Paris 25 November 1696   You will have heard all about the reception of our little bride. She has been given the rank of Duchesse de Bourgogne, though she doesn't yet bear the name—she is just called *la princesse*. Since she will have to take precedence over me in the end, it hardly signifies whether it starts this year or next, and apart from precedence I have never had the slightest advantage out of being the first lady.

The King's passion for the Maintenon is quite incredible: the whole of Paris says that their marriage will be publicly announced as soon as the peace is made. The lady will then take her rank, and this is why I am very happy no longer to be the first at Court; at least I'll not have to present her chemise or gloves, and will have something decent preceding me.

I don't know if the future Duchesse de Bourgogne will be luckier than Mme la Dauphine, Mme la Grande Duchesse or I were. When we arrived, we were all thought marvellous in turn, but they soon tired of us.

However, says Liselotte, none of the three ladies ever had the advantage of the great man's interest and affection to the same degree, and the little princess's popularity might well turn out to be more lasting. 'What a calculating child she is, clearly very well-instructed by her father and quite unlike her mother, who was always so frank and open. You can see the child's intelligence in her eyes.' Though she is not as pretty as she seemed at first, Liselotte thinks her far less hideous than some people would have one believe.

Versailles 17 January 1697 I take care not to talk much with the princess. She dines with the King at Marly today, so you see how well she is being entertained. But she isn't allowed to amuse herself with anyone but the King and Mme de Maintenon. I expect that the plays which are performed for her at St Cyr[1] will make her so disgusted with any other kind that she won't be able to sit through them once she is grown-up. When she is alone with the King and Mme de Maintenon they allow her to do whatever she likes; she can behave just as she pleases.

Versailles 18 January 1697 Monsieur thinks only of what is best for his young men, and of nothing else. No one can be trusted, grooms and lackeys are master everywhere. Only last week, Monsieur gave away 100,000 francs. All his beautiful jewels and diamonds are being sold piece by piece.

My son isn't much better than his father, except that he gives everything he owns to his mistress.[2] He lets himself be entirely ruled by his valet, and I fear that his debauches will cost him his life. Monsieur won't speak to him about it; he doesn't want to raise the subject because of his own behaviour.

[1] Inevitably religious in character.
[2] La Florence, whom he shortly afterwards removed from the Opéra and installed in Paris in a smart house of her own.

Monsieur le Dauphin takes no interest in anything at all. He spends his entire time at the Princesse de Conti's. For all his laughing at her, he is ruled by her as surely as his father is ruled by Mme de Maintenon. He is in love with an actress[1] whom he brings out to Meudon for the night. During the day he looks on while work is being done in the garden. He takes his evening meal at four o'clock in the afternoon. He eats nothing at midday, but at four he sits down with all the gentlemen of his household, spends two hours at table, and that's all he does.

Versailles 2 May 1697 I am truly sorry to hear that you have nothing better to amuse yourself with than my old letters. While papa was still alive, you won't find anything but praise for Monsieur; I didn't want His Grace to find out the real state of affairs. When you were here, though, I didn't hide anything from you. I concealed the truth from the Elector because I heard as soon as I had gone that he was most distressed at my having left against my own wish, out of pure obedience to him and feeling quite certain that I could never be happy here. I hid all my troubles for as long as I could. In the end (though I don't know how) the Elector learned the truth and gave me a good scolding for not having told him all about it in the first place. But when I gave him the reason he accepted my apology.

We used to have a man here called Dalancé. He made microscopes and once, in a drop of water on the point of a knife, he showed me a whole oceanful of sole. There were long serpents in the vinegar. It seems to me that we know both too much and too little for our happiness: enough to want to know more, but too little to do us any good.

Liselotte also accurately observed that the skins of eels were thinner than those of other creatures, as with the aid of a lens she was able to watch the circulation of their blood. 'A fine art has been invented by means of those glasses,' she wrote later in the month. 'I think it will make the doctors cleverer.' Many years later she asked her sister Luise to find out if M Hartsoeker, the distinguished Dutch scientist, famous for his work on optical instruments, ever sold any of his glasses 'that make a louse look so big', and fondly remembers the many happy hours spent examining moths at various stages of their development in her old sables and the upholstery of her carriage.

[1] Known as La Raisin. When she visited Meudon on fast-days she was given nothing but a meagre salad and some bread fried in oil because the Dauphin, considering it a mortal offence to eat meat on fast-days, 'intended to commit only one sin, not two'.

St Cloud 16 May 1697 The day before yesterday I went to Paris, where the poor child, Mlle de Chartres,[1] was lying deathly ill. Her end was expected at any moment. I felt greatly distressed, but when I saw that her mother, without shedding a single tear, allowed herself to be served with a collation consisting of four *entrées*, and that her grandfather, thinking only of gambling, took himself to Seissac[2] for the purpose, I considered it foolish to grieve alone. Since I found the spectacle harrowing to watch, I climbed into my coach and returned here.

Port Royal 19 May 1697 The Tsar of Muscovy[3] must be a likeable fellow, though I fear that we shan't see him here. I've been told that the Muscovite envoys won't come to France, as those who were here ten or twelve years ago behaved in such an extraordinary fashion that the King had them thrown out. This gentleman, however, seems so good-humoured that I'm sure he can't be as bad as the others, who did nothing but steal, drink, fight and misbehave themselves with animals. Still, this Tsar can't be so very noble after all, if he is so familiar with the tradespeople.

St Cloud 9 June 1697 Isn't it an amazing idea of the Tsar's to leave his realm and go flitting about the world? If German emperors or French kings did such a thing, people would think their heads had been turned through reading too many romances.

I wish the Tsar would take a fancy to see France, too. I should so much like to see him and his Circassian prince. Thank you for the stories about him. You can't imagine how useful they have been. I have to see a good many people nowadays, and when I run out of conversation I tell them about the Tsar. Then they listen to me as if I were an oracle, and leave well satisfied with their visit.

LUISE
St Cloud 21 June 1697 I couldn't answer your letter of a fortnight ago until now, because I wasn't skilful enough in writing with my left

[1] Mlle de Chartres, Madame's eldest granddaughter, pulled through this illness owing to the treatment prescribed by her father after the doctors had despaired of her life. He nursed her devotedly through this and a subsequent disease, and it has been suggested that the inordinate attachment between father and daughter which was to become such a scandal had its roots in the fact that he twice saved her life.

[2] A famous Parisian gambler.

[3] Peter the Great, on a working visit to Western Europe.

hand, and dictating to Fräulein von Rathsamshausen was not much use, her spelling is so dreadful. Perhaps you will say, dear Luise, that this lady's hand couldn't be harder to read than my left-handed scrawl, and that may well be so, though all in all I think you will prefer to puzzle out my own writing to anyone else's, and I'll tell you myself what happened.

Four weeks ago I was hunting wolves with M le Dauphin. It had been raining and the ground was very slippery. We had been searching for two hours, found nothing, and were on the point of going to another part of the forest. We were walking quite slowly, when suddenly someone passed me at a gallop. This gave my horse the idea of galloping too, he reared, slipped on the wet grass and fell on his side, and my elbow landed on a stone which dislocated the big bone in my arm.

They looked for the King's surgeon, but he was nowhere to be found. His horse had lost a shoe, and he had gone on to a village to have it seen to. Then a peasant who happened to be passing told us that a very clever barber lived less than two miles away, who was accustomed to setting arms and legs every day. When I heard how experienced he was, I got into my calèche to go to him. On the way there I was in great pain, but as soon as he had set my arm I felt no discomfort at all, and came back here at a trot.

The following day, though, Monsieur arrived with surgeons who wanted to look at my arm. (I think their interest was mixed with envy because the peasant had done so well.) They pretended that gangrene would set in unless they examined it straight away, and took off the bandage, which shouldn't have been touched for another nine days. They moved the arm about and bandaged it up again so badly that everything had to be redone the next day. The result is that my arm is now so swollen that I can't either close my hand or raise it to my mouth. I could do all this quite comfortably before those damned surgeons took the first dressing off. Yesterday the swelling started to go down a little, but if they had only left the barber alone I should have been quite cured by now. As it is, I shall be in the doctors' hands for at least another month.

SOPHIE
St Cloud 27 June 1697 Entertaining the Tsar seems to be a very expensive pleasure for the Elector of Brandenburg; a hundred thousand thalers for presents alone is strong stuff. Blowing one's nose with one's hand must be the height of fashion in Moscow if the Tsar himself goes

in for it. It must save handkerchiefs. Thank you for the Tsar's portrait. It served for two evenings' conversation and *divertissement*. The gentleman is not ugly, but he should have his scaramouche-moustache taken off. He would be much handsomer then.

St Cloud 8 August 1697   All Paris, the army and the Court say that King William is considering my daughter, but I can't believe it. Even if it were true, Mme Whore would never permit it. I have never received anything but ill from that one, and I don't see her disposed to do anything to please me now. I can't imagine he has any desire to re-marry, and even if he did I don't think Parliament would allow him to take a Frenchwoman and a Catholic, so I have no illusions.

I never thought there would be much difficulty in having King William recognized here, it is no more than his good right. Almost everyone has spoken of him as *le roi Guillaume*[1] for a long time now.

St Cloud 15 August 1697   Last Monday I went to dine with *ma tante* at Maubuisson. We built castles in the air: I wished that my daughter could become Queen of England, then King William could take her with him to The Hague, I would meet you there, and stay with you forever. I know quite well that nothing can ever come of it, but it gives me such pleasure to speak of it as if it might all come true. My aunt had to warn me not to shock the nuns, who were under the impression that I had come to Maubuisson to find comfort because my daughter was to marry a Huguenot.[2]

St Cloud 18 August 1697   It must have seemed like a dream, eating at the same table as the great Tsar. It sounds just like a romance to me, and to make it quite perfect he should have fallen in love with the Electress of Brandenburg. I hope that the dancing amused you a little. If I had danced with the ambassador, it would have been a very funny sight: I look like a pagoda with clothes on. With my thick hips, belly and behind (by your leave, by your leave), my broad shoulders, large face and double-chin I am so exactly like a pagoda that I have to laugh whenever I happen to pass a looking-glass.

Marly 22 August 1697   Russian women can't be wearing stays, if these people have never come across whalebone before.

[1] One of the conditions of the peace treaty of Ryswick, which was then being negotiated, was the recognition of William III by France.
[2] Religious considerations quite apart, William III had no intention of remarrying.

Madame wearing her hair dressed high, by Nicolas de Largillière.

Louis XIV, by Hyacinthe Rigaud.

It was after dancing with the well-laced ladies of the Court of Branden-burg that the Tsar remarked that 'the German ladies have devilish hard bones'.

St Cloud 15 September 1697 The great man and his whore are really vile to my girl. You know that we had a chamberlain from the Viennese Court here. He had been given a passport and was allowed to come and go as he liked. Among other things, he bought a good many fine clothes for the imperial princesses and his master, but the moment after he had ordered a portrait of my daughter he was turfed out of bed and thrown into prison, where he was kept for a full twenty-four hours in spite of the envoy of Parma's protests. As soon as he was released he was sent back to Austria, so we didn't get a chance to have the portrait painted. There you see the whore's duplicity; she was never more amiable to me than when she played this trick on my daughter.

Fontainebleau 9 October 1697 I am afraid my daughter will have to take the Duc de Lorraine after all. I would prefer to see her marry the Roman King, because Lorraine is so very much under the thumb of the French. The only good thing about it is that she will neither remain an old maid nor be made to marry the bastard.[1]

LUISE
Paris 10 November 1697 My arm is better now, for I can move it again, though my shoulder still acts like a barometer and aches when-ever it rains.

You will have heard that the peace with the Empire has been con-cluded.[2] There seems to be a strange curse on this peace; the news of it was received without any joy although everyone has wanted it for so long. Even the people of Paris weren't pleased, they had almost to be forced to rejoice.

Now we are at peace, there is a chance that we might see each other again. If the rumours of the past few months are true and my daughter is really to become the Duchesse de Lorraine, we could easily arrange a rendez-vous.

Do tell me, dear Luise, what the Duc de Lorraine looks like and what manner of man he is. Though you remark that he danced a lot, you don't say whether he danced well or if his bearing was good. The

[1] The Comte de Toulouse had been mentioned in this connection for the last few years.
[2] The Treaty of Ryswick.

F

gentleman who suggested blind-man's buff cannot, I'm sure, be one of those wicked fellows. He must be one of our sort, for these were the sort of games we used to play in our day. Some adventures are amusing whether or not one knows the people concerned, so keep on writing the news.

SOPHIE

Paris 22 December 1697 The envoy from Lorraine has come. He goes to Versailles today, and M le Grand[1] tells me that he has orders to ask for my daughter's hand.

It is a very middling match, not grand enough to warrant great rejoicing, on the other hand not so unreasonable as to cause any real displeasure. As I say, it seems middling to me. I'm glad, though, that we have given the little stinker[2] the slip. According to Luise, the Duc de Lorraine is not handsome, but short and stout with a typical Austrian mouth.

Versailles 2 February 1698 I'm sure the insane life my son leads will soon be the death of him, tearing about all night and never any sleep until eight o'clock in the morning. He often looks as though he's been dragged out of the grave. I'm certain it will kill him in the end, but his father refuses to speak to him about it. Nothing I could say would do any good, so I shan't pursue the subject except to add that it is a shame to see him so steeped in debauchery. Had he been brought up to something better and more worthwhile, he would be quite a different person. He doesn't lack intelligence, knows a great deal and from early childhood has inclined to all that is good and noble. However, since he has become his own master so many low fellows have attached themselves to him, and introduced him to such very vulgar whores (by your leave), that his face and his character are quite changed, and he is hardly recognizable any longer.

Leading the sort of life he does, he's no longer interested in anything at all; even his love of music, which used to be such a passion, has quite disappeared. In short, they have made him utterly insufferable.

Port Royal 25 September 1698 We go to Fontainebleau for my daughter's betrothal on the 2nd, the ceremony will take place on the 12th, and the nuptials on the 13th.

[1] Louis de Lorraine, of the Guise family, a secondary branch of the House of Lorraine.
[2] The Comte de Toulouse.

My daughter will receive nine times a hundred thousand francs from Monsieur and me, and twenty thousand thalers for her *toilette* from the King, who is also giving her a *parure* of diamonds. And Monsieur is giving her a lot of jewellery. All in all it will add up to sixteen, almost seventeen, times a hundred thousand francs.

Paris 1 October 1698 The Duke's wedding present to my daughter was delivered yesterday. It is extremely beautiful, and consists of diamond eardrops which could not be lovelier; a string of pearls, not particularly large but of excellent whiteness and perfectly round and even; two bracelets of five rows of pearls a little larger than green sugar peas; another diamond bracelet, quite perfect; and two rings. My daughter's pleasure is indescribable. Following the custom here, all her clothes are displayed in Monsieur's gallery.

Monsieur was in his element, and enjoyed showing the trousseau to visitors. There were fifteen dresses—two of them so heavy that Liselotte thought her daughter would never be able to wear them—all splendidly embroidered. One of them, black velvet bordered by golden garlands over a foot deep and worn over an underskirt of cloth of silver decorated with two sorts of gold, was so delicately embroidered that it looked as though it had been worked by a goldsmith.

The linen was trimmed with *pointe de Venise*, embroidered with the bride's and her Duke's *chiffre* surmounted by crowns. There was a large chest entirely filled with ribbons, and a dressing-set in silver-gilt, made by the famous Losné, from the King, who also presented his niece with a bed, six armchairs and twenty-four chairs.

Paris 15 October 1698 However my daughter's marriage may turn out, it certainly began sadly enough. When they were married, everyone in the chapel wept. Our King, the King and Queen of England, all the princesses, the clerics and the courtiers, even the soldiers and the Swiss guards, the ambassadors and the ordinary people —all of them wept bitterly. Only the Dauphin didn't shed a single tear, he behaved as though he was at an entertainment. The Duchesse de Bourgogne showed at last that she has a good heart. She couldn't eat a thing, and went on weeping bitterly after she had said goodbye to her aunt.

I don't think the Duc de Lorraine will consider my daughter ill-provided for; she has twenty thousand crowns' worth of linen, and great quantities of laces and embroidery. It is all very handsome, and fills four huge chests.

Fontainebleau 22 October 1698 My goodness, how badly they are
bringing up the Duchesse de Bourgogne.[1] I feel quite sorry for her.
She is allowed to do whatever she likes. In the middle of dinner she
starts to sing, dances about on her chair, and pretends to salute people.
She pulls frightful faces, tears dishes of chickens and partridge apart
with her hands, sticks her fingers into the sauces, in short, no one could
be naughtier. And the people standing behind her chair cry, 'Oh, how
graceful she is, how pretty!' She treats her father-in-law without any
respect and calls him '*tu*', which enchants him and makes him think he
is in favour. She is said to be even more familiar with the King.

Fontainebleau 25 October 1698 My daughter's journey is progressing
happily. I had a letter from her today which she wrote in Châlons. It
will be a hard day for her today, because this is where she officially
leaves the King's house and becomes a wife in earnest. She and her
husband are to sleep together tonight. That will seem very peculiar to
her. Although my daughter finds her Duke attractive, she says she is
feeling very apprehensive at his coming to collect her; she says she's so
beside herself with fear about the night that she is all of a tremble and
hardly knows what she is saying. She may not be all that wrong, one
hears such strange reports of our son-in-law. Apparently once, when he
was taking a bath, the man who was washing him said, 'Would His
Grace move his arm so that I can wash His Grace?' It turned out that
it wasn't his arm that was in the way at all, but, by your leave, quite a
different thing. I am incredibly impatient to hear how the first night
passed.

Fontainebleau 5 November 1698 The Duc de Lorraine seems very
fond of my daughter, and if only their love lasts they should be happy
enough. '*Mais hélas, il n'est point d'éternelles amours*', as they say in
Clélie.[2]

Young Liselotte was very happy indeed, and remained in love with her
Duke all her life. Referring to the bridegroom's frequent and ardent
attentions to her daughter, Liselotte declares, 'I shall take more pleasure
in becoming a grandmother on this side than on the other. My son's

[1] The Duchesse de Bourgogne had been married to the King's grandson on December 7th of the previous year, shortly after her twelfth birthday. For the time being, however, the sixteen-year-old groom was under the King's strict instructions not to touch so much as her little finger.
[2] A novel by Mlle de Scudéry.

children' (another daughter had recently arrived) 'seem too much like
bastards to me.'

Paris 16 November 1698 My daughter has soon become used to her
new state, and it is reported from Nancy that the Duke is extraordinarily keen on married life. After the entry into the town, my
daughter was obliged to change her clothes because her dress was so
heavy that she couldn't stand up in it, and just as she had taken off her
skirts, along came the Duke and paid her one of his visits. She's quite
used to it by now, and doesn't dislike that business as much as I did.

It isn't at all surprising that Monsieur had the dressing-table things
melted down, for they were his own property. But one day, although I
implored him not to, he took all the silver that had come from Heidelberg,
as well as all the silver things that used to decorate my rooms and look so
pretty, and had them melted down too. He put the money into his own
pocket. He hasn't left me so much as one poor little box for my bits
and pieces.

Versailles 11 January 1699

> *In dulci jubilohoho*
> *nun singet und seid frohoho*
> *unsers Herzens Wohohonne*
> *liegt in praesipiohoho*
> *und leuchtet einst die Sohohonne*
> *matris in gremiohoho*
> *alpha es et ohoho*
> *alpha es et o.*

If you haven't sung this yourself, I'm sure it has been played to you on
the trumpets and cymbals, because today is your New Year's day. I
wish you all the joy and happiness that you could wish yourself.

The Raugravine Amalie Elisabeth von Degenfeld, whom Madame
called Ameliese, was another of Liselotte's half-sisters. Like her elder sister
Luise she never married, and the two ladies lived and travelled together.

AMELIESE
Marly 6 February 1699 I enjoy your letters very much. Do go on
writing like that, quite naturally and *sans façon*: I can't stand compliments. If only you could write something to make me laugh! Laughter

has become rare in my life during the last few years, I am quite getting out of the habit and my spleen is none the better for it. Do not think, dear Ameliese, that cleverness consists in being able to pay compliments. The silliest people in the world can memorize compliments and write them down, but to write well on ordinary subjects and to have a readable style is far rarer than you seem to think, and it is your great humility that is at fault if you think you don't write well.

Your life, as you describe it, sounds quite pleasant to me. Here one soon regrets frank speaking, and that is why I live in solitude.

LUISE

Versailles 3 April 1699   Hunting is not my favourite amusement, but the theatre is. I only go hunting now for the sake of my health, for without exercise my spleen aches quite dreadfully. I remember well that His Grace the Elector would never hear of us hunting, and I didn't even learn to ride until I came here. I must have had twenty-four or -five falls, but that has never frightened me off.

However much I may dislike the French marriage laws, I shall have to submit as I have been married according to them. I'll tell you something even worse, dear Luise: it may come about that, although I am credited with having a great deal of property, I may still be reduced to living on the King's charity, for if Monsieur squanders his fortune and mine and dies before me, I shall have no income from any source. His appanage[1] cannot come to me. One must be a bit of a philosopher, else I should live in constant anxiety and never know any peace at all.

St Cloud 23 June 1699   Nobody talks about anything but the Councillor's wife who had her husband murdered, and of her courage when she went to her death. But she suffered horribly, because the executioner struck five or six times before her head came off. There were such crowds of people anxious to watch the execution that windows were rented at fifty louis d'Or.

SOPHIE

St Cloud 25 June 1699   We have this moment returned from the most tedious devotions imaginable. We marched along, taking tiny steps, for two long hours on the hot pavement, kneeling every quarter-of-an hour for a quarter-of-an-hour. My knees are so bruised that they're black and blue, because every time I knelt down I landed on the buttons of my riding habit.

[1] The allowance made by the King to his brother and younger sons.

Marly 2 July 1699   Yesterday I called on all the favourites—first the Duchesse de Bourgogne and then the Maintenon, whom I found in royal state. She was sitting at table in a large armchair; M le Duc de Bourbon, his daughter and the others, who were eating with her, were on tabourets. They did me the honour of bringing me a tabouret too, but I assured them that I wasn't in the least tired. I had to bite my tongue to keep from laughing. How different from the time when the King came to ask me to let Mme de Scarron eat with me just for once, and then only to cut up the food for the Duc du Maine, who was still a child.

When the King walks in the gardens here, the lady sits in a chair mounted on four wheels, pulled by four men. His Majesty walks alongside like her lackey, and the others follow on. The Duchesse de Bourgogne walks in front, arm-in-arm with the Maintenon's niece, whom she calls 'sister'. It seems an upside-down world to me, and I don't like anything but the place. No one could deny that Marly is really beautiful, much lovelier than Versailles. The upkeep costs the King a good deal of money, it comes to 70,000 francs. There are fine marble statues everywhere, and more fountains than I can count.

AMELIESE
St Cloud 10 July 1699   I hope that you and Luise will enjoy yourselves in Schwalbach-Spa. It is a dear, happy place where people can live without restrictions and without being criticized. You couldn't find anywhere like it in France. Let the French ladies laugh at your innocent enjoyments if they have a mind to. They know nothing of real pleasure; you only have to see them at their twenty-four-hour-long gambling sessions to realize how desperate they are, like creatures possessed.

SOPHIE
Port Royal 19 July 1699   I asked Monsieur why I was only offered a tabouret at the Maintenon's. He says no one ever has a chair there because the King calls so often. What a splendid excuse for not allowing anybody to have one except the lady, who has one because of her health. In this way, nothing is said about her being queen or not, and at the same time she takes that rank.

St Cloud 24 July 1699   It is not a bad thing to be forced to take violent exercise occasionally, it shakes up the spleen, makes one sweat and prevents illness. It is impossible to get overheated on a rabbit-hunt. The little animals that are used for catching them are not weasels, they are bigger and browner and have more pointed faces. In French they are called *les furets*.

I can't eat rabbit. I much prefer English food to French. I have never been able to get used to French cooking, and can't touch *ragoût*, soup or *bouillon*. There isn't much that I can eat here, only roast mutton, roast chicken, roast veal, roast beef and salad. I once had plovers' eggs in Holland, but I ate so many that I was sick, and I've never been able to look at them since.

It seems to me that knowing about the winds and the stars is more suitable for a mathematician than for a nobleman, and a duke at that. In general, scholars have no idea how to live. However learned they may be in their own field, when they move in society they seem like fools. It is not at all suitable for people of great quality to be very learned, but highly necessary for them to know the world and be able to deal with people, and they can't learn that from books but only from experience.

Port Royal 26 July 1699 Certainly, if Monsieur were less weak and didn't let the worthless people he loves and esteems so much lead him by the nose, he would be the best man in the world. Indeed, even when he harms one he is more to be pitied than detested.

My son is full of good sense, I'm sure you would enjoy his conversation. He knows a lot, has a good memory and expresses himself well and without pedantry. But his mind is not sufficiently lofty, and he would rather mix with common painters and musicians than with the right people.

He is hard at work on a historical picture for you. Painting is the reason he gives for going to Paris in the mornings, but between ourselves our *cavalier* is in love with a girl of sixteen,[1] an actress, whom he meets there. If he uses her face for your Antigone, she should be very pretty.

Fontainebleau 16 September 1699 No girl could have a more sheltered upbringing than our three princes. Every evening at nine o'clock the two younger ones are sent to bed, although the Duc d'Anjou is sixteen and the Duc de Berry thirteen, and would be wide enough awake if he were allowed to be. He is a very nice child and always cheerful. His eldest brother is intelligent but less cheerful, he is supposed to worry about being so badly made. It quite upsets me. The Duc d'Anjou is the

[1] Not Mlle Florence, who had given birth to his son in 1698, but Mlle Charlotte Desmares, who was to bear him a daughter in 1702.

best-natured person in the world, not very good-looking, but I think he'll be as strong as the King of Poland.[1] No one can make him bend his arm or unclench his fist.

Let us hope that the Duchesse de Bourgogne, who has a pretty figure, will pass it on to her children. She has become much steadier since last year, and no longer behaves like a child at table but quite like a grown-up.

Fontainebleau 23 September 1699 If anyone had listened to me, the Heidelberg tapestries would now be in Berlin and the medal collection in my possession, but in France the only thing that counts is the wish of the *maître de la communauté*.

The colours of the Julius Caesar tapestry caught Monsieur's fancy, and he really doesn't know the first thing about engraving.

AMELIESE

Fontainebleau 1 October 1699 It would be a blessing for the whole of Europe if the Queen of Spain were to have a child. Boy or girl, it hardly matters which, if only it were a child and stayed alive. You don't need to be a prophet to see that there will be a war if the King of Spain dies without an heir. After all, it's well known that neither of the crowned heads who claim the succession will yield; it is bound to be settled by fighting.

The death of Charles II of Spain was expected at any moment, as indeed it had been from the time of his birth. The Austrian Habsburgs and the French Bourbons were related to him in the same degree, and each house was proposing its own candidate for the succession.

LUISE

Fontainebleau 1 October 1699 Of my wretched journey to Bar,[2] which is now cancelled, I'll say no more than thank you for taking such an interest. The King wouldn't let us try to find a way round the question of etiquette, by which the Duc de Lorraine claims the right to an armchair in our presence because he has one at the Imperial Court. The King replied that the Emperor has one etiquette and he has another.

[1] Augustus the Strong of Saxony, who succeeded John Sobieski on the throne of Poland. He could bend iron bars with his bare hands, and roll up silver plates at dinner parties.

[2] Liselotte had wanted to be with her daughter at Bar-le-Duc for the birth of her first baby.

For instance, the Emperor lets cardinals have armchairs in his presence, while in the King's they may not sit down at all. Monsieur was quite willing to agree to a chair with a back to it, and the King agreed, but the Duke claims the right to be treated like an elector and the King wouldn't allow that. Monsieur proposed that it should be done as the King of England does:[1] he doesn't offer us armchairs in his presence, although we say we are entitled to them, so when we are there he sits on a *tabouret*. That's what we suggested doing too, but the King wouldn't hear of it, so rather than offend our Duke we have given up the journey.

SOPHIE

Paris 1 November 1699 The Queen of England does not, of course, treat the Maintenon like a sister-queen, nor does that lady expect to be treated according to this rank, but she does demand the same consideration as if she were actually queen—more, in fact. She expects to be consulted about everything, and nothing must be done without her advice or at her command. That isn't my way at all. If, as she did at first, she had gone on allowing me to give her messages for the King on subjects which I couldn't mention to him myself, I might have been weak enough to confide in her completely, and ask her for advice. But how can she expect that now, when she has made the King publicly, in front of all the world, forbid me to give her any message for him ever again? I have obeyed the King's orders, nothing can be said against that, and if the King had commanded me to call on her since I should of course have done so. Only it seems to me she shouldn't be offended if I carry out the King's orders.

Port Royal 5 November 1699 The King admits himself that there are faults in the architecture of Versailles. The reason is that he didn't at first intend to build such a vast palace, but only to enlarge the existing *château*. But then he liked the place so much that he had to provide more accommodation in order to be able to stay there, and instead of starting with a new design, and tearing down the original *château*, he kept it and, so to speak, put a fine new mantle around it, and that spoilt everything.

In June 1710 Liselotte writes to Sophie, 'Everyone fond of building is fond of making alterations. Our King is no exception. There is not a corner in Versailles that hasn't been altered at least ten times, and not always for the better!'

[1] James II at St Germain.

Versailles 24 January 1700 I must tell you what happened at Marly. On Thursday, immediately after supper, when the King was sitting in the salon which had been prepared for the ball, the Duchesse de Bourgogne came in, very prettily dressed as Flora. She was wearing a great many silk flowers which suited her beautifully. With her were a number of ladies to whom, in truth, this costume was rather less becoming. Among the other Floras was the Duchesse de Sully, who is short and stout. When all the masks had taken their places we heard cymbals, a Sarmatian[1] entered followed by a camel carrying a negro who was striking the cymbals, then came a group of Amazons, and when this parade had passed everyone danced countless minuets.

The following day, on the Friday, I drove to Paris at half-past eleven, heard Mass with Monsieur and afterwards went with him to St Eustache for the christening of a bell. I almost laughed out loud; the bell was covered with flowers, there was a bit of brocade draped round the top, and I said to Monsieur, 'The bell is dressed like Flora too,' it looked so exactly like the Duchesse de Sully.

Golden ropes with golden tassels were hanging from the clapper of the bell. We were given these to hold, and we had to pull three times to make the bell ring. Confidentially, it's a very peculiar ceremony.

The church was filled with people who had come to watch this fine ritual, and afterwards the *canaille* rushed in to ring the bell. They imagine it will protect them from thunderstorms.

It was only fitting that Monsieur should have been invited to the christening of the bell, as the sound of their ringing was the only music ever to give him any pleasure. Liselotte says that he used to spend the night of All Saints in town on purpose to hear the massed church-bells of Paris.

Marly 3 February 1700 Now that a way has been found to take trees as tall as houses from the woods, gardens will soon be made. Today we met more than thirty wagons with trees this size. We hear that when they're transplanted they do well and don't die.

Marly 6 May 1700 I used to play tricks on Jungfer Kolb too, secretly eating at night. Only we didn't go in for such delicacies as chocolate, coffee or tea, but feasted on a good salad of *Sauerkraut mit Speck*.

I remember once, when the door of my room was being rehung, our beds were moved to a room next to my maids'. The Kolb had

[1] Sarmatia was the ancient name for the district north of the Black Sea.

forbidden me to go into their room during the night. I promised her not to cross the threshold, and begged her to go to bed. I told her that as I wasn't sleepy I would look out of the window at the stars. She refused to trust me and kept sitting about in her nightgown, till I said I was concerned for her and suggested that if she lay on her bed, leaving the curtains undrawn, she would still be able to see me. She agreed, and as soon as she was in bed my ladies opened their door and put a plate of salad just inside. I pretended to drop my handkerchief, picked it up and the plate with it, and went straight to the window. I had hardly swallowed three mouthfuls when they started firing the cannon outside my window: a fire had broken out in the town. The Kolb was terrified and jumped out of bed, and I was so afraid of being found out that in a flash I hurled my handkerchief, the silver plate and the salad out of the window. Now I had nothing to wipe my mouth on. Then I heard steps on the wooden staircase; it was our late papa the Elector, come to see where the fire was. He noticed my greasy mouth and chin and began swearing at me: '*Sakrament*, Liselotte, I do believe you've rubbed some mess on to your face.' I said, 'No, only some ointment, my lips are chapped,' and he said, 'You look disgustingly dirty.' I started to laugh then, and papa and the others thought I had gone out of my mind. Then the Raugravine appeared. She had walked in through the maids' room, and remarked that it smelled strongly of *Speck-salat*, which made the Elector realize what had happened. He was not angry, but only said, 'So that is your lip-salve, Liselotte,' and laughed. It took the Kolb a long time to forgive me.

This is a very old story, which I only tell you to prove that I know very well what fun it is to spite one's governess and eat at night when one is young.

St Cloud 12 August 1700   I expect you know that the Duke of Gloucester[1] is dead. If the English decided not to allow our Prince of Wales to succeed King William, you would be the person closest to the crown. It would be nice if you became a queen. I wish it more for you than for myself.

Here everything goes on much the same. The King likes no one except his old frump and the Duchesse de Bourgogne.

The Duc d'Anjou, who is seventeen, is treated like a child of eight. They are bringing him up so idiotically that it amuses the Duc de Berry, who is more intelligent.

[1] The Duke of Gloucester had been the only child of Princess Anne, heiress to the English throne, and George of Denmark to survive infancy.

My son is living his life of debauchery, he is forever in Paris in bad company.

His wife thinks that she is the most beautiful object in the whole world; I find her very unpleasant. My son doesn't notice what a coquette she is. He is so clever in everything else, but in this he is like a child. As I see that he isn't concerned about it, I shan't disabuse him.

The Duchesse de Bourgogne does entirely as she pleases. If she has a sudden fancy to take a four- or five-league drive, she goes even if it means returning in the middle of the night. At Versailles she runs all over the palace day and night, and everyone finds it charming. If the late Dauphine or I had behaved like that, we should have been thrown out.

Fontainebleau 6 October 1700   Our King and Queen of England, whom I visited yesterday, talked about you all evening. The good King of England, with tears of love for you welling up in his eyes, and raising both hands in the air, said, 'O-o-o pour-pour cela eh-eh-eh-elle me-m'a tou-toujours aimé.' His stutter is worse than ever.

Fontainebleau 10 November 1700   I have great news for you today. It arrived yesterday morning, though it had long been expected: the King of Spain is dead. The Queen is said to be ill with grief. The King died on the first of the month at three o'clock. Our King has received a copy of the will; the Duc d'Anjou is the chosen heir. A grandee of Spain is supposed to be on his way to present the original to the Duke and to claim him as his king. In case the King refuses to let the Duc d'Anjou go, this same grandee is to go straight on to Vienna and offer the Spanish crown to the Emperor.

Fontainebleau 13 November 1700   People went about whispering to each other yesterday, 'Don't tell anyone, but the King has accepted the crown of Spain for the Duc d'Anjou.' I kept quiet, but when I heard the Duc d'Anjou coming up behind me in a narrow path during the hunt I pulled up and said, 'Pass, great King! May your Majesty pass.' You should have seen his surprise at my knowing about it. His little brother, the Duc de Berry, almost died, he laughed so hard.

The Duc d'Anjou looks like a proper king of Spain; he seldom laughs, he is always serious. Our King is said to have told him secretly that he was to be king, but that he was not to let anyone know. He was playing *ombre* in his room at the time, and before he could stop himself he jumped up, but sat down again at once with his former gravity as though nothing had happened.

This young King may not be as lively as his youngest brother, or as intelligent, but he has exceptionally fine qualities. He is good-natured, generous (unlike most other members of his family), and truthful; he would not tell a lie for anything in the world. No one could have a greater horror of lies. He is a man of his word, charitable, courageous, in short, a really virtuous gentleman with no vice in him. If he had been an ordinary nobleman, he would truly be called an *honnête homme*. I imagine the people around him will be very happy.

He looks rather Austrian, and always has his mouth open. I have spoken to him about it a hundred times. When he is told to close his mouth he closes it, for he is very docile, but as soon as he stops concentrating on keeping it shut he opens it again. His voice is harsh and he speaks very slowly. He talks very little, except to me, because I give him no peace and am always badgering him. Sometimes I manage to make him laugh. I like him better than the Duc de Bourgogne, he is not so easily offended and is much nicer-looking. But the one I love the best is the Duc de Berry. He is such a pleasant child and is always cheerful; laughing and talking are one and the same to him, very amusing. A few days ago he said, 'I am really miserable. I have no chance of becoming a king like my brothers, and now the Duc d'Anjou is leaving I shall inherit all his governors and under-governors. I have more than enough of my own already—what is to become of me when I get all the others as well? I can only hope they will make me quite perfect!' He doesn't say any of this by way of complaint but with a laugh. But this is enough about our prince.

Paris 18 November 1700 The King summoned the Duc d'Anjou to his closet on Tuesday morning and said to him, 'You are the King of Spain.' Then he admitted the Spanish ambassador and all the Spaniards who live here. They fell at their King's feet, kissed his hand one after the other and lined up behind him. Our King then led the young King of Spain into the salon, where all the Court had assembled, and said, 'Gentlemen, behold the King of Spain.' Immediately there was great rejoicing and everyone came up to kiss the young King's hand. The King then said, 'Let us go to Mass and thank the Lord', gave the young King his right hand and took him to Mass, where he made him kneel at his right on his own hassock. After Mass our King accompanied him to his apartments, the large ones, and afterwards his brothers came to visit him. My Duc de Berry was so happy that he kissed the hand of his brother, the King of Spain, in his joy.

In the afternoon the young King drove out to Meudon to visit his father, who is staying there. Monseigneur came out to the antechamber to meet his son. He had been out in the garden, not expecting his son the King of Spain so early, and was puffing and panting when he arrived. He said, 'I see one must never swear to anything. I could have sworn I would never make myself short of wind coming to meet my son, but here I am, quite out of breath.' The good young King was quite taken aback to be treated like foreign royalty by his father, who accompanied him to his coach on leaving.

> Philippe d'Anjou, now Philip V of Spain, took leave of his family among the usual floods of tears. This time even the Dauphin was affected. He embraced his son with such tenderness that Liselotte was still quite distressed when she reported the scene on the following day to her dearest *tante*. The only person not to cry was the Duc de Bourgogne, though Liselotte said his eyes looked red.

Versailles 23 January 1701 When I was ill all France, from the King to the lowest in the land, called to enquire after me. Mme de Maintenon was the sole exception; she didn't even send to ask how I was. However, this didn't prevent me from recovering, and I would much rather suffer the old prune's dislike than the fever, which would do me more harm.

I hear the coronation in Prussia[1] is held up because the ice has delayed all the baggage. In my view, an elector who is richer in land and people than any royal highness ought to be content with his title. But from your description this King must like glitter and formality, since he is so fond of ceremonies, and I'm not surprised that he wanted to be king.

St Cloud 27 March 1701 I think your last letter must have been held up for so long because of their curiosity to see if you mentioned the news that is all over Paris: that the English Parliament have chosen you to succeed the Princess of Denmark[2] on the throne of England, and your son the Elector after you.

People talk of nothing else. They add that King William is about to invite you to live in England and become a member of his Council, because of your great wisdom.

[1] Frederick III of Brandenburg, who was married to Sophie Charlotte, Sophie's daughter, became King Frederick I of Prussia on January 18th.
[2] Later Queen Anne.

Versailles 17 April 1701   You see, I was not mistaken when I assured you that you and your sons would be called to the English throne.[1]

The Princess of Denmark is said to drink so heavily that her body is quite burnt up. She will never have any living children, and King William's health is so delicate that he can't live long. So you will soon sit on your grandfather's throne, and I shall be overjoyed, much more pleased than if it had been my children and myself, because I love my dearest *tante* more than anyone: when the time comes I will send you a compliment as wide as it is long, and stick 'Your Majesty' all over it, although for the time being I shan't write any compliments, for you are now what you always were: the one person in all the world worthy of being a great queen. Now I am happy to be here and a Catholic, so that there is no obstacle between you and the crown.

St Cloud 9 June 1701   This is written by the most unhappy of all living creatures. Monsieur had a stroke at ten o'clock last night, he is on his deathbed and I am in the greatest distress in the world, but shall remain until death your niece and devoted servant Elisabeth Charlotte.

> Liselotte does not say, and at this point possibly did not know, that a furious quarrel between the royal brothers had preceded their dinner, triggered off by the Duc de Chartres' behaviour. For all that he was married to the King's own daughter, Philippe was conducting an open, tactless love-affair with Mlle de Séry, one of Liselotte's ladies in waiting. The King regarded this as an insult, and angrily asked Monsieur to see that his son mended his ways. In reply Monsieur had several pertinent things to say about the King's own conduct. The quarrel continued until the meal was announced, and when Monsieur sat down to eat his usual prodigious quantities of food his face was so red that people remarked upon it.

Versailles 12 June 1701   Now that I have recovered a little from the first shock, I will tell my beloved *tante*, whom I love most in all the world, the only being to whom I can turn for comfort, everything that has happened.

Last Wednesday Monsieur was still hale and well. He went to Marly and ate a hearty dinner with the King. Afterwards he went on to St Germain. He returned in high spirits and told us how many tabourets he had seen at the Queen of England's. At about nine o'clock I was

[1] Sophie of Hanover was now the recognized heir by Parliament's Act of Settlement of 1701.

Sophie, Electress of Hanover, by Andreas Scheit.

Monsieur in middle-age, by Charles Lebrun.

called to supper, but as I was still suffering from fever I didn't feel like eating. Monsieur said, 'I shan't follow your example, I shall go and eat, I'm very hungry', and went.

Half-an-hour later I heard a noise and Mme de Ventadour came into the room. She looked as pale as death and said, 'Monsieur is unwell.' I rushed to his room at once. He still knew me, but he wasn't able to speak clearly. I could only make out, 'You are ill, don't stay.'

He was bled three times, given eleven ounces of emetic, a quantity of Schaffhausen-water and two whole bottles of *goutte d'Angleterre*, but at six o'clock in the morning the end was plain to see. They dragged me out of the room by force, barely conscious. They put me to bed, but I got up again, for it was impossible to rest. Since in joy or sorrow my thoughts fly to you I wrote to you, though I don't remember what I said. When I had sent your letter off the King came to see me, very upset, and did all he could to comfort me. He showed me great kindness. Mme de Maintenon was also much moved and full of sympathy. Then the King left, and at noon Monsieur died. I got into my coach at once and came straight here. The King sent M le Premier to ask how I was, and I found that the shock had driven the fever away. Mme de Maintenon sent a message by my son to say that the moment had come to make up any differences with the King. I reflected upon this, remembered that you had often advised me to make my peace with the lady herself, and asked the Duc de Noailles to tell her on my behalf that I was so touched by the friendship she had shown me during my grief that I begged her to take the trouble to come to see me, as I was not yet able to go out.

She came yesterday at six o'clock. I quickly repeated how grateful I felt and how much I longed for her friendship. I also admitted that I had been angry, because I had been under the impression that she loathed me and had turned the King against me. I had heard this from Mme la Dauphine, but should be very ready to forget it if she would now be my friend. She then said many eloquent and beautiful things and promised me her friendship, and we embraced.

Afterwards I said that it was not enough to tell me that the King had been displeased with me; she must also tell me how to win him over again. She advised me to speak to him quite frankly, to tell him that I had disliked her because I thought that she had set him against me, for which I had disliked him too.

I took her advice, and, since Monsieur had told me that the King did not like my writing to you so frankly, I tackled that subject as well. The King said he knew nothing of any letters, had never seen any,

G

and that it must have been Monsieur's imagination, but mentioned that Your Grace detested him. I said that His Majesty's great qualities had always been admired by you, and that, if His Majesty so wished, he would be loved by you, too.

When I had explained everything, and shown him clearly that, however badly he had treated me, I had always loved and respected him, and moreover had been grateful simply to be allowed to live near him, he embraced me, begged me to forget the past and promised me his favour. He even laughed when I said, quite artlessly, 'If I hadn't loved you, I shouldn't have hated Mme de Maintenon when I thought that she was depriving me of your kindness.' Everything ended most graciously.

It will be another sad day for me today, for the King is coming at three o'clock to open Monsieur's will. This will upset me dreadfully.

From a letter written twenty years later to Caroline of Wales, it is plain that the interview also decided Madame's future residence. After Monsieur's death Madame had been heard to cry at the top of her voice, 'No convent for me, I'll go to no convent. Let no one speak to me of convents!' According to her marriage contract, Liselotte had to choose between spending her widowhood at a convent of her choice or at the château de Montargis, her dower-house. She had no intention of doing either, and from the later letter it becomes clear that the little speech about the happiness she felt at being allowed to live near the King was more than idle sentiment, and directly referred to her future. She won her point, for no more was said of convents (Maubuisson had been the one suggested because of Aunt Louise Hollandine, its abbess) or of Montargis.

St Cloud 26 June 1701   I had to receive the ceremonial visit of the King and Queen of England wearing the strangest apparel: a white linen band across my forehead, above it a cap which tied under my chin like a veil, over the cap *les cornettes*, and over them a piece of linen that was fastened to the shoulders like a mourning-coat, with a train seven ells long. I was dressed in a coat of black cloth with very long sleeves; ermine, two hands wide, bordered the cuffs. There was more ermine of the same width down the front of the coat from throat to floor, and a girdle of black crêpe reaching to the ground in front and a train of ermine, seven ells long.

In this get-up, with the train arranged to show the ermine, I was placed on a black bed in an entirely blackened room. Even the parquet was covered in black and the windows hung with crêpe. A great candelabrum of twelve candles was lit, and there were ten or twelve candles burning on the chimney-piece. All my domestics, short and tall, were in long mourning-coats: forty or fifty ladies, all in crêpe, it was a ghastly sight.

Versailles 30 June 1701 You know already that the King is going to look after me. Monsieur left debts worth seven and a half million. Rich I shall never be; I only hope to God that I shall be able to manage. I think it would have been better to die than to go through what is happening to me now.

Monsieur really felt his death; for twelve hours he was made to suffer quite unnecessarily, with emetics, blood-lettings, leeches, and a hundred similar things as well as all kinds of purges. He lost consciousness only just before he died.

Before Monsieur fell into this unhappy state he was hale, well and gay. He was eating with great appetite, laughing and chatting, and when he began to speak indistinctly the ladies thought he was doing it in fun. Unhappily, it was all too much in earnest.

If those in the next world could know what goes on in this one, poor Monsieur ought to be very pleased with me: I have found all the letters that he received from his young men and burnt them unread, so that they can't fall into the hands of strangers.

These letters, which Monsieur kept in strong-boxes, were so violently perfumed that Madame, who was no friend of scent, was overcome by the vapours and found herself suffering from another bout of fever.

Versailles 7 July 1701 It isn't surprising that Monsieur did not mention me in his will. He could not have done so, for in this country no husband can leave anything to his wife, or she to him. Only what he gives her during his lifetime is hers, but Monsieur preferred to give presents to those who amused him. It appears that three young men alone drew 100,000 thalers apiece per annum. I admit that Monsieur often plagued and worried me, but only out of weakness and too great a devotion to those who assisted his pleasures.

The fever has left me. I believe I cured it myself by eating cherries. I had been forbidden to touch them, but then I received such a beautiful basketful from St Cloud that I guzzled them in secret, and the fever disappeared.

I envy people who can go to the play. I shan't be able to go for two years now.

AMELIESE

Versailles 15 July 1701   I am not such a fool as to shut myself up in a convent, that is not my way at all. Fate has surely destined me to live out my life here briefly, and then die. I know the world too well to have any great plans; my only ambition is to live in tranquillity, and if I am left in peace your kind wishes for me will be fulfilled.

In this country children care very little for their parents. It is rare to find a son who loves his mother and does not scorn her after his father's death, so my son has more merit in this respect than you may think.

Now I have had my dinner and will finish answering your letter. We were talking about my son. Believe me, it is a great thing that he loves me. He hasn't been brought up to do so, for since he was quite small people have always been busily at work to estrange us. But his good nature has prevailed. There is too much to say on the subject, so it will be better to say nothing.

SOPHIE

Versailles 21 July 1701   Mme de Maintenon continues to be very friendly, and I am very pleased with her: if she goes on like this I shall certainly remain her friend. And I am too old to be bored in her and the King's company, like the Duchesse de Bourgogne, who can think of nothing but singing and dancing. But I am racking my brains to find the reason for the Maintenon's sudden liking for me. The more I think about it, the less I can understand it, but one thing is certain—that woman does nothing without forethought and a reason behind it. I imagine she has chosen me to make the Duchesse de Bourgogne jealous, so as to draw her closer to herself again. It is simply not natural for a person to change from one hour to the next as she has done, and I shall have to be careful about what I do or say. One can't be certain of anything.

Marly 28 July 1701   I have been here since Sunday night. The King received me with great kindness. He came to meet me, and then took me for a walk. He has made many improvements since I was last here; there is a new *mail*[1] so shady that one can play at high noon without feeling the sun. We made a tour of the entire garden, and climbed a

[1] A mall where a game resembling *boules* was played.

small hill to see the new waterfall. It is very fine, and constructed in quite a new way: it has three steps right at the top, a large fountain spurts a great gush of water, and the heads of sea-monsters spit out more. This water forms the cascade. In the centre of each step there is a low jet, and on each side, at the top, bronze children play with the sea-creatures.

In the distance there are more cascades; the water bubbles up as from natural springs.

Meudon 1 September 1701 This place is really lovely. M le Dauphin has built a fine fountain and made many improvements. Yesterday the King was kind enough to take me for a drive. Mme de Maintenon and the Duchesse de Bourgogne were in another *calèche*, for they had both taken quinquina[1] and did not want to be out as late as the King. We didn't return until it grew dark.

I don't think there can be a finer view in all the world than there is here from the Belvedere. You can see as far as the Mont-Valerian, and all St Cloud with the Bois de Boulogne and Madrid.[2] On the right you can see Paris with a long stretch of the Seine and all the bordering villages, behind you is the house with its garden, and to the left you see five avenues *à la perte de vue*, studded with fountains. You can't imagine how beautiful it is.

Fontainebleau 4 September 1701 Good King James will do himself a mischief one day with his boundless piety. The day before yesterday he spent so long kneeling and praying that he fainted clean away, and he was unconscious for so long that everyone thought his last hour had come.

King James died at St Germain less than a fortnight later, on September 16th. Louis promised him on his deathbed that he would proclaim James Francis Edward Stuart as King James III, and lost no time in doing so, although he was bound by the Treaty of Ryswick to recognize William of Orange as King of England, Scotland and Ireland.

AMELIESE

Fontainebleau 12 October 1701 Everyone here goes hunting every day and to the theatre twice a week except, of course, for me. Between

---

[1] China rind, an aperient.
[2] A *château* by the Bois.

ourselves, I must admit that it is no small mortification for me to have to miss both entertainments. I go for long walks, usually a good French mile through the woods, and this chases away the melancholy thoughts that pursue me, especially since I have to listen to talk about business affairs, which I've never had anything to do with in my life. When I'm told things I can't understand, I become dreadfully bad-tempered and as cross as a bedbug.

Apropos of bugs: they almost ate the young Queen of Spain[1] alive. She had to be guarded all night long. She arrived in Toulon a few days ago, and will continue to Barcelona by land. Her Majesty wrote to me that she couldn't bear to be at sea any longer. I shouldn't like to change places with her. To be a queen is hard anywhere, but to be a queen in Spain is surely worse than anything else.

SOPHIE

Fontainebleau 15 October 1701 If my marriage-contract had been drawn up in the ordinary way like all the others here, I should be better off. But in order to prevent me from getting anything at all, they put in a number of unusual clauses. This is why I think papa can't have understood it, or else he wouldn't have made me sign such a document. But poor dear papa had me on his hands, and he was afraid I might remain an old maid, so he got rid of me as fast as he could.

I am sorry to hear that Frau von Harling is so ill. It makes me very sad because I love her, and am so grateful for all the care and trouble she took with me when I was a child.

AMELIESE

Fontainebleau 4 November 1701 I assure you, dear Ameliese, I have no ambition—indeed, the last thing I want is to be Queen of England. The higher the place, the greater the constraint, and if the position of Madame were an appointment to be put up for sale I should have let it go very cheaply long ago, let alone wanting to be a queen.

The Princess of Savoy does not come to her kingdom green. She is truly of the stuff that queens are made of, and can't be faulted on either her father's or her mother's side. She is Monsieur's grandchild but not, as you know, mine, though the good child writes to me with such affection that she might be my own granddaughter. The reason is that her mother was barely two years old when I came to France and didn't remember her real mother at all, so she grew as fond of me as if

---

[1] Liselotte's younger step-granddaughter, Marie-Louise of Savoy, who had been married by proxy to Philip V, and was on the way to Spain to join her new husband.

she had been my own daughter. I, too, love her with all my heart, and make no great distinction between her and my own children.

SOPHIE
Versailles 17 November 1701 Nobody had warned the Queen of Spain that all her people were to be sent away, and when the child got up in the morning she found herself surrounded by repulsive old women instead of her own people. She cried and asked to go back home with them, and the King, who is fond of her already and is still a bit childish himself, began to weep at the thought of having his wife taken away from him. But they consoled him by telling him that there was no possibility of this as the marriage had already been consummated.

The palace-ladies that the Queen has about her are absolute beasts. The Queen asked to be served with French food as she couldn't eat Spanish cooking. The King ordered his French chefs to prepare their dishes for her, but the ladies just left the French food on one side and served her only the Spanish. That made the King angry, and he forbade the Spanish people to cook anything at all, and had her meals prepared entirely by the French kitchens. At this, the ladies took the *soupes*,[1] poured away all the broth, saying it might spoil their clothes, and gave them to the Queen without any liquid, likewise the *ragoûts*. They refused to touch the great *entrées*, such as the legs of mutton and loins of veal, because, they said, their hands were too delicate to carry such dishes, but pulled out three chickens from among the other roasts, flung them on a plate, and set them before the Queen like that. You could not find more horrible people anywhere, and so hideously ugly too.

Versailles 27 November 1701 I am well-treated in a general way, but not really wanted in particular. Yesterday, when I went to Mme de Maintenon's to speak to the King, I was very politely sent away, and told that any command I wished to give would be collected by the lady from my apartments. I could see quite well that it meant she didn't want me there, and I wrote what I had intended to say. Although the King lets me come into his closet after supper, he sends me away as soon as I have finished speaking.

Versailles 4 December 1701 I have never in my life heard of an eider-down-blanket. Personally I am kept snug and warm in bed by six little

[1] The name then used for the great dishes of boiled meats and vegetables. The word was not used for the liquid itself.

dogs, who arrange themselves round me. No eiderdown could ever be as cosy.

The little Queen of Spain is beginning to feel more at home. She has resigned herself to her fate. I pity the poor child. She writes to me so often and so affectionately that I quite love her for it.

Mme de Bracciano, who is now called the Princesse des Ursins,[1] is to remain *camerera majore*. The King of Spain is supposed to think the world of her. She has some very peculiar duties: she has to help the King in and out of his dressing-gown when he comes to sleep with the Queen, and to carry his sword and chamber-pot after him. It makes the Queen laugh; she describes the palace etiquette most amusingly.

Versailles 29 December 1701 I'm sure you have fewer wrinkles than I have. Mine come from many years of exposure to the sun while hunting, but I don't mind about them at all. Never having had good looks, I didn't have much to lose, and I see that those who used to be beauties in the past are now as plain as I am. Not a soul could recognize Mme de la Vallière now, and Mme de Montespan's skin looks like paper which children have folded over and over, for her face is covered with minute lines, so close together that it is astonishing. Her beautiful hair is as white as snow, and her face is quite red, no longer pretty at all. I am quite content never to have had what after all passes so quickly.

You possess more lasting beauty: your intelligence, your vivacity, your generosity and goodness, your constancy to those to whom you have once given your friendship, are all qualities that serve to make your friends' attachment to you so strong that they remain devoted to you all their lives.

Versailles 12 January 1702 I haven't forgotten the Lutheran hymns because I sing them every year with Frau von Rathsamshausen when she is here. My memory, alas, isn't as good as you think.

I don't think it will be possible for the King of Spain to do away with the Inquisition. The monks, especially the Dominicans, are too dangerous. If he attacked them, his life would be in danger.

Versailles 19 January 1702 Mme de Maintenon is quite unchanged, she is exactly as she was thirty years ago. She is still very polite to me and so is the King, but that is all. So far as the King is concerned, the proverb that 'familiarity breeds contempt' works in reverse, because those

---

[1] Anne Marie de la Trémoïlle. Her husband, the Duke of Bracciano, had become the Prince Orsini, which, translated into French, made her the Princesse des Ursins.

with whom he is the most familiar love him the most. I assure you that my letters to you have nothing to do with my not being asked into his closet. No, the real reason is that people think I am too frank and natural. They fear that he might learn truths from me which would really open his eyes, that is the true reason.

Marly 26 January 1702 Mme de Maintenon did me the honour of sending me a ticket for the performance of *Absalom*. I went, and can assure you that they all act extremely well. I should have thought that my son's voice was too rough to sound well on the stage, but it sounds splendid. I had already been told that he's not a bad actor, but I never dreamt he could be so good.

> Liselotte furiously regretted that etiquette prevented her from visiting the theatre or the opera during her two years of official mourning. She had already missed no fewer than six new plays and three new operas since Monsieur had died.
>   *Absalom, Tragic Saint*, an opera by Duché, with the new Duc d'Orléans in the title-role, was privately presented. It was by no means the Duc's debut: he had already played Alceste in 1699 and sung in a motet before the King in 1700. In 1703, when he was to interest himself in the music of ancient Greece, his own opera *Panthée* was to be performed in Versailles.

Versailles 19 February 1702 I think the fashions here will change soon, because the Queen of Spain has sent her sister, the Duchesse de Bourgogne, a Spanish dress which everyone greatly admires. It is made of cherry-coloured satin with a mass of silver lace, the bodice is cut like a child's coat, the shoulders are covered and the neckline is square. The sleeves are narrow down to the elbows, the lower part trimmed with wide flounces of lace such as actors wear, silver-lace mixed with *point de Venise*. The bodice laces at the back like proper stays. The underskirt is mounted on iron hoops, very wide at the hem and getting smaller and smaller towards the top, which makes the waist look tiny. The overskirt is looped up like an ordinary overskirt, and has a small rounded train. For the head there is a little cap made of lace, entirely covered in bows of wide ribbon. It suits the Duchesse de Bourgogne wonderfully well.

LUISE
Versailles 12 March 1702 Frau von Harling's death has really upset me. It has made me very sad although it is the best thing that could

have happened, because she could never have recovered completely. I imagine her Majesty the Queen of Prussia will be very much affected too, as the good woman was her governess after she was mine.

SOPHIE
Versailles 23 March 1702   Yesterday I took a fancy to see the apartment of M Moreau, the Duc de Bourgogne's first groom of the chamber. He arranged it himself. I had heard a lot about it and went to see it instead of hearing the sermon.

It was small, but neat and very curious.

He has four little rooms, full of portraits and paintings. First there are some large paintings by Poussin, as good as any belonging to the King. There are three of them, two of the death of Phocion and one of Moses being pulled out of the water by the Egyptian king's daughter. Then there is a Caracci, a Mignard, a Van Dyck, a Bassano, and the works of two others whose names I have forgotten. Everything is in carved gilt frames. As well as the large pictures there are small ones, all the same size, showing every ruler of France from François I to our present King. Under each king are the great men of that reign, the warriors as well as the scholars. He has portraits of every single poet from that day to this. Malherbe has a horrible beard. All the kings' mistresses are there, as well as all the queens of the entire period.

Our own epoch is in a separate cabinet. Mme de Montespan, Mme de la Vallière and Mme de Ludre are all there. Mme de Maintenon is dressed as a saint. The entire royal family is there too, and the people who have won battles hang side by side. Below Cardinal de Richelieu are all his victims.

There are also beautiful, costly porcelains and bronzes: Le Brun, Mignard, M le Notre, also Racine, Corneille and all the *fausemots*. Mme de Guyon is there too.[1] I wanted him to put her between M de Cambrai and M de Meaux, but he said he had already thought of it and decided it was too risky.

Versailles 26 March 1702   A banker in Paris, Samuel Bernard, had a letter from England telling him that King William died last week. Now you are one step nearer the throne, with only a single person

---

[1] Mme de Guyon preached Quietism, a mystic religious doctrine which caused a great rift in France. She was responsible for the breach between the archbishops of Cambrai and Meaux, Fénelon and Bossuet. Liselotte said that she took care to preserve the strictest neutrality in this spiritual war.

before you, and it looks as though she is almost ready for the next world too.[1]

Versailles 9 April 1702 I was not surprised that King William died with such *fermeté*. One usually dies in the way one has lived. Mlle de Malauze writes that Milord Albemarle was on the point of following his master, he was ill to death with grief. I am sorry to say there were no such displays of friendship when Monsieur died.

LUISE

Versailles 22 April 1702 I couldn't answer your letter because of the Easter feast, which in this country obliges one to be in church for days on end. After the holidays, in order to make up a little for the boredom I had to endure from all that Latin whining, I admit I took advantage of the fine weather and went for an outing to the Trianon, where the gardens are surely the loveliest one's eyes could wish to see.

King William's death has made me sad. Last autumn Lenor sent me an almanach for this year, and King William's death is clearly predicted as follows: 'NB♂♄☉[2] March 20th 1702; A potentate goes to his grave/this pleases not a few/that's how it goes when one departs/to make room for the new'.

I can imagine how the Allies must grieve. You hear of nothing but war and rumours of war. The Court will soon be deserted, but that is the least of my worries, I shan't be deprived of any company on that account. I am on my own in my rooms day in, day out, without ever being bored. I find the days too short. There are a great many flowers in front of my windows, many little dogs of whom I am fond about me, I have my books, my engraved stones, and with all this I can amuse myself very well without troubling God or the world. One of my most beautiful bitches is whelping here in my room at this very moment.

This was far from being a unique occasion, for Liselotte was frequently announcing similar happy events. 'I amused myself by watching one of my bitches pup. She has already produced two offspring in half-an-hour, and M Titti, not yet twenty-five months old, now has thirty-two children, and all this without any admonitions to be fruitful and multiply!'

[1] William III had died at Kensington on March 19th, and Queen Anne was known to be ailing.
[2] Signs of Mars, Saturn and Sun.

And once, 'One of my dogs jumped up behind me on to the divan where I was entertaining the Princesse de Conti. I felt it turn round and put out my hand to make it settle down. Something felt moist, and when I took a look there was a pup on my skirts, and afterwards three more made their appearance. How the Princess laughed at this adventure.' The first puppy was suitably named 'Robe'.

SOPHIE

Versailles 7 May 1702 The King took me stag-hunting in his *calèche* last Friday, and how I needed it: my heart was so heavy from the loss of my poor little Mione. Yesterday, when I arrived from Marly, it still hurt me to see all her sisters coming to welcome me, without her. I miss her constantly; in my bed, on my walk, in the morning during my *toilette* when she used to lie on my lap, and whenever I was writing she used to sit behind me in my chair. She was with me all the time, such a beautiful little animal with eyes full of fire and intelligence.

You will think your Liselotte has gone mad over her dog, but, my dearest *tante*, I can't help it, I must always tell you all that happens, good or bad, and I had to let you know that I have lost my poor Mione and how it has upset me.

Before leaving Marly yesterday, I walked for an hour-and-a-half looking at the King's admirable tulipans, which all the *curieux* come to see. A Scottish milord who called the day before yesterday expressly to look at them said that one of them was worth 2,000 francs. He is an *amateur* of flowers and has travelled to every spot that has a reputation for growing them, England, Holland, but he says that none are rarer and finer than those at Marly.[1]

Marly 6 July 1702 People here think that fighting will soon begin in Flanders. The two armies are standing in readiness, separated only by a small bog. It seems as if something is brewing in Italy, too. Is it not a dreadful thing that men, whose lifespan is so very short as it is, should be so eager to shorten it further by killing each other like flies?

Apropos of insects: the damned mosquitoes don't give me a minute's peace. They have bitten me to pieces—I look as though I have the smallpox all over again. We are plagued by wasps, too. Not a day passes without someone being stung. There was fiendish laughter here the other day: a wasp had got under a lady's skirts and stung her high up on her leg. She rushed round like a madwoman, crying as she raced

[1] Tulips were still something of a rarity a good century after their first arrival had made—and lost—enormous fortunes in Holland.

about, '*Ah, fermez les yeux et prenez-le moi.*' It sounded very funny.

This morning I went walking with the King. It is as though the fairies had been at work here, for where I had left a pond I saw a wood, and where I had left a clearing there is now a great artificial lake. This evening it will be stocked with more than a hundred carp. These are extremely handsome, some gold, some silver, others are a beautiful deep blue, or yellow-spotted, or black and white, blue and white, gold and white, or white-gold with red spots or black spots, in short, so many kinds that it makes one marvel.

I have no news, and if I did I shouldn't be able to write it. I have been told that the people who examine my letters are making some very strange comments in order to get me into trouble with the King. Should his Majesty do me the honour of taking me to task, I should be perfectly capable of answering for myself, and I only wish I could confront the laughing little Minister: I am positive he wouldn't be able to face me with his lying constructions. I would ask the Herr Interpreter of German letters to translate this very faithfully, so that the Minister may know exactly what I think. Should I ever hear the like again, he need not trouble to speak to the King. I shall myself ask for an audience, and ask his Majesty if he has ordered my letters to be opened and commented on. What I write is no secret from anyone, provided it is transmitted without lies or falsification. I can't think what the little man has against me: I've never harmed him in my life, and I should have thought that in view of the present state of affairs he would have better things to do than to scrutinize my letters to my closest relatives.

The 'little man' to whom Liselotte refers was Torcy, one of Louis' trusted ministers. He was in charge of the post office, but had many other duties on all of which, in Liselotte's opinion, he would have been more profitably employed now that the War of the Spanish Succession had been officially declared. France was facing England, Holland and the Empire, who had formed the Grand Alliance in order to preserve the balance of power in Europe.

AMELIESE

Versailles 22 July 1702 Oh, that the French Court were as it used to be, how one could have learnt the art of living then! But now, when no one but the King and Monseigneur knows the meaning of *politesse*, when the young people think of nothing but frightful debauches and the grossest are the most admired, I shouldn't advise anyone to send his children here, they would acquire only vices instead of virtues; you are so right to disapprove when Germans send their children to France nowadays.

It is certainly right and proper to admire those who sacrifice life and limb for their country. How I wish that both of us were men and in the fighting now. An idle wish, perhaps, but I can't help myself.

SOPHIE
Versailles 23 July 1702   The Dutch understand cleanliness better than anyone in the world. Things are very different in France. There is one dirty thing at Court that I shall never get used to: the people stationed in the galleries in front of our rooms piss into all the corners. It is impossible to leave one's apartments without seeing somebody pissing. This would be a better thing to abolish than plays and operas.

LUISE
Versailles 9 August 1702   The French proverb says '*L'homme propose et Dieu dispose*', and that's how it was with me. I meant to finish my letter to you last Thursday, but the hunt lasted for more than two hours and it was half-past six before we got back. I have such a bad memory that I forgot I've told you already that I always have to change all my clothes afterwards, so I have crossed it out here, God knows if you can read it. It was eight o'clock before I was ready, and then I had to write to *ma tante* and my son, to tell them the good news that M Vendôme has beaten 3,000 troops led by General Hannibal Visconti. They call him *l'animal* Visconti here, because he has been whipped so thoroughly.

For the Sunday post I wrote twenty sheets, I mean pages, to *ma tante* the Electress, ten to Lorraine, ten on business, twelve to my friends; and all this made me so tired that I could write no more. On Sunday I had to reply to Mme de Savoie's four sheets written on both sides, and then I had to receive visitors, which kept me from your letter.

Yesterday, both before and after dinner, we were out in the garden with the King and watched two beautiful statues being put up. They cost 100,000 francs for the pair. One is the *Renommée*[1] on a winged horse, carved from a single block of marble, the other a Mercury, also on horseback, the most splendid thing you could ever wish to see.

When one is happy and contented, one does well not to change one's condition. If the King of Poland had observed this maxim, he wouldn't be caught up in disaster now. We hear that the King of Sweden, with 12,000 men, won a crushing victory over the King of Poland's army,

[1] This statue, by Coysevox, is now in the Jardin des Tuileries.

which was half as strong again. If he had quietly remained Elector of Saxony, none of this would have happened to him. Lenor comments: When the goat is feeling frisky, he goes on to the ice and breaks a leg.

There is no point in wondering which watering-place would do me the most good, for I'm in no position to go to any of them. The rash now covers my entire neck and back; it has reached my chest too, and God knows what will become of it. Otherwise I am well, thank the Lord, and not in any pain.

Believe me, dear Luise, if we had nothing to worry about except our sins, we should be very gay indeed. Do you know what makes us sad? When fate sends us one misery after another and our temperament is inclined towards spleen, then we take everything to heart and become melancholy. Whether we are cheerful or sad depends very little on ourselves. For example, Lenor's disposition is cheerful and sorrow never clings to her, the witch. When she is at home, she can amuse herself with her friends as much as she likes, and although she endures boredom here for my sake, she makes up for it in her own house during the winter. Here she sits, spinning her silks, laughing at everything I write.

At a well-conducted royal Court, no one can possibly appear *en manteau* without showing a lack of proper respect. I am surprised that the Queen of Denmark should have allowed such a thing. As she and her ladies were travelling, they were quite in order, but unless people are travelling they should never appear like that. When we are at Versailles, which counts as a royal residence, everyone appearing before the King or us is *en grand habit*, but at Marly, Meudon and St Cloud people are always *en manteau*, and it's the same on journeys. I find the *grand habit* much more comfortable than the *manteau*, which I can't stand—such a double-layer of clothing. And I hate the head-dress too: there is nothing pretty about it, and it catches on everything.

AMELIESE

Versailles 18 August 1702 No wonder you make occasional mistakes if you seldom speak French. I am keeping my promise to correct them for you, but neither you nor Luise ever corrects my German, which I am sure is often in need of it. I hardly ever speak German, and can feel that it doesn't come as easily as it used to. I read a psalm and a chapter from the New and Old Testaments every day, but it isn't the same thing as daily conversation. I can't learn anything from the Rathsamshausen either, her German is dreadful, and she is more likely to learn some from me than vice versa.

There is no need to be embarrassed if you don't know a foreign language properly: just take courage and talk away and let yourself be corrected, and you will learn it all the sooner. What surprises me is that the Germans, all of whom seem so anxious to express themselves in French now, should bother so little about spelling.

How do you come to have a French Fräulein now? People like that are usually of very low nobility, and can't compare with our German aristocracy.

Here, as soon as a bourgeois has bought a *charge de secrétaire de roi* he counts for a gentleman. Moreover, they never think twice about unsuitable matches, and marry all sorts of tradesmen's daughters and sometimes even peasant girls, provided they're rich. Consequently they are related to all kinds of artisans. The common nobility is little respected, even here.

Fontainebleau 12 October 1702 With regard to the people whom you describe as noblemen, one could well quote the saying: *Ils sont des princes à gros grains.* And yet, though we Princesses Palatine have provided the world, so to speak, with some of its greatest rulers, people here will scarcely admit that we are of good lineage. Any lousy, tattered duke is thought grander than a Palatine count, however ancient his descent. It drives me mad, though my son's wife thinks it is quite proper. I have had several arguments with her on the subject.

SOPHIE
Versailles 4 January 1703 When M de Créqui returned from his embassy in Rome, he brought back the body of a saint which he intended to present to a church or convent.

Such a relic, especially a saint's entire body, is always moved with great ceremony and lifted from the casket by a bishop in full pontifical robes before being placed in the reliquary.

When all the preparations had been made, the case was brought in and opened with all the usual rites, but they had made a mistake, and all the bishop found were great *saucisses* and *cervelas de Boulogne*. Everyone laughed when the sausages were taken out so solemnly, and the bishop left in a state of embarrassment.

Versailles 21 January 1703 I have never had a bad time in labour, but still, it stands to reason that it hurts less to push a small object out of the body than a large one. For many years now I have been quite safe from any such inconvenience. I have been entirely out of danger ever since the birth of my daughter. Monsieur made *lit à part* very soon after-wards, and I never enjoyed the business sufficiently to ask him to return to my bed.

When Monsieur slept in my bed, I was always obliged to lie on the very edge, and often fell out in my sleep. Monsieur couldn't bear to be touched, and if I stretched out my foot and accidentally brushed against him in my sleep he would wake me up and berate me for half-an-hour. Really, I was very glad when he decided to sleep in his own room and let me lie peacefully in my own bed without fear of falling out or being scolded.

Versailles 1 February 1703 Nothing pleases me more than your letters. And what else would you write about except whatever is happening from day to day? Philosophy I don't understand, theology even less, and of affairs of state I know just as little. So please let me off learned dis-courses, or else I couldn't write to you any longer, for fear you might say: Silly Liselotte, what stupid, boring things she chatters on about, and how much better it would be if she kept quiet.

Versailles 17 May 1703 My little dogs try to please me harder than you imagine. They are jealous of one another, and each of them tries to think of something to win special privileges. Rachille usually sits behind me in my chair, Titti lies near me on the table where I write, Mille Millette lies under my skirts on my feet and Charmion, her mother, cries until a chair for her is placed close to mine. Charmante lies on my skirts on the other side, Stabdille sits on the chair opposite mine making faces at me, Charmille lies under my arm, and this is how they spend almost all the day.

Versailles 11 November 1703 After dinner I had a conversation with a much-travelled merchant who has journeyed all over Egypt, Persia and Judaea. He tells such marvels that I think I should have listened to him all day if I hadn't had to write to you. He says there are four-legged animals in the Nile which are the enemies of the crocodiles. They pursue the people who swim the Nile, which is usual there, tear off all their clothes, but beyond that touch nothing belonging to man.

He also says that he saw flying creatures with human faces in Egypt. He shot one down, but an Arab he had with him warned him not to touch it, it was too vicious and poisonous. And then between Damascus and Jerusalem he tasted some fruit which has made it impossible for him to eat any other kind: he can chew it quite well, but can't swallow

H

it. Also, he saw a crowned serpent which is believed to be the devil in that country.

He has many other marvellous stories; they are going to be put into a book which he is dedicating to me.

Versailles 18 December 1703   I always said that my marriage would serve no purpose, but neither you nor the Elector would listen. Now my company seems to have been made so disgusting to the King that he can't bear to have me about him at all. At Marly he lets me follow the hunt because each of us is in a *calèche à part*, but here he has been out twice without taking me, because I should have to be in his coach. I admit that at first I was rather hurt by this disdainful treatment, but now I have made up my mind not to torture myself any more.

I have too much affection for our King and Queen of Spain to be able to call any other man 'King of Spain'. The Holy Scriptures say 'He who has the bride is the groom', and since our King is in Spain, and acclaimed as king by all the Spanish, he is bound to be their rightful king, not the Archduke. I don't dispute his good qualities, and quite believe that he is intelligent, well-mannered and good looking. I only wish he would manage to chase away the Turks and become emperor of all Asia, but Spain must remain our young King's.

The Archduke Charles, the Allies' candidate for the Spanish throne, was soon to be acknowledged as Carlos III of Spain by a number of Spanish provinces after a series of Allied victories led by Marlborough and Eugene of Savoy.

AMELIESE
Versailles 30 March 1704   I have left the good work of fasting undone: fish doesn't agree with me, and in my opinion there are more useful things to be done than to ruin one's stomach by eating too much of it.

What harm could there be in my knowing or not knowing who came to the Fair in Frankfurt? They must be in a great state of anxiety there if they disapprove of that. I have no difficulty at all in reading a list that you didn't send, but if you fear that sending it would get you into difficulties you do well not to include it. I couldn't bear to think I was the cause of your getting into trouble.

SOPHIE
Versailles 21 April 1704   I was under the impression that Herrenhausen was your dower-house, and that no work could be done there except

by your orders. The only house I have left is my dower, Montargis. It is three or four days' journey from here, but if I were to go and live there I should be stranded, and have to lead an extremely boring country life without anyone taking any notice of me. No, that wouldn't suit me. I prefer to jog along here, although I'm not one of the chosen, nor am I admitted to the Holy of Holies.[1]

Versailles on Ascension Day, 1 May 1704   Today we have a holiday, just like you, and have to go to Vespers this afternoon, which is a boring pastime. You will be singing 'And peace will reign eternally' (I can't think where) and 'All feuds are at an en-hen-hend' (though it seems to me that there is still quite enough fighting everywhere). What a miserable state of affairs.

If I had to read romances for long stretches at a time, I should find them tiresome; but I only read three or four pages in the mornings and evenings when I sit (by your leave) on my close-stool, and then it is neither fatiguing nor dull.

Marly 10 August 1704   Here I am, like a person in limbo: I hear the sounds of rejoicing in heaven without being able to take part.

Last Thursday the King sent presents to the Duchesse de Bourgogne from each of his pavilions. From the first a Flora delivered flowers and verses. From the second and third came a collation of fruit, sweet-meats, ices and liqueurs, despatched by Pomona and brought by Love. There was a basket from the fourth, filled with beautiful ribbons of every sort, sashes and every kind of fan set with diamonds, rubies and emeralds. These were presented by another deity, but I've forgotten which.

In the sixth pavilion there was a spinning-wheel and a table of Chinese lacquer with two hundred pounds of silk because she likes to spin. In the seventh, the one with the celestial globe, there were all sorts of rarities from India, from the ninth came perspectives through which to gaze at the stars, the tenth contained a table set with an extra-ordinarily fine Indian silver service, the eleventh a gold one, and in the twelfth pavilion there was a painting, magnificently framed, of the Duchesse de Bourgogne herself, with the Duc de Bretagne in her lap.

I should have gone to visit my son and his wife yesterday to hear an opera that my son has composed, but it didn't start until nine, and as I never see the King except at table I couldn't miss the meal.

[1] Liselotte's name for the King's closet, which she also calls the Sanctum Sanctorum.

In spite of the war the fêtes, for which the birth of the Duchess's new baby (who, however, died some months later) in this instance provided the occasion, grew more and more splendid. Although Liselotte was in mourning, she was bidden to a sumptuous entertainment arranged to show off the splendours of Marly to the English Court at St Germain. Her letters contain descriptions of the royal repast, served in a grassy clearing, *une véritable salle verte*, where the different coloured ices were arranged in pyramids on tiered banks, making a fine effect in their crystal dishes of various sizes. The party sat at a huge marble horseshoe table, 'covered with a tablecloth that looked so exactly like marble that you could only tell the difference by touching it'. She also writes of the party's astonishment at the magnificence of the marble Galatea on her raised island in the centre of the lake that had recently welcomed the multicoloured fish, and the sculptured marvels surrounding the statue: 'golden children, some carrying golden fish in golden nets, others picking the beautifully worked flowers that were placed about, and the most life-like waterfowls everywhere.'

After the festivities had concluded with a breathtaking fireworks display, lasting for a good half-hour, and another meal, the English Court went home, the King and his family retired to his closet, and Liselotte went to her rooms and to bed.

Meudon 28 August 1704 Again my grateful thanks for the eye-ointment that you so kindly sent me. The Comtesse de Gramont was delighted to have it, though I think I shall soon be needing it myself. My eyesight has got so much worse that I can hardly read the Dutch gazettes any longer, it makes me quite miserable. I do so dislike spectacles and can't see through them properly. But soon there'll be no way out, I'm afraid.

Ma tante, the abbess of Maubuisson, still has very good eyesight, thank God. I had dinner with her the day before yesterday. I found her sense of humour and her understanding as good as ever. She looks well, only her legs are changed for the worse. She walks very badly. To see her totter about, looking as if she might fall at any moment, makes one tremble with anxiety, but she isn't pleased when her nuns offer to help her. Still, I hope she will have a long life in spite of this disability for, as I say, her five senses are in perfect order and her repartee is full of wit, quite as it ought to be.

We came here last night. First I went to St Cloud to see my grandchildren. I thought my grandson was so pretty that I begged my son to have him painted, and when I have his portrait I'll send you a copy of it.

After I had played with all the children for a while I came here to see the most beautiful spectacle one could wish for, namely, an illumination.

There was a great archway like a dome, a real *arc de triomphe*, twelve porticos on each side, with coats of arms painted on pyramids between the portals. In front of the triumphal arch there was a huge plinth with *la Renommée* on top. At the base, which appeared to be made of marble, there were four inscriptions. Right in front of the column, as on a stage made of turf, the great *bassin d'eau* was so thickly studded with lights that it seemed to be on fire. The palace of the sun itself could not have been more splendid.

The fireworks, too, were magnificent. I can't imagine that Paris had a finer show that evening, but it was over all too soon.

Versailles 26 October 1704 Last Thursday we arrived at Sceaux. The King attended a private concert at Mme de Maintenon's and I amused myself in my rooms by playing backgammon, which I play very badly.

On Friday I went to look at the Duc du Maine's new fountains. They are very fine, made of stone to look like pierced rocks, with shell, coral and mother-of-pearl, and rushes with gilded heads. Then I went to the kitchen garden, which is large and beautiful. I wanted to see what M de Navailles, my son's old governor, had so greatly admired. He came to see the gardens at Sceaux in M Colbert's day. He was shown the splendid waterfall, the *galerie d'eau*, which is unbeliev-ably lovely, the *salle des marroniers*, the *berceaux*, in short, he was shown all that is most beautiful at Sceaux, yet he didn't utter one word of praise. But when he came to the lettuces in the kitchen garden he exclaimed at the top of his voice, '*Franchement la vérité, voilà une belle chicorée!*' So I also went to see *la belle chicorée*.

Marly 14 December 1704 Here, beauties are the greatest rarity; to be beautiful is quite out of fashion. The ladies themselves help this state of affairs along: with their whitened ears and their hair pulled tightly back off their faces, they look like rabbits held up by the ears to stop them from escaping. Rather ugly, to my way of thinking. Also, they have become lazy, and walk about without stays all day long. This makes their bodies grow thick; waistlines have disappeared. There is nothing pretty to be seen, of body or of face.

A little later: 'They all look as if they had escaped from a mad-house. It couldn't be worse if they did it on purpose. I'm not surprised that the

menfolk despise the women, who have become really too despicable
now, with their clothes, their drunkenness and their tobacco, which
makes them stink to high heaven.'

AMELIESE
Marly 28 January 1705   The cavaliers don't care whether they drink
with ladies or with chambermaids, provided they are *coquettes* and
fond of hard drinking. Truth to tell, it isn't the chambermaids but
people of the very highest quality who get rolling drunk.

LUISE
Versailles 14 February 1705   Dearest Luise, I grieve with all my heart,[1]
and worry so much about *ma tante* the Electress that I can find no rest or
comfort. I cannot think of your bereavement without horror, and feel
so distressed for you that it nearly breaks my heart! Oh my God, why
didn't the Almighty take me instead of this dear Queen, in whom *ma
tante* could still have found comfort and pleasure for a long time to
come? I am no use to anyone, and have lived long enough.

AMELIESE
Versailles 26 March 1705   It was a good idea to send the three learned
men to talk to *ma tante*, to take her mind off the frightful ceremony
when the late Queen of Prussia's body was removed. I hope that, God
willing, all this is behind us now. No one could say you were useless.
Really, dear Ameliese! In any case, no one dies before their appointed
time.

   The end of your letter is what is called here *une belle chute de fin*.
Seriously, it is elegant. I am not so accomplished, and shall only state
quite flatly that I shall always love you, and I embrace you with all my
heart.

SOPHIE
Versailles 9 April 1705   These are the days we have to spend stuck in
church—I've already been there for a good five hours. I should have
gone to the *Salut*, too, but then I shouldn't have been able to answer
your letter. When I came away from the Great Man I was delighted to
find your two letters: the Almighty has thus already repaid me for the
tedium I endured in His service.

   [1] Sophie's daughter, the Queen of Prussia, had died on February 1st, aged thirty-six.

Versailles 12 April 1705 My son, who is up to his ears in music, more than ever before, is looking out all the old ballets to discover how music used to sound. In a ballet going back to the days of Charles VII he found the melody of the Lutheran hymn that goes, 'Oh God I'll cleave to thee as Thou willst cleave to me'. I'm sure you'll never be able to sing that again without thinking that you are singing an air from Charles VII's ballet.

My son can sightread any music. Last night I made him give me a recital of the music that Henri III had performed at the nuptials of his sister-in-law and the Duc de Joyeuse.

LUISE
Marly 2 May 1705 My cough has gone, just as I thought it would. I'm not worried about irritating the doctors. When I appointed mine, I told him straight out that he was not to expect blind obedience from me. While I should permit him to state his opinion, he was not to be offended if I sometimes took no notice of it. My health and body were my own, and I proposed to deal with them as I considered apropos.

The doctors, I suppose, have to hold forth upon their art in order to make themselves indispensable, but in my experience there is nothing wiser than nature, which I allow to take its course. Should that fail and help be needed, there is still time enough to trouble oneself with quackeries. The doctors are scarcely able to heal diseases, how on earth could they expect to prevent them?

I loathe all medicines, and when I am forced to take any I get no sleep all night long and feel as cross as a cockroach.

AMELIESE
Marly 16 May 1705 No Carthusian monk could live more quietly or in greater seclusion than I do. Eventually I think I shall forget how to speak at all, though soon I shall talk a little more: Frau von Rathsamshausen arrives today or to-morrow, and I expect that we shall recall together the old stories of our youth.

Let me tell you about my life: every morning, except on Sundays and Thursdays, I rise at nine. I kneel, say my prayers, read my psalm and bible-chapter, then I wash as thoroughly as I can and ring for my women, who come and dress me. At a quarter to eleven I am ready, then I read or write. At twelve I go to Mass, which in my case lasts just under half-an-hour, and afterwards I talk to the ladies, mine and others. Dinner is at one o'clock sharp, and directly afterwards I spend a quarter of an hour walking up and down in my rooms. Then I sit

down at my table and write letters until half-past six, when I send for
my ladies and go out walking for an hour to an hour-and-a-half, then
back to my rooms until supper. Is that not truly the life of a recluse?

> Carthusians are bound by vows of solitude and silence. Liselotte had
> earlier said about her life of loneliness: 'What prevents me from making
> friends is that as soon as you do, there is talk of your being in love with
> them and they with you, and that has made me break off all *commerce*.
> I have no friends left, I spend my life by myself, it may be dull but at
> least it is peaceful.' She added that she was in any case not much troubled
> by *galants*, owing to her shape and lack of money.

SOPHIE
Versailles 7 June 1705   In the gardens, the King never says outright,
'Do not accompany me'. When you meet him he halts, and if he bows
after saying a few words you must walk on. If he wishes you to stay, he
asks you to walk with him, otherwise you simply can't.

Trianon 21 June 1705   I am very well lodged here. I have four rooms,
and the closet where I am writing this looks out on to what we call
'*les sources*'. This is a little wood, which is so thick that the sunlight can't
penetrate it even at midday. There are more than fifty springs in it.
They make little rivulets, some of them no more than a foot wide and
easily crossed. Their grassy banks form little islands, large enough for
chairs and a table where one can play card games in the shade.

Marly 30 July 1705   From all I hear of Leibniz[1] he must be very
intelligent, and pleasant company in consequence. It is rare to find
learned men who are clean, do not stink and have a sense of humour.

Marly 2 August 1705   Mme la Duchesse de Bourgogne must have
recovered, for yesterday she was out hunting with the King. I see her
every day, but she hardly says two words to me in a fortnight; she
only bows, and then she looks at me over her shoulder. However, I
know where I stand and don't let it worry me. It is more to her dis-
credit than mine, and only proves what an ill-mannered child she is.

One hardly knows who one is any more. When the King passes
by, people don't raise their hats. When the Duchesse de Bourgogne

---

[1] Gottfried Wilhelm von Leibniz (1646–1716), the German philosopher, who had
been one of the 'learned men' to take Sophie's mind off her loss. His thoughts had
often been quoted in the Electress's letters to Liselotte, who dutifully ordered copies of
his works for her son.

goes walking, she is arm-in-arm with one of her ladies and the others walk by her side, and no one can tell who she is. In the drawing-room here and in the gallery at the Trianon the menfolk sit in the presence of M le Dauphin and the Duchesse de Bourgogne; some even lie full-length on the divans. I find it difficult to get used to this muddle, it seems very odd to me and not like a Court any more, I can't really say what it seems like.

AMELIESE
Marly 6 August 1705   The Trianon is quite close to Versailles, just a cannon shot away, and the gardens are the loveliest in the world. How surprising that you had never heard of it. No one ever comes to Versailles without seeing the Trianon.

If you had this heat and horrible dust in Hanover, you wouldn't think that driving about was such a pleasure. I went to St Germain yesterday to visit the Royals, and when I came back I had to change every stitch I was wearing and wash my face. I looked as though I was wearing a grey mask. A sailor tells me that even India is no hotter than this. There has been no rain for over two months, and the leaves are scorched on the trees. Adieu. I have changed my clothes from head to foot. The heat is terrible, and one sweats as though one were in an oven.

Marly 20 August 1705   A great many people here have seen the Princess of Ansbach,[1] and they are all full of praise. I hope the marriage will be a happy one, it started off so gaily. Of course, a wedding like this is bound to cheer up the Court. There is a time for everything, as King Solomon said, a time for grieving and a time for rejoicing. Their grief has lasted a long while, now it is time for joy. It is very lucky when such a marriage gives everyone pleasure: it is not often the case, as I know all too well.

My son has given me a fine fright: he has made himself ill with his crazy life, playing tennis, bathing, and paying too many visits to his mistress. It began violently but was soon over, thank God. He is, thank God, quite well again now.

Versailles 3 December 1705   Where can you and Luise have been hiding, to know so little of the ways of the world? I should have thought it was quite impossible to spend any time at all at any Court without getting quite a good idea of it. If one were to detest every man who is

[1] Caroline of Ansbach's betrothal to George Augustus of Hanover, Sophie's grandson, had been announced at the end of July.

fond of young fellows, it would be impossible to find even six people
to like, or at least not to dislike. They come in every sort of variation.
Some of them hate women and only love men, others like both men
and women, some only like children of ten or eleven, others young
men between seventeen and twenty-five. Most are in this category.
Other debauchees, who love neither men nor women, amuse themselves all alone, but there are only a few of those. And then there are
those who don't mind what they have, human or animal; they take
whatever comes along. I know someone here who brags that he has
had relations with everything under the sun except toads. Since I
heard this I can hardly look at the fellow without feeling sick. He used
to be in Monsieur's service, a really vicious piece, and no brains at all.
So you see, dear Ameliese, the world is much worse than you supposed.

Versailles 25 February 1706   Our Carnival is over. Even I, at my time
of life, had to put on fancy-dress in the end. All I used was a piece of
green taffeta. I tied it to a forked stick with a great rosette of rose-
coloured ribbon at the top. The disguise was open from head to waist, I
slipped into it, fastened it round my neck and held the stick in my hand.
You couldn't see the lines of my figure underneath, for the height of
the stick made me appear slim, and not a soul recognized me. Whenever the King looked at me I inclined the stick and seemed to be bow-
ing. He grew quite irritated, and at last asked the Duchesse de Bourgogne, 'Who on earth is that tall mask, eternally saluting me?' She
laughed, and said at last, 'That is Madame.' I thought he would die of
laughter.

The Duc de Bourgogne and three others, le Vidame, the Prince
de Rohan and young Seignelay, were wittily dressed: they were in gold
with golden masks and silver sashes to look like the carved gilt *guéridons*.
They wore candelabra on their heads and stationed themselves at the
four corners of the room. M le Dauphin was *en cornettes et andriennes*,
as were many of the ladies. It was most amusing—I had to laugh whenever I looked at him.

LUISE
Marly 22 April 1706   The story about the valet Harsch was very funny.
It reminds me of something that once happened to my son. I had
engaged a German teacher for him, and after he had studied the
language for four solid years I told him that in order to learn a language
it was necessary to practise conversation, and asked him to speak to me
in German every now and then.

Once when we were in the gallery, where you never know what might be going on, my son, intending to quote the German proverb *Art lässt nicht von Art*,[1] exclaimed with emphasis, as though pronouncing judgement, '*Arsch lässt nicht von Arsch*'.[2] I was utterly shocked. Thinking that he had meant to say this dreadful thing, I cried, 'Boy, be silent!' I really thought he had noticed some beastliness, which wouldn't have been at all uncommon here. But when he explained in French what he had meant to say and I had explained the difference between *Art* and arse, he laughed fit to die. But this showed, he said, that he would never learn German, and he has since given it up.

A M E L I E S E
Marly 20 May 1706 How can you possibly think that our young King[3] of England is a changeling, and not the Queen's son? I would stake my head on his being the rightful child. For one thing, he and his mother resemble each other like two drops of water. For another, a lady not at all partial to the Queen was present at the birth and told me, for the sake of simple truth, that she saw this child still attached to the umbilical cord. She has no doubt at all that he is the Queen's son.

The English treat their monarchs so curiously that it's not surprising there is no rush to become their ruler. *Ma tante* is quite right when she regards this child as the true heir.

S O P H I E
Versailles 10 June 1706 The upheavals of the last twenty years are unbelievable: the kingdoms of England, Holland and Spain have been transformed as fast as the scenery in a theatre. When later generations come to read about our history they will think they are reading a romance, and not believe a word of it.

A M E L I E S E
Marly 17 June 1706 The seals may look quite undamaged, but our letters are none the safer for all that. It is quite easy to open and close them up again, my son showed me this art.[4]

[1] Like is drawn to like.   [2] Arse is drawn to arse.

[3] James III, the Old Pretender, whose birth had been subject to a good deal of gossip. Evidently the rumour that he had been smuggled into the Queen's bed in a warming-pan was not yet forgotten.

[4] The Duc d'Orléans was keenly interested in science, as well as in the arts, and spent a good deal of his time with his German chemist/physician, Wilhelm von Homberg, in his laboratory conducting experiments.

Ma tante wrote that the King of Prussia was bringing his Crown Prince to Hanover, but not a word about a betrothal, so I pretend to know nothing.[1] I hope, dear Ameliese, that you will keep me informed.

Marly 29 July 1706 I can't understand why the King of Prussia goes out of his way to find more and more occasions for ceremony. As you know, I am the arch-enemy of all ceremonial. But it is hardly surprising that Court dress should be worn for the royal nuptials: it would be ridiculous otherwise, like the marriage of a chambermaid.

In the meantime, I have chosen an underskirt for *ma tante*, not bad at all: natural-looking blue flowers and gold festoons on a black background. German figures are no different from French ones, after all—the same dress is worn here and over there.

How funny that you should call my son the Duc de Chartres. That is the name of his son, my grandson. My son is called the Duc d'Orléans.

SOPHIE
Versailles 1 August 1706 It is now the greatest fashion to complain about the air. The Princesse de Conti no longer cares to leave the house at all, and never takes a walk. Nor does Mme d'Orléans, and they are forever in need of purging, bleeding, baths and mineral waters. Worst of all, they all exclaim about my health. I tell them every day that if I lived as they do I should be even sicker than they are, and that it is precisely because I don't use medicines, go out into the fresh air and take frequent exercise that I am well. However, they don't believe me. I can't even bear my curtains to be closed, I always keep them open —otherwise I should suffocate.

Versailles 2 September 1706 I'll tell you what we saw yesterday. We left here at half-past nine—Monseigneur was kind enough to let me sit next to the King—and arrived at the Invalides at eleven o'clock. The field was filled with coaches, and up at the church stood M. Mansart[2] with a troop of painters and workmen who had been employed in the building. He made a short speech, and presented the King with the freedom of the Invalides, handing him a mighty gilded key, beauti-

---

[1] Crown Prince Frederick William, Sophie Charlotte's son, came to marry Sophie Dorothea of Celle.

[2] Jules Hardouin Mansart, who was in charge of most of Louis' buildings, including Versailles, Marly and the Trianon. He had just completed the chapel in the Dôme des Invalides. The main building, the Hôtel des Invalides, which was to house the veterans of Louis' wars, had been begun in 1670.

fully worked. Then we entered the great church. It was quite over-whelming at first sight: gold, marble, and more marble in beautiful white squares.

When you stand in the exact centre under the dome, you can see seven golden altars. There are four chapels, dedicated to the four fathers of the church, and in the dome of each chapel is painted the life of the saint concerned. There are a St Gregory, a St Ambrose, a St Augustin and a St Jerome in the middle. Directly underneath the great dome are the four evangelists, one in each corner. Above, inside the dome, is the Holy Trinity. The martyrs are at the sides, and I think the Saints are up there with the Trinity. The dome is enormously high, and the figures look smaller than life-size although they are sixteen foot tall. But I must send you a book about this church—I'm afraid I may spoil the beautiful impression with my stupid description.

There is not a word of truth in the story that my son refused to accept the army command. They are now, unfortunately, lying outside Turin, and I am very much afraid that he and Prince Eugene, who is in hot pursuit, will get infernally into one another's hair.

AMELIESE
Versailles 9 September 1706 My daughter is losing no time in having babies, she has been married eight years now, and is pregnant with her eighth.

The wedding-skirt and all the other things will soon be on their way. Dear Ameliese, in your account of the presents you forgot to mention the bouquet with the ruby ring that the King of Prussia gave to his son's bride, *ma tante* writes of it.

I don't feel very cheerful because I am worried about my son, who is up to his ears in the siege of Turin.

SOPHIE
Versailles 16 September 1706 My heart is heavy. The very day when you last wrote was a most unhappy one for me, and all because the Maréchal de Marsin and the other generals refused to listen to my son. He wanted his army to leave the lines to attack the enemy, but neither Marsin nor the others would consent. They issued an order expressly forbidding it, which my son, unhappily, was forced to obey.

The enemy attacked the entrenchment at a spot which the Maréchal de la Feuillade had neglected to fortify, relying on two rivers that flow nearby, and never realizing that the water dried up in the hot weather.

So the enemy crossed over, 35,000 against 8,000 men, forced their way through and of course relieved Turin.

My son defended his position as long as he could, and was wounded in two places. He was hit in the hip by a musket-ball, and his left arm was injured between the elbow and the hand, though his barber wrote to assure me that he is in no danger. Maréchal de Marsin paid for his bad counsel with his life.[1]

Versailles 23 September 1706 This is how my son's misfortune came about. The King had expressly commanded him not to make a move without the Maréchal de Marsin, a timid fellow who doesn't stir without consulting Mme de Maintenon, and she understands no more about warfare than my Titti. How is it to end?

LUISE
Versailles 7 October 1706 Thank you for your concern about my son. The wound in his side was not dangerous, but he almost died of the one in his arm. My poor son didn't take enough care of himself, he kept on riding, his low spirits prevented him from resting night or day, and the wound became inflamed. But it was cut so *à propos* that it didn't come to anything terrible. Thank God, he has an excellent doctor and barber.

My son will remain with his army and not come home this winter. Fortunately for him, it is well known that had his advice been followed the King would now be in possession of Turin, and the enemy defeated.

Versailles 28 October 1706 As I have been saying for a long time, it would have been far better to let the two Spanish kings fight it out between themselves. Ours would have had the advantage, for his fists are terrifying. But I should consider it more Christian if the two kings fought for their kingdom instead of spilling so much blood.

AMELIESE
Versailles 18 November 1706 I had to laugh, dear Ameliese, because you find me good-looking in the portrait that I sent to *ma tante*. If a great fat face, flat lips and small, narrow eyes are things of beauty, then I certainly am good-looking, and getting more so every day, since every day I grow fatter.

Dearest Ameliese, we must all follow our destiny. Mine has led me to

[1] The Orléans army was destroyed by the Imperial forces under the command of Prince Eugene of Savoy at the Battle of Turin on 7 September 1706.

France, here I live and here I shall probably die. Germany is still dear to me, and I am so little part of France that I live out my life in solitude in the midst of all the Court, but I see that it is God's will.

What foolishness to think that no pretty and elegant objects can be made outside France. The very best of our craftsmen were amongst the Protestants who were driven out, and it is obvious that it must be possible to obtain equally beautiful things in Germany now.

LUISE

Versailles 2 December 1706 Thank you for sharing my pleasure in my son's arrival. Since he has been playing tennis again his arm is much improved, he can move all his fingers and even play the flute. And even if one of his fingers is always stiff, it is to be counted for nothing compared with what might have happened.[1]

AMELIESE

Versailles 3 February 1707 I'm glad you liked the little silver box, though it hardly deserves the honour of being called a rarity. I see that you and Luise don't exchange New Year presents, as this is the first present you had this year. Do you carry tobacco in your pocket? I shouldn't have thought so, it is an ugly habit, and I didn't imagine that you were so much *à la mode*.

I am glad you enjoyed yourself so much. That is more than I can say of my life here. All the year round I eat my midday meal on my own, and hurry through it as fast as I can, because it's annoying to eat by oneself surrounded by twenty fellows who count every mouthful and watch one chew. I never take longer than half-an-hour. In the evenings I eat with the King. There are five or six of us at table, but people swallow their food without taking much notice of anyone else, it is like eating in a convent, and there is no conversation except for occasional whispered words to a neighbour.

SOPHIE

Versailles 10 February 1707 I can't get used to the idea of the Elector of Brunswick, whose birth and childhood I remember as though it were yesterday, being a grandfather.[2] I am exactly eight years older than

---

[1] The field-surgeons had been in favour of the immediate amputation of the hand, so Liselotte's suspicion of doctors was once more shown to be well-founded.

[2] George Louis of Hanover had become a grandfather through the birth of Frederick, the future Prince of Wales, remembered as 'poor Fred'.

he is; I was born on 27 May 1652, and he on 28 May 1660. I
remember how I watched everyone rush about, worrying. Then I ran
up to your room and lay down quite flat by the door so as to hear
what was being said inside. Soon afterwards Frau von Harling came to
look for me and took me to you. The prince was being bathed behind a
screen, I looked all round at everything that was happening, and it
seems to me that I can see it yet.[1]

ANELIESE
Versailles 27 March 1707   Although I have a dreadful cough and such a
cold that I can neither hear nor speak, I must write to you today to
correct a mistake that you made. I see you are under the impression
that my son is a prince of the blood, but that is not so. He is a Grandson
of France, which is the greater rank, with many more privileges.
Grandsons of France may salute queens, sit in their presence and ride
with them in their coaches. None of this is possible for princes of the
blood. They are served like *les enfants de France, par quartier*, they have a
master of the horse, a chief almoner, a chief controller of the household,
none of which princes of the blood have, nor do they have a bodyguard,
like my son, nor a Swiss guard; so you see there is a great difference in
everything.

I always like hearing how things are going in Germany. I am like an
old coachman who still takes pleasure in hearing the crack of the whip
even though he can no longer drive.

SOPHIE
Marly 21 July 1707 5 a.m.   Here I sit, writing to you in my shift, for
at this hour there is no danger of a surprise visit. The heat is so great
that even the very oldest can't remember anything like it. You hear of
nothing but dogs and horses dropping dead, of labourers losing consciousness and dying in the fields, and of huntsmen fainting and falling
like mosquitoes. We all stayed in our rooms, wearing nothing but
shifts, until seven o'clock yesterday. One had to change continuously,
I used up eight shifts in a single day, they were soaked. During meals
one wipes and wipes, it is terrible. If Spain is any hotter than this, my
son and his army will surely melt.

----

[1] Liselotte often referred to the occasion of her cousin's birth, remembering such
details as the doll in swaddling-clothes placed in a gilded urn on the terrace, and her
governess's efforts to convince her that it had grown there. 'But,' she said, 'I knew
better. Afterward they showed me the real prince. He was a beautiful child with large
eyes.'

AMELIESE

Fontainebleau 14 September 1707 Naturally, I write more than one letter a day. Not a day passes when I don't write at least four, and on Sundays often twelve. I am glad you are back from your visit to Brunswick, because nothing is sadder than to see everyone depart and be left behind on one's own.

Many honest lives are being lost in the Turkish wars, too. I think a general peace would be the best thing. Wherever you look, the clerics are corrupting the Christians with their quarrelling. It makes any faith impossible, and if people had faith they would lead better, more Christian lives.

I expect you know that our princes aren't leaving for the wars. Toulon has been relieved without their help. The French proverb says '*Qui trop embrasse, mal étreint*'. They tried to gobble up Toulon and Marseilles in one mouthful, and failed on both counts.[1]

Versailles 12 January 1708 My God, how lucky you are to be able to travel wherever you like, there is nothing I like better than to travel.

It did my heart good to hear you say that Heidelberg has been rebuilt so well. God save it from further disaster. There is not so much burning and scorching as there used to be in M Louvois' lifetime, and I hope it will be safe.

Please tell me where you are lodged and which street you are in. And I should like to hear whether the Heiligengeist church and the Neckar Bridge have been rebuilt. Why won't the Elector repair the castle? Surely it would be worth the trouble. The air is good in Heidelberg, but by the castle it is even better than in the town.

SOPHIE

Versailles 28 January 1708 8 p.m. I came back here at three o'clock. Before the meal I walked in the garden for a good hour, it was the finest weather in the world. The sun is so hot that all the flowers are in bud, the honeysuckle is quite green and the almonds and peach-trees are in full flower.

Last night the King ate an omelette filled with tiny champignons, the sort that are called *mousserons* here. They have never in living memory been found until April or the end of March at the earliest.

I'm sure M de Louvois must be burning in the next world because

[1] The Maréchal de Tessé defeated the Imperial forces in their two-pronged attack.

I

of the Palatinate, he was so horribly cruel and quite incapable of feeling any pity. It seems to me that Villars[1] should be satisfied with what he has collected from Germany already; no one in France is richer than he is. Heroes are greatly at fault when they are avaricious; sooner or later it leads to trouble, as it must cause injustice, which does no one any good. For this reason I don't think things will end well for Milord Marlborough.

Versailles 29 March 1708 We expect to hear any day now that our young King of England has arrived in Scotland.[2] So far we only know that His Majesty sailed with a good wind from Ostend. A frigate that encountered him off Dunkirk has brought the news that the whole of Scotland has declared for him; he is expected with longing, and will be proclaimed as soon as he disembarks. It serves Queen Anne right, she was so eager for war, and now she will have it.

Versailles 5 April 1708 There is no news at all of our young King of England, we don't know what has become of him. I was amused that you called him King *in partibus*, like the bishops. But I should be sorry if anything had happened to him. It would be too dreadful if he had been taken prisoner, and Queen Anne were to order the execution of her own brother.

Versailles 13 May 1708 The King experienced a great loss last Friday, he lost a good, honest man, the *Contrôleur des Bâtiments*, M Mansart. On Thursday he was still with us, taking part in the promenade with the English Court. He walked next to me until half-past seven. Then, as he was very hungry, he begged leave to go home. When he got there he drank a great deal of iced water and ate enormous quantities of all kinds of food: a ham omelette, green peas, strawberries, cream, cucumber salad, then drank more water, and so gave himself indigestion. At two o'clock in the morning he had a stomach-ache, at six o'clock that evening he was dead. The King loses much in this man, he really knew his job.

Versailles 9 June 1708 Here comes the news that M d'Antin, the legal and legitimate son of Mme de Montespan, is to have Mansart's office,

[1] Claude Louis Hector, Maréchal Duc de Villars, commander of Louis' Rhine army.
[2] The Old Pretender had tried to return to England with the help of the French fleet. He had hoped for a rising in his favour, but this did not materialize, and he was back in France before the end of the month.

which brings in 50,000 francs, and when the King spends ten million on building, the superintendent has one for himself, as well as two or three hundred to hand out in commissions, from which he can draw money. To be *Surintendant des Bâtiments* is one of the most profitable positions at Court.

Prince Eugene is far too intelligent for you not to admire him. Since you want to know why he used to be called Mme l'Ancienne and Mme Simon, it was because these were the names of two very common whores (by your leave, by your leave). People used to say that he, too, used to give *à tout venant beau jeu* by acting the lady, but he may have lost the knack in Germany.

> Prince Eugene of Savoy was in Hanover on behalf of the Allies. His military genius, which first attracted attention during the Turkish wars, rather surprised the French Court, where he had been brought up. Liselotte remembers him as a dirty, thin little boy with straight, greasy hair. Nothing much had been expected of him. 'Had you seen him then, you wouldn't have been surprised that our King didn't do very much for him,' wrote Liselotte to Sophie. And later, 'The handsomest thing about him must be the diamond-studded sword presented by Queen Anne.'

Fontainebleau 1 August 1708 I knew that a battle[1] had been lost, but didn't know where. Now I do know: but none of the details because one mayn't discuss it here, and the men who are in the fighting aren't allowed to write of it. All our princes in the army are unharmed, thank God, and have done well. M de Vendôme blames two of the Duc de Bourgogne's people for the loss of the battle. He is a clever man and his heart is in the right place, but he is always being accused of laziness, and of lying in bed and, by your leave, sitting on his close-stool for too much of the time. It's more than ten years since someone who saw the Duc de Bourgogne's horoscope said that he would be unlucky in war and lose a battle. Funny, how that's come true. People talk as much about this battle as they do where you are, but only in whispers and not out loud.

Versailles 20 September 1708 The old woman is more horrible than ever, and she is training the Duchesse de Bourgogne to be malicious

---

[1] The Battle of Oudenarde, in which Prince Eugene and Marlborough once again joined forces to inflict a crushing defeat on the French. The Duc de Bourgogne had a command under Vendôme.

and insincere. The Duchesse de Bourgogne goes to Mass wrapped in a great hood in order to appear pious, and pretends to cry at the *Salut*, but she can drink two whole bottles of undiluted wine without showing any effect, and is such a *coquette* that she even runs after her own *écuyer*. So you see. The old woman tells the King that the Duchess has no equal in piety and virtue, and he believes her faithfully. She is rude to me every single day. When I am about to help myself at the King's table she has the dishes whisked away from under my nose, and when I call on her she looks at me over her shoulder without a word, or laughs at me with her ladies. The old woman has arranged this on purpose, in the hope of provoking me to protest, and then she will say that there is no living with me and have me sent to Montargis. But I am up to her tricks, I say nothing, do not complain, laugh at whatever they may do, and tell myself that she is not immortal, that everything in the world changes, and that they won't get rid of me except by my death.

Versailles 23 September 1708   Every evening Mme de Maintenon receives five or six large packets from the Court spies, accounts of all that goes on at Court. The spies are all people of quality. Their underlings, members of the Swiss guard, are posted by the doors, and observe all the comings and goings and who eats meat on fast-days. This information is then placed on the lady's dressing-table, and she makes use of it to entertain the King.

Yesterday at supper M le Dauphin talked to me for the first time in a long while. He told me about his new palace at Meudon. The panelling alone cost him 110,000 francs, quite apart from the building, which cost three times as much. He seems more concerned about that than about what is happening in Flanders.[1]

AMELIESE
Versailles 1 December 1708   I am very busy today. We have just arrived from Marly, and today is the first of December. First, we have to get settled in, and secondly, this is the day when the creditors come to call for their money. I have already paid out 150 pistoles.

We travelled from Marly in the gentlest spring weather, but today it is beginning to freeze. M le Dauphin remarked that hard frost before Martinmas means a mild winter.

[1] Lille, the capital of French Flanders, was under siege, and surrendered to Marlborough and Eugene in December.

SOPHIE

Versailles 10 January 1709 The cold is so grim that words fail me. I am sitting in front of a roaring fire, there is a screen in front of the door, my neck is wrapped in sables and my feet are in a bearskin sack, but all the same I am trembling with cold and can hardly hold my pen. I have never known such a dreadful winter in all my life; the wine is frozen solid in the bottles.

I must thank you for the beautiful coins, I spend entire days poring over them. Last Monday I bought 150 with the King's New Year present, and now I have a cabinet of gold coins, a suit of emperors from Julius Caesar to Heraclius, with no gaps. Amongst them there are some quite rare pieces that even the King himself hasn't got. I got them all quite cheaply, and now have 410 coins.

> In the morning of that same day Liselotte had written to Ameliese, 'It is so cold that my ink is turning to ice, and I can hardly move although my stove is blazing and I am still in bed.'

AMELIESE

Versailles 19 January 1709 You hear nothing but complaints about the cold, there has not been such a winter in living memory. During the last fortnight people have been found dead of cold every morning, and the partridges are picked up frozen in the fields. All the plays have been stopped and so have all the law-suits, for the judges and the advocates can't sit in their chambers because of the cold.

SOPHIE

Marly 7 February 1709 We arrived here yesterday, although it is still dreadfully cold. Last week it began to thaw a little, but since Sunday the frost has been worse than ever. We had some music here last night, but it didn't work out very well, half the coaches couldn't make their way up here because the roads were covered in ice. A great many people have broken their arms or legs.

The Duc de Berry and the Duc de Bourgogne may have been brought up together in the same manner, but their characters are entirely different. The Duc de Berry is anything but pious. He has no consideration for God or man, no principles, and nothing worries him as long as he can enjoy himself, it hardly matters how. He loves shooting, playing cards, chatting to young women devoid of common sense, eating well, all that is much to his taste. Skating must be added.

My son is very different. He likes warfare, and understands it. He enjoys neither hunting, shooting nor gambling, but loves all the arts, especially painting. The painters say that his judgement is very good.[1] He loves chemistry, he loves conversation and talks well. He has studied hard, and knows a lot because his memory is good. He loves music and he loves women. I often wish there were a little less of the latter, because it takes him into such bad company and makes him ruin himself and his children.

Marly 14 February 1709   The whole of Marly, great and small, comes to me with condolences,[2] and those who don't call write. Only Mme de Maintenon, who lives no more than ten paces away, hasn't called or sent word.

LUISE

Versailles 2 March 1709   The misery has hit the flour-mills too, and many people in Paris have died of hunger. I was told such a pitiable story yesterday, of a woman who stole a loaf of bread from a baker's shop. The baker caught the woman, who said, weeping, 'If you knew what misery we are living in, you wouldn't take the bread away from me. I have three children with no clothes, no fire and no bread. I couldn't bear it any longer, and that's why I took the bread.' She was taken before a *commissionaire*, who said, 'Mind what you say, for I'm going back home with you', and went along with her. In the room were three little children, dressed in rags, cowering in a corner trembling with cold. He asked the eldest, 'Where is your father?' 'Behind the door,' said the child. The *commissionaire* looked behind the door to see what the father was doing, and was horrified to find that the man had hanged himself in desperation.

Versailles 20 April 1709   I do so entirely agree with you, nothing in this life is more important than one's health. Tell me, dear Luise, what do the doctors call Ameliese's illness? I can imagine how you feel, it is a frightful thing to see a beloved sister suffer so.

You must not say 'by your leave' when you mention feet. That is considered very bourgeois here, we say 'feet' without any 'by your leave'.[3]

---

[1] His painting master was Antoine Coypel.

[2] Liselotte's aunt, the Abbess of Maubuisson, had died at the age of eighty-six.

[3] When Liselotte uses this phrase, as she often does, and nearly always twice over, she is using it in inverted commas, quoting an old Heidelberg retainer who used to say in the broadest *patois* '*mit Verlöff, mit Verlöff*'.

SOPHIE

Marly 2 May 1709 Queen Anne is certainly well advised not to be looking for a new husband. From what I have heard of the last one, so far as his company and conversation were concerned, the Queen's loss didn't seem to be great.[1]

If all confessors resembled my first two, superstition would soon be abolished. But there must be vast numbers like my present one, who has the beliefs of an old nun. He admires everything that is not admirable in this religion, but he can't make me change my views. I tell him that I won't be persuaded against my better judgement, and we have many a quarrel, though we always remain good friends, as, religion apart, he is the best, most honest man on earth.

Next Saturday will see the arrival of a certain lady, Frau von Rathsamshausen. I hope she will bring me new anecdotes to pass on to you, for here you hear of nothing but sadness, how bread is dearer every day, how people are dying of hunger.

Versailles 19 May 1709 Our King in Spain has assured all his subjects that he will live and die amongst them, while they have promised His Majesty to fight for him to their last breath. This King, it seems, will not be dethroned easily.

Versailles 23 May 1709 If the famine gets any worse, perhaps they will send all the extra mouths away, including me. Then I would come to you, for you would not let me want for bread. I wish I could say there was no famine here, but it is, alas, only too true.

> The terrible winter, the famine ('They say that little children are devouring each other'), and the ruinous war led France to sue for peace. The Allies agreed to negotiate only on condition that Louis himself removed Philip from the throne of Spain. 'While our King could make his grandson accept the kingdom of Spain,' wrote Liselotte, 'he cannot force him to leave it when his subjects want to keep him.' Louis refused the Allies' demand, saying that, if fight he must, he would fight his enemies rather than his own flesh and blood.

Versailles 9 June 1709 The King has sent all his gold tableware to the mint. Golden dishes, set with diamonds and rubies, extremely beautiful, the *nef* where the napkins were kept, of the finest possible workmanship, everything, everything is melted down. Many of the courtiers

[1] Prince George of Denmark had died in 1708.

have sent the King their silver plate, and will eat off earthenware now.
The Comte de Toulouse alone sent 200,000 francs' worth; the Duc de
Gramont was the first to send. I shan't follow his example, for I have too
little silver to amount to anything much, but so that no one can say I
flout the King's wishes I no longer eat off gold, only silver; I have no
gold on my table at all.

> A few weeks later Madame writes, 'My son has given all his gold plate
> and some of his silver, but not all. He has, to be sure, spent such a fortune
> on his campaigns that they ought to be very grateful.'

LUISE
Marly 15 June 1709 The Allied proposals are really too barbaric.
Better to go to rack and ruin than accept such conditions. I can't think
how anyone could have imagined that our King would agree. Since,
as the proverb has it, pride comes before a fall, I hope the insolence of
Milord Marlborough and Prince Eugene won't go unpunished. The
latter would do well to remember that France is his mother country,
and that he was born the King's subject. I am really angry with him for
having prevented the peace.

I often reflect how strangely Our Lord divides His good gifts. You
two have your freedom, but you are ill; I on the other hand live in
slavery, but am hale and hearty.

There has been a lot of news during the last week. The Minister of
War, who is called M de Chamillart, has been dismissed, and his place
has been filled by a Councillor of State, the *Surintendant* of St Cyr.[1]
This shows who was behind it. I am sorry about M Chamillart's misfortune because he used to do his best to please me. This new one may
well do the opposite in order to pay court to his benefactress.

Versailles 13 July 1709 I feel irritable today, I have so many disagreeable things on my mind. My treasurer has robbed me abominably, and
this has given me a lot of work. People here are really too full of self-
interest. It comes from all this buying and selling of appointments, in
the end it makes villains of them all.

> M Avoust had defrauded Liselotte of 50,000 thaler. He threw himself
> out of a second floor window to escape arrest, and later died from his
> injuries, 'too squashed to live'.

[1] The new Minister of War was Daniel François Voisin.

The buying and selling of appointments (called *charges*) greatly pre-judiced the loyalty of servants, who did all they could to enrich them-selves while they were in office. The *charges* died with the employers, but the employees, as a matter of right, collected the objects under their care.

SOPHIE

Versailles 15 August 1709 I have had a new carriage only four times in all my thirty-eight years in France, but all the linen is renewed every four years, and the old things go to the first woman of the bedchamber. There is nothing that one can truly call one's own. Linen, nightshirts and petticoats belong to the woman of the bedchamber, and the *dame d'atour* takes possession of my clothes from one year to the next, as well as all my lace; the carriages are the property of the *premier écuyer*, and when I die all my silver goes to the *premier maître d'hôtel* unless he is paid the equivalent in money.

Versailles 22 August 1709 When I came through the Porte St Honoré just now I saw the people rushing about; they looked terrified, and there were cries of '*Ah, mon Dieu!*' Every window was black with people; some of them had climbed on to the roofs, and down below the shops were being shut up and doors locked. Even the Palais-Royal was closed.

I couldn't think what it all meant, but when I reached the inner courtyard a woman, a complete stranger, came up and said, 'Did you know, Madame, that there is a revolt in Paris?' I thought she must be out of her mind, but she said, 'I'm not mad, Madame. It's true—so true, in fact, that forty people have been killed already.' When I asked my people if this was true they said, 'Only too true', and that was why they had closed the gates of the Palais-Royal.

I asked what had caused the revolt. It was because the labourers working on St Martin's wall had each been promised three sous and a loaf of bread. There had been two thousand of them, but that morning there were suddenly four thousand people demanding money and bread in no uncertain terms.

When supplies ran out, an especially insolent woman was arrested and put into the pillory. That started the uproar. Suddenly there were six thousand people. The woman was dragged from the pillory. A lot of servants who had been dismissed from their posts joined in, shouting for loot, and broke into the bakers' shops, which they plund-ered. The soldiers were called out to fire at the mob, but the people soon noticed that they were shooting only to frighten, and that there was no lead in the muskets. The rioters called, 'Let us attack them, their guns aren't loaded.' This forced the soldiers to shoot some of them down. This went on from four o'clock in the morning until about midday.

The Maréchal de Boufflers and the Duc de Gramont happened to drive by while the revolt was taking place and the stones were flying. They alighted, addressed the mob, threw down some money and promised to tell the King that the men had been promised bread and pay which they hadn't been given. Instantly the tumult died down, and people threw their hats up in the air, crying '*Vive le roi et du pain*'. Aren't they good, the Parisians, to calm down so quickly?

Yesterday, when they held their market, all was peaceful, but dearly though they love their King and the royal house they hate Mme de Maintenon. I needed a breath of fresh air because it was hot in my low-ceilinged closet, but I had hardly appeared when a whole crowd of people collected; they showered me with blessings, but spoke so horribly of the lady that I was forced to return indoors and close my windows. They shouted that they wanted to get their hands on her and burn her for a witch.

LUISE
Marly 31 August 1709   I wish to God, dear Luise, that there were something I could say to comfort you.[1] Poor Ameliese often delighted me with her letters, she used to write so amusingly and naturally, I was so fond of her.

I think you are quite right not to have her opened up. We only die when our hour has come, and not before, and there is no evidence that a single life has yet been saved, though so many people are being opened up now. I have forbidden it in my will.

Versailles 14 September 1709   You will now have many companions in grief. Four days ago our troops lost a battle near Mons,[2] but this time they defended themselves so valiantly that there were a great many dead on both sides. You see nothing but sadness and tears.

I fear that the affair of my treasurer will not be settled without loss to myself, because the rogue has stolen more than he can ever pay back.

[1] The Raugravine Ameliese von Degenfeld had died in July, and of the Elector's many children only Liselotte and Luise were still living.
[2] At Malplaquet, where Villars and Boufflers were beaten by Marlborough and Eugene on 11 September 1709. There were 33,000 casualties.

My son, far from being able to advance me any money, can't even give me what he owes me. He has almost ruined himself with his Spanish campaigns. He had to use his own money, it is dreadful what he spent. The King never sent him a penny. Everything—journeys, campaigns, sieges—everything was at his own expense.

Never in my life have I seen such wretched, miserable times. God grant that a good peace may change all that.

SOPHIE
Versailles 28 September 1709   It is very true that the lady[1] is the cause of the universal misery. The famine is so great that you see people drop dead of hunger, there is grief and suffering everywhere, it affects the greatest and the lowest.

The court is filled with intrigue, some to gain the powerful lady's favour, some M le Dauphin's, and others the Duc de Bourgogne's. It is a great muddle, and I can say in the words of the song '*Si on ne mourrait pas de faim, il en faudrait mourir de rire*'.

LUISE
Versailles 26 October 1709   These are indeed sad times. As soon as you leave the house you are followed by the poor, black with hunger. Everyone is paid with notes now, there is no money anywhere.

SOPHIE
Versailles 19 January 1710   You probably know that the Duc de Bourgogne is so pious that he won't look at anyone but his wife. To tease him, she once asked Mme de la Vrillière[2] to get into bed in her place. The Duchesse pretended to be very tired that evening. He was delighted to find her ready for bed first for once, and undressed as quickly as possible. When he came into the room he asked, 'Where is madame?', she answered 'Here' from behind the curtain, and he flung off his dressing-gown and leapt into bed. As soon as he was under the bedclothes she came out and made a great pretence of being angry. 'You claim to be devout,' she said, 'yet here you are, between the sheets with one of the prettiest ladies in the kingdom!' He asked her what she was talking about. She told him to take a look at the person who was lying beside him, and he fell into a fury. He took his 'bedwarmer' by the shoulders and threw her out of bed, without

---

[1] Mme de Maintenon, who in Liselotte's opinion was making a fortune out of the shortages by buying up food and selling it to the army at extortionate prices.
[2] Françoise de Mailly, Marquise de la Vrillière.

giving her time to catch her breath or put on her slippers. Then he
set about her with his own slippers. She escaped barefoot, he couldn't
catch her, but called her every sort of name—*effrontée* and *vilaine* were
the least of them. They tried to calm him, but they were laughing so
much that they could hardly speak. In the end he cooled down.

A few days ago, when the Maréchale de Coeuvres tried to kiss him
he defended himself with all his might. When he saw he was losing the
struggle he stuck a pin into her head so hard that she has had to keep to
her bed ever since. Even Joseph himself didn't go to such lengths—he
only ran away and left his coat behind, but neither did he flail about him
nor jab pins in. Such chastity as this has not been seen before.

LUISE
Versailles 26 January 1710   We have a charming novelty here, a picture
that a Carmelite made for the King. In case you don't know what a
Carmelite is, it's a kind of monk. He is called Père Sebastien, and he
made this picture with more than a hundred pieces that can be moved
about. Women wash and beat their laundry, men chop wood and shoe
their horses, and two of them are sawing. Others, in carriages, are
saluting : one waves his hand, another pulls off his hat. A beggar doffs his
hat and begs, and when the people have passed by he puts it on again.

Liselotte goes on to describe how ladies in a coach cross a bridge and
acknowledge greetings with bows. Above the castle-gate a clock keeps
proper time. There are windmills and a watermill, and ships in full sail
move across the sea in the background. It must have been toys like this
that made Liselotte say later, 'Oh, that the King were still alive! There
was something interesting to see every evening, for whatever was new
and pretty was sent to Court for us to admire.'

Versailles 15 February 1710   My grandson is too delicate, I don't think
he will live long. Though he may be large for his age, he is altogether
too weak and sickly. I prefer children to be a little headstrong, that is a
sign of intelligence.

I never boxed my son's ears when he was small, though I whipped
him so thoroughly that he remembers it today. A box on the ear can be
dangerous, as it may injure the head.

FREIHERR VON HARLING
Versailles 27 February 1710   Of course I remember the good Meyer
and all her stories, and how I once thrust a brand-new candle-trimmer

into her behind (by your leave, by your leave). Please make no apology for reminding me of the old days, there is nothing I like better than thinking of them. I was never happier than in Hanover.

> Further tomboyish deeds came to Liselotte's mind around this period. 'Stories over fifty years old, my God, how quickly time passes and everything changes. . . . That must have been the house where I once shot one of the maids in the behind with an arrow from my crossbow, which caused a great row, but a thaler soon calmed everything down again.' And, 'If things are still done in Hanover as they used to be, you will have found the church filled with flowers and foliage. I always used to get into trouble because I could never resist making the foxgloves click.'

SOPHIE
Versailles 5 March 1710 I once had an amusing conversation with the poor Archbishop of Rheims.[1] As you know, he used to be *premier duc et pair*. Once, when we were walking together in the *val* at St Germain, he said to me, 'It seems to me, Madame, that you don't think too highly of us, the French dukes, and have a much higher opinion of your German princes.' I answered, quite drily, 'That is so.' 'If you don't want to compare us to them, who would you compare us to?' 'To the pashas and viziers of Turkey,' I replied. 'How is that?' he asked, and I said, 'Like them, you have all the dignities, but no birth. The King has made you what you are, just as the Great Turk created his pashas and viziers. But our German princes are made only by God and their mothers and fathers, so there can be no comparison. What is more, they are free while you are subjects.' I thought the poor man would jump out of his skin, he was so furious.

Versailles 9 March 1710 It is hardly surprising that the Duc de Berry is like a child. He never talks to clever people, but sticks day and night in the Duchesse de Bourgogne's apartments, where he plays the lackey for the ladies. They make him fetch and carry for them—their work, their little tables, whatever it might be—and while they are lying *en écharpe* in armchairs or on divans he stands, or sometimes sits on a small tabouret.

Versailles 3 April 1710 I assure you that even at Mass there are distinctions of rank. For example, only the *petites filles de France* have the

[1] Le Tellier, Louvois' brother, who had died on February 23rd.

right to have *clercs de chapelle* to make their responses and hold the torch from the *sanctus* in the *préface* to the *domine, non sum dignus*. The *princesses du sang* may not have torches or separate *clercs*, and have their responses made by pages instead. And at the end of Mass the Host only goes to be kissed to the *enfants de France*, and the goblet is not offered to the *princesses du sang*, either. So you see, there is something worldly in spiritual affairs; and should matters fail to have the desired effect on our Lord, a worldly purpose always remains and all is not lost.

Versailles 27 April 1710 New medals are rarer than antique ones, which I often find in Paris. If that rogue of a treasurer hadn't robbed me, I could buy any number of gold medals, but as it is I can't buy more than five or six at a time. Still, I manage to add to my cabinet every month. To begin with I only had 160, now I have 511, and I hope in time to have a fine cabinet full of rare medals.

I don't think there can be a country in the world where the people revolt as often and as easily as England. The Germans love their masters more than other nation, and the French, while fond of saying and singing every kind of slander, allow them to do as they like.

Marly 5 June 1710 The Duchesse de Bourgogne came rushing into my room with her husband and all her ladies and cried, 'Madame, we bring you the Duc de Berry, the King has just announced that he is to marry Mademoiselle.' I said to the Duchesse de Bourgogne, 'Now that I am at liberty to speak let me assure you, Madame, that I shall be eternally grateful for all the trouble you have taken in this matter', and to the Duc de Berry, 'Come, let me embrace you, because you are now more than ever what Mme la Dauphine used to call you.' His mother always called him 'le Berry de Madame', as he well knows.

The proposed marriage between the Duc de Berry and her son's eldest daughter was no surprise to Liselotte, who had been informed of it by the King under seal of secrecy. With this marriage, each of the King's grandsons now had a wife who was a granddaughter of Monsieur. The Queen of Spain and the Duchesse de Bourgogne were the children of his younger daughter by his first wife, and the future Mme de Berry was the eldest daughter of the Duc d'Orléans. The Duchesse de Bourgogne had been largely responsible for this project, and this was why she was the first to announce the news. The King and the Dauphin arrived soon afterwards, followed by the whole of Marly, offering congratulations.

Versailles 29 June 1710   You are very kind to share in our joy, which is considerable, in my grandchild's marriage. My son is busy with his daughter's finery, just like the late Monsieur. There was a funny scene that made me laugh. I expect you remember the splendid diamond earrings, a mass of diamond drops, that Monsieur used to own. Since his death Mme d'Orléans has worn them all the time, but my son intended to give them to his daughter. When he handed them over and the mother realized he was in earnest, she began to weep bitterly. The daughter, seeing her mother cry, brought them back at once. The mother was all smiles, but when the daughter saw that the mother meant to keep them *she* burst into tears. My son and I laughed so much that we nearly split our sides.

LUISE

Versailles 5 July 1710   Tonight at 5 o'clock the betrothal and signing of the contract will take place in the King's closet. Mademoiselle my grandchild will not be a Royal Highness until tomorrow; today she is still *Altesse Sérénissime*, for *Altesse Royale* goes no further than the grandson and granddaughter of France. All the others are only 'of the blood', and not royal highnesses but only serene.

Marly 24 August 1710   Since yesterday it has been quite cool, but we don't think the grape harvest will be spoilt. Of course I know that hops, not vines, are grown in Hanover. What do you drink there, beer or wine? When I was there I used to drink small beer, but towards the end of my stay I drank a little wine, which agreed with me very well.

Since we arrived here last Wednesday we have been out stag-hunting twice. I went in a *calèche* and the young men were on horseback. My goodness, how everything changes! When I was young I should never have dreamt that I shouldn't mind watching people ride without being able to join them. Now I don't care a straw, and hardly remember that I ever sat on a horse.

SOPHIE

Marly 13 November 1710   It is the foolishness of Frenchwomen that they always stick in dark corners. Mme de Maintenon has had proper little niches built, which she uses when she lies down. She has made a sort of house round a small divan, a pavilion of boards that can be closed up tight. The Duchesse de Bourgogne has one, and so has the Princesse de Conti. I should suffocate if I had to sit or lie in such a thing.

LUISE
Versailles 14 December 1710   The Duchesse de Berry fainted dead away.
We thought it was a stroke, but when the Duchesse de Bourgogne
poured some vinegar over her face she returned to her senses and began
to vomit abominably. Small wonder, after hours of continuous stuffing
during the play—*pêches au caramel*, chestnuts, a confection of red-
currants and cranberries, dried cherries with quantities of lemon—
and then she ate some fish for supper and drank on top of that. She felt
sick, tried to keep it back, and fainted. Today she is well again, and
although I tell her she is bound to make herself very ill one day with
all that terrible overeating, she won't listen.

SOPHIE
Versailles 23 December 1710   The King is more charmed than ever with
his little old sweetheart; everything is done through her, and everything
goes like the old lady's figure, crooked and crisscross. She has every
intention of feathering her own nest, makes money out of everything
she does, and is teaching the Duchesse de Bourgogne the same trade.
Also, she knows all the State secrets and communicates them to the
Duchesse de Bourgogne; this is why nothing remains secret for long.
    The Dauphin is still in love with his Choin;[1] I am sure he must have
married her. She is a clever woman and takes care never to appear at
Court, as she would then be under the thumb of her step-mother-in-
law. She only shows herself to the Duchesse de Bourgogne and her
favourites, but has her creatures everywhere. They form a *cabale* in op-
position to the other two, so the Court is now divided into three parties.
    Also we have a comedy in our own house. My son has such a passion
(in all honour) for his daughter that she rules him as surely as the
Maintenon the King and the Choin the Dauphin. But my son's wife,
who is selfish, ambitious and scheming, has grown jealous. Now the
two of them try to make one another appear ridiculous, which would
be funny enough to watch if only it were not so close to home.
    My son comes to me at eight or nine o'clock in the evening, and
sometimes his wife comes too. Afterwards I go to eat with the King,
but I often have to wait because he and the entire royal family are at
Mme de Maintenon's. This waiting about is tedious. After supper we

    [1] Liselotte says of Marie Emilie Jolie de Choin, 'She looked like a bull-terrier, with
short legs, round face, upturned nose, and a large mouth filled with rotten teeth which
stank to high heaven. You could smell her right across the room. She had monstrously
large breasts which seemed to charm Monseigneur, as he used to beat on them as if
they were kettledrums.'

La Maison Royalle de France.

1. Loüis Le Grand Roy de France, et de Navarre, né en 1638, avoit Epousé Marie
   Therese Infante d'Espagne, dont il a eu en 1661,
2. Loüis Dauphin de France, qui avoit espousé, en 1680, Marie Victoire Princesse de
   Barviere, dont il a eu
3. Monseigneur le Duc de Bourgogne né en 1682, qui a epousé, le 7e. décembre 1697,
   Madame la Princesse de Savoye née, en 1685.
4. Monseign.r le Duc D'Anjou né en 1683. 5. Monseign.r le Duc de Berry, né en 1686.

The royal house of France, by Bonnart.

Mme du Maine in fancy-dress, eighteenth-century French School.

always go straight to the King's room and stand there in rank and file until every one of the royal ladies has arrived. Then the King makes his great bow and takes the whole royal party into his closet, and I have to go home.

At table the King doesn't speak at all except when he wants to be kind to someone, and then he will offer some dish and say, '*En voulez-vous?*' He is still supposed to show some of his old gaiety in his closet, but I see none of it. Three or four days may pass without his speaking to me at all; he only bows.

Marly 11 January 1711   I remember that in Hanover Christmas was always celebrated for three days. I am sure the box trees must have been decorated with candles for your grandchildren. How I should have loved to see it. Here they have no idea of it at all. I wanted to introduce it, but Monsieur said, '*Vous voulez nous donner de vos modes allemandes pour nous faire la dépense, je vous baise les mains.*' I love seeing children enjoying themselves, but my son's children enjoy absolutely nothing. I never saw such children in all my days.

The Duc de Berry is very much in love with his wife, but since she is certainly no beauty I'm afraid it won't last.

Marly 5 February 1711   There is no conversation anywhere. They may be talking to one another at Meudon, but the Dauphin hardly ever opens his mouth, and I'm sure the King counts his words and takes care not to exceed the number. There is no conversation at St Cloud either. My son doesn't go there any longer, and the ladies are so frightened of giving offence that they don't talk of anything but clothes or gambling, which seems rather boring to me.

LUISE
Versailles 28 February 1711   Here is a bottle of the *baume blanc*. I know several ladies who put this white balsam, which is prepared with *esprit-de-vin*, on their faces.

Monsieur wanted to rub some on my face once, but I wouldn't let him. I'd rather put up with all my wrinkles than have white messes smeared over my face. I hate paint, and can't endure rouge either.

Versailles 5 April 1711   My breath is shorter than ever it was, and all that kneeling during Holy Week didn't do my knees much good. But one must be patient. I treat my knees with nothing but English plaster, which is supposed to be beneficial; it is more convenient than ointment

K

SOPHIE

Marly 16 April 1711 I must tell you of the great sorrow that has over-whelmed the whole of France, and all of us here—the Dauphin's death, which was quite unexpected.

I told you last Sunday that he had the smallpox and that things were going well; there was every hope of his complete recovery. These hopes continued until Tuesday morning, and when the people of Paris, who adore the Dauphin, sent a deputation of fishwives to embrace him and tell him that they were planning to have a Te Deum sung for him he said, 'Not yet, wait until I am quite well again.'

The same day I went to Meudon, to congratulate the King because the Dauphin was getting on so well. I arrived at 5 o'clock in the evening, and because I knew that the King was in Council I walked in the garden until the meeting was over. Then I went to the King, who received me very graciously. He was in a very good humour, reproached me for having complained so much when I had smallpox and said that M le Dauphin was not in any pain. I said that was still to come, and the spots were bound to become inflamed, which would be painful.

At six o'clock, just as I was about to leave, word came that the Dauphin was restless and that his head was swelling. Everyone thought this was the beginning of the suppuration, and considered it a good sign. When I arrived at Versailles the entire English Court called, and left again at 8 o'clock. At nine there came news that all was well, but at ten there was a message that M le Dauphin was growing restless; his face was so swollen that it was unrecognizable, and the pocks were gathering on his eyes. This didn't seem alarming; I had my supper as usual at ten o'clock, at eleven I was still chatting to the Maréchale de Clérembault, and then I meant to say my prayers and go to bed.

At midnight I was surprised to see the Maréchale come back. She was quite stunned, and told me that the Dauphin was at death's door, and that the King was at this moment passing through Versailles on the way to Marly, and the Duchesse de Bourgogne had called for her carriage to follow him. Immediately afterwards the message came that all was over, and the Dauphin was dead.

You can imagine the ghastly shock. I dressed quickly and rushed over to the Duchesse de Bourgogne. There I found the most harrowing spectacle. The Duc and Duchesse de Bourgogne were completely dazed, and pale as death. Neither of them uttered a single word. The Duc and Duchesse de Berry were lying on the floor with their elbows on a divan, sobbing so loudly that they could be heard three rooms away. My son and Mme d'Orléans wept silently and did what they could to calm the Duc and Duchesse de Berry. All the ladies sitting on the floor around the Duchesse de Bourgogne were weeping too. I accompanied the Duc de Berry and his wife to their apartments and they went to bed, but didn't stop crying. Mme la Duchesse de Bourgogne had told me as I went out that the King had forbidden any of us to leave for Marly that night; we were to go the next morning. It was half-past two by the time I was back in my room and in bed, but I only slept for an hour, between five and six. At seven I got up again, and drove here at half-past eight.

When I arrived, everything was still quiet at the King's. I went to Mme de Maintenon, who told me that at ten o'clock they still had hope, but at half-past ten things had changed and death appeared imminent, so they quickly sent out for Extreme Unction, and that the King was eating his dessert when they told him. You can imagine the King's shock. He wanted to go straight to the Dauphin's room, but they restrained him. He immediately sent for his coach, but before he had entered it with Mme de Maintenon, Mme la Duchesse and the Princesse de Conti, poor M le Dauphin had gone. Immediately after his death he turned pitch-black, which shows that he had had purple fever as well as smallpox. Everything had stayed in his head, there were no pocks at all on his body, but the nose was quite filled with them, so that he actually suffocated, and at once began to stink so abominably that they were obliged to take his body straight to St Denis without any ceremony.

I saw the King yesterday at eleven o'clock. His grief would melt a stone. He acts with such patience, speaks to everyone with such gentleness and gives all his sad orders with such firmness, yet all the while his eyes fill with tears and he is choked with sighs. I am terribly afraid he will fall sick himself, he looks so ill. I pity him from the bottom of my heart. The people who thought they were doing me great harm by estranging me from the Dauphin have now perhaps saved my life, because, if we had still been on the same terms as we were before Monsieur died, I might now have fallen ill or even died of grief, but as it is I bear the misfortune with equanimity and worry only about the King; of course, I am very sorry about M le Dauphin, only I cannot grieve over someone who didn't love me in the least and entirely forsook me, as I would over someone who had always been my friend. In the meantime, I have been told how things are to be with the new Dauphin, the former Duc de Bourgogne. He is not to be called simply Monseigneur, like his father, but Monsieur when one talks to

him and M le Dauphin when one speaks of him. When one writes to
him, however, the letters are to be addressed to Monseigneur.

I am not skilled in the art of saying much in a few words, which is
why I write such long letters.

Marly 18 April 1711 All Paris and the provinces are in despair. It
must have been a dreadful poison that killed the poor man, because
they told me yesterday that when he died black vapours were seen
coming from his mouth, and his face turned, and remained, pitch-black.

Marly 26 April 1711 Last night around midnight we had the news that
the Emperor died of smallpox on the 17th of this month. What a good
thing it would be if this could bring us peace. Time will tell what will
become of that. There is nothing but sadness on all sides.

> Joseph I's death was a turning point in the war of the Spanish succession.
> The Allies' candidate, the Archduke Charles—at present in Madrid as
> Carlos III—was obliged to return to Vienna to succeed his brother as
> Charles VI. To see Spain governed from Vienna was as unpalatable to
> England and the United Provinces as to see her, as it were, ruled from
> Paris.

LUISE
Marly 7 May 1711 Never has there been so much smallpox about as
there is now. All my grandchildren in Lorraine are ill, at least the two
boys and the eldest girl are.

Among the common people there are still a few who love their
wives. For instance, one of my lackeys here was married to one of the
ugliest women in the world. She had the voice of a duck and the face
of a squashed toad; she was wider than she was tall, but in spite of all
that the poor man is in despair because she died last week.

SOPHIE
Marly 9 May 1711 You are very right when you say that the King
has good cause to regret M le Dauphin: he always behaved perfectly
to the King, no son could have shown greater respect, obedience and
filial love, one has to admit that: this is also the best thing that can be
said about him. If I could find the opportunity to talk to the King, I
would certainly deliver your condolences, but it is difficult at table,

because His Majesty doesn't say a single word and nobody speaks out, and that is the only time I ever see him.

The late M le Dauphin had never thought himself healthier: Mme la Duchesse has not yet got over it at all, nor has the Princesse de Conti; Mlle de Choin is supposed to be very sad. The King is giving her a pension of 12,000 francs and she is keeping her house in Paris. The Dauphin has a bastard-daughter, never recognized, by the actress,[1] she's now a girl of seventeen or eighteen—face and figure lovely as an angel—and she's in despair. He had her called Mlle de Fleury, because there is a village of that name in the park at Meudon.

There is not much love lost between me and the present Dauphin,[2] but he is very polite to me, which is all I ask of him. His wife, too, is more polite than she used to be. Since the bedding of the Duc de Berry she has changed very much for the better, and lives on good terms with her husband. He is not so much ugly as ill-made, he limps and is hunch-backed, but his face is not bad, he has fine eyes with intelligence in them, and very beautiful hair like a periwig; it is true, he is a bit too bigoted, but at least he doesn't preach.

I have this moment received the sad news that my daughter's eldest son and dear second daughter are dead too, and that the other two princes aren't out of danger yet. I'm frightened that my daughter may die or lose her reason, because the unhappiness of losing all one's children at once is unbearable. In Lorraine the disease seems to have turned into a veritable plague.

Marly 31 May 1711 Today I have drunk your health in Rhine wine that my poor daughter sent me last year. I made a proper May cup with herbs—pimpernel, dragon's blood, mugwort, liverwort, strawberrywort and violetwort.

My poor daughter is inconsolable, and only wishes to die and join her children and Monsieur. But I told her I was convinced that there could be no reunion after death, and that it was pointless to die in order to be with those one had lost. My poor daughter has already lost eight children.

Marly 20 July 1711 I have heard a rumour that Milord Marlborough's wife has been insolent to Queen Anne. It was well done to dismiss her. What business is it of Milord Sunderland whether Queen Anne is well served by Mrs Masham or not? He is a dangerous fellow, that

---

[1] La Raisin.   [2] The Duc de Bourgogne, the late Dauphin's eldest son.

Sunderland. To look at him, he appears so modest and quiet that he hardly seems able to count up to three.

Fontainebleau 25 July 1711   I am rather tired, but nothing is going to stop me from answering your letter, which arrived yesterday after I had been bled. They took 16 oz, which is why I am so tired today. The reason I have been bled is this: last night I felt (by your leave, by your leave) a sudden urge. I got up, and as I'm used to reading on this throne I lit a candle and placed it on one of the *guéridons*. But the floors in old houses like Fontainebleau aren't smooth. My slipper twisted in the uneven parquet, I tried to hold on to the *guéridon*, but it was too light, and we crashed to the floor together. As I was embracing the *guéridon* I couldn't even break my fall, and landed flat on my nose, which is so swollen that it deserves the name of 'badgernose', which is what my brother used to call me.

Fontainebleau 2 September 1711   I like Fontainebleau better than anywhere else in France. I am well lodged, and have all my people about me, which is more than I can say for Marly. Here I have the hunt, and walks through the wood better than anywhere else in the world, and your letters arrive earlier than at Versailles.

Mme la Dauphine often gets cross and impatient because the Duc de Berry loves his wife so much. She says he's becoming a bore. The Duc de Berry is not in the least devout, and doesn't hold with praying, which he does as little as possible. But he used to be kept fairly short, and now he has a wife with whom he may and can do what he likes he is absolutely charmed. He thinks that no one in the world can equal her in beauty, which is not at all the case regarding her face or figure. She has a short, thick body with long arms, walks badly, and is *de mauvaise grâce* in all she does. She pulls horrible grimaces, and always looks as if she's about to burst into tears. Her eyes are pale blue with pink rims, her face is red, and she looks a great deal older than her years. But her neck, arms and hands are flawless, very white and well made. Her legs and feet are nice too, and I can't understand why her walk is so tottery and ugly. Nevertheless, with all her attributes, her husband and her father are convinced that Helen was never as beautiful as the Duchesse de Berry.

Versailles 30 September 1711   I am beginning my letter today for a great and rare reason, which is that the King has invited me to hunt with him tomorrow—the first time for twenty years that this has happened.

Mme de Maintenon doesn't look her age in the slightest. She has grown a bit thinner, but she still looks very fine. I haven't seen her at close quarters for six months. Whenever I send to her she is out—I sent eight times when we were at Marly. Still, I can't force myself on her.

P.S. Thursday 1 October 1711, 8.30 in the evening.

We have this instant arrived from Marly. The hunt only lasted for an hour, then we all went in to change. The King showed me great courtesy, and said that he wanted to visit my rooms to see how I had arranged everything and to have any inconveniences put right, which I must say is very polite.

Marly 10 October 1711   When anyone is put in the Bastille no one hears anything about it, either at Court or in Paris. There is an even stranger thing: for many years a man was imprisoned there who lived and died wearing a mask. He always had two musketeers at his side with orders to shoot him if he ever took it off. He ate and slept with his mask on. He must have been of some importance, because in every other respect he was very well-treated and well-lodged, and given everything he asked for. He was devout, and always reading. No one could ever find out who he was.[1]

Marly 14 October 1711   Last Tuesday I went to call on the almighty lady, who told me to send my own ladies into another room. She was so stern that my heart began to thump; I thought she was going to lecture me. I briefly examined my conscience but found nothing. Then she told me that the King had spoken to my son and his wife regarding the conduct of their daughter, but had said nothing to me as he was firmly convinced that I would, naturally, do what I could of my own accord. But since His Majesty had given this commission to the father and mother, he learned that I have stopped saying anything to the girl; now he had commanded her, Mme de Maintenon, to charge me, on his behalf, to lecture the young woman. Then she listed the points on which I was to preach. I said that lecturing people was a disagreeable thing, but that I would nevertheless accept the commission and prove to His Majesty that I always obeyed him, no matter what he ordered me to do. But I begged that he would tell the Duchesse de

[1] This, according to Helmont's note in his collection of Liselotte's letters, is the first reference to the mysterious 'man in the iron mask'. The mask is now thought to have been of black velvet, and the prisoner, whose identity was so carefully kept secret, Count Ercole Antonio Mattioli of Mantua, incarcerated for unknown crimes against the state.

Berry that he had asked me to speak to her, so that the impression might be the deeper. This the King did. That evening mother and daughter came to see me. I started at once, 'My dear child, you know very well that I have lectured you only once since your marriage; it was my intention never to do so again, but only today I have received orders from the King, which I cannot disobey, to explain to you why he did not take you to the hunt in his *calèche* last Monday. The reason is that your entire behaviour displeases him.'

Then I recited every point, one after another, and added that, if she wished to be perfectly miserable, all she had to do was to carry on as she did now. But if she wished to be happy she would have to begin by making herself as well-loved 'as you have made yourself disliked up to now. When the King hears from every side how you have corrected all your faults, he will certainly be kind to you again. So cheer up, consider what you can do to improve, and do it, and you will make yourself and us happy.' I said a lot more, but it would take too long to tell. She cried bitterly, and faithfully promised to change.

Versailles 15 November 1711 The pupil in my charge is behaving better now, thank the Lord, and seems to have profited from my remonstrances. I hope to God it may last. Neither father nor mother says a word; they were quite moved by my lecture and the daughter cried bitterly. I didn't use a single harsh word; on the contrary, I heartily sympathized with her because she had been so badly brought up, a sensible girl like her, that she had not learned where her duty lay, nor what her duties demanded. My harangue was long, but I am too afraid of boring you. My son often spoils the good I do.

Marly 14 February 1712 We are full of grief. The day before yesterday, at a quarter past eight, poor Mme la Dauphine departed this life. I am as convinced that the doctors killed her as I know that I am telling you about it. They had given her a little Milady Kent powder, only a few grains. She began to sweat hard, but they didn't have enough patience to let her sweat it out. Halfway through, when she was as red as fire from the measles, they put her in a bath of warm water and bled her four times. This drove the rash inwards again and now everything is over. Every time I look at the King my eyes fill with tears, for he is so grieved that it would move a rock. Monsieur le Dauphin grieves with all his heart, but he is young, he can marry again and make up for his loss, but Mme de Savoie's[1] loss is irreparable and so is the King's, as the Dauphine had been brought up entirely to his liking. She was his comfort and joy, and had such gay spirits that she could always find something to cheer him up.

Milady Kent's powder was a medicinal concoction said to encourage sweating, and Liselotte herself seems to have introduced it at Court. When she first took it her entire entourage, including her doctors, flocked round her to see her die. 'Madame is poisoning herself,' they cried, 'it is certain that Madame is dead.' Her survival seems to have encouraged them to use it in the treatment of their other patients. Liselotte swore by this powder to the end of her days, and believed that it had often saved her life. She even went so far as to recommend it— one grain to be taken with the milk of the wet-nurse—for a sick English baby.

Marly 18 February 1712 I thought that today I should write only of the unhappy ceremony which I had to watch at Versailles yesterday, but disaster has struck once again, because today M le Dauphin has followed his wife, and left this life at 9.30 this morning. It is an abominable loss for the whole kingdom, for he was a virtuous, just man, and intelligent. France could not have suffered a greater blow. They didn't wake the King, as he has a cold and a cough, but he soon heard the news. He loses much in this man, because since his father's death he used to come to the Council and work with the ministers. He comforted the King whenever he could, he was charitable and gave many alms, he sold all his mother's jewellery to help wounded officers, he did as much good as he could and never harmed anyone. I don't think the world has ever seen what we are about to see now: a man and his wife being taken together to St Denis. I can't get over the shock. The grief is indescribable, I almost think that all of us here will die, one after the other.

Marly 20 February 1712 Although the post doesn't leave today, I can think of nothing which will give me greater comfort than to tell my dearest *tante* how frightened, sad and heavy my heart is. Malicious tongues have spread all over Paris a rumour that my son poisoned the Dauphin and Dauphine. As I would go to the stake for his innocence, I didn't take it seriously at first, for I simply couldn't imagine that such a thing could be said in earnest. Some say that this wicked rumour comes from Spain. If so, the Princesse des Ursins must be a veritable devil to

[1] The Dauphine's mother, Madame's step-granddaughter.

carry her revenge against my son so far, and he pays a high price for annoying her.

The Duc d'Orléans, whose chemical experiments with his friend Dr Homberg were well known, was the chief suspect in the poison rumours that followed the death of the second Dauphin as he appeared to have most to gain from eliminating all who stood between himself and the throne of France.

The stories may well have originated in Spain, where Orléans had long been regarded as an audacious plotter. At a time when Philip V seemed to be considering abdication, the anti-Habsburgs had adopted Orléans as their candidate for the throne of Spain, and Mme des Ursins, the power behind the Spanish throne, was convinced that this was an Orléans plot. (He had in fact not been personally involved.) Liselotte, however, attributes Mme des Ursins' libels to motives of revenge, for apparently Orléans had repulsed her advances—she was said to have 'the morals of a hussar'—finding her too old and ugly to be able to play the *galant*.

The post-mortem showed that the Dauphin had died from natural causes, variously described as measles, scarlet fever or *Fleck-Fieber* (spot-fever, Liselotte's diagnosis). This is a variety of typhus causing a scarlet rash, severe nervous symptoms and dreadful bowel disturbances. The bacteria are carried by clothes-lice, and it is extremely contagious.

Marly 21 February 1712 I must tell you the end of yesterday's affair. When my son sent his Homberg to the Bastille to be interrogated, the king forbade him to enter, not only because His Majesty doesn't believe my son capable of such a thing, but also because not a trace of poison was found in either body when they were opened. All the doctors present are ready to swear that Mme la Dauphine died of the measles and M le Dauphin of grief and the polluted air.

Versailles 5 March 1712 I feel deeply sorry for the King. He forces himself to appear calm, but you can see how much he is suffering. God preserve him, there is no telling what might otherwise happen.

People are beginning to fear that my son will play his part in a future reign, and this is why they are trying to make his name odious at Court and spread the rumour of the poisoning, as I told you. Whoever dies at Court, my son is blamed. There is no crime that he is not accused of.

Versailles 10 March 1712 You will be horrified to hear how our disasters continue. The doctors have repeated the mistake they made with Mme la Dauphine, because when the little Dauphin[1] was red from the measles and in a sweat they bled him and gave him an emetic, and during this operation the poor child died.

And there is good proof that the doctors murdered this Dauphin. While all nine of them were occupied with him the younger prince,[2] who is suffering from the same illness, was hidden away by his ladies, who locked themselves in with him and gave him biscuits and wine. Yesterday there were plans to have him bled, but Mme de Ventadour and the Prince's under-governess, Mme de Villefort, stoutly resisted the doctors and wouldn't allow it. They simply kept the Prince nice and warm, and saved him, thank God, to the doctors' shame. I am sure that, if they had had their way, he would have died too.

And now I must tell you how horribly malicious people are here. Although neither my son nor any of his people had ever been anywhere near the elder child, people are saying quite openly that he killed this one too, but that he spared the younger one for fear that the King of Spain, who hates my son, might return. Yesterday, quite reliable people have heard *'qu'on laisse mourir aussi le petit Duc d'Anjou, afin que le Royaume ne demeure pas après le roi minorité'*. There is no country in the world where you could hear such insolent talk.

Our King bears his grief with such composure and firmness that I cannot admire him enough. One can truthfully say that, except for Mme de Maintenon, he has lost everything that he most loved.

Versailles 13 March 1712 I am sure there must be a hundred saints who deserve their canonization less than our second Dauphin, for, sad to say, in eleven months we have lost three, one of forty-nine, one of twenty-six and one of five. I don't believe such a thing can be found in the whole of history. It is certain that M le Dauphin died of grief. He loved his wife to an extraordinary degree, and the grief over her loss must have brought on the fever. It came irregularly at first, but then it came every fourth day. They bled him. After his wife's death, spots appeared on his forehead, but that didn't prevent him from going out and about. He didn't take to his bed until Sunday night. Then he came out in a purple rash, and spots which were larger and different from ordinary measles. They gave him cordials and tried to make him sweat, but it was no use.

The autopsy showed that all his organs had putrified, and his heart was shrunken and flat. From this they judged that he had died of grief.

Versailles 17 March 1712 Yesterday M le Dauphin's little dog made

---

[1] Louis, the third Dauphin.   [2] The future Louis XV.

me cry. The poor beast came into the tribune of the chapel to look for his master, whom he last saw kneeling there. He sadly looked at everyone as though to ask where his master had gone. It made me so sad.

There are two reasons why I am pleased to go to the Sanctum. The first is that this is the only place where the King ever talks, and since I have always loved and respected him it has always hurt me not to be able to speak to him except during an audience; and for another it seemed really hard to be the only exception in the whole royal family.

Versailles 19 March 1712   I can't think why all Paris hates my son, when he has never harmed anyone in his life. Monsieur and I were well liked in Paris, and I am still popular. But I think that the people of his household, who were jealous of Homberg, really began it all, because, in order to harm him, they spread the rumour that Homberg was working on poisons. Here, when *cabales* want to start anything, they are usually successful.

I need you to be where you can have a long, healthy and peaceful life, and since it is my conviction that the English are mad and difficult, London is unhealthy and the sea dangerous, I cannot wish that you were there. You are used to the air and the food in Hanover, and to get used to a change of air is always difficult, and often causes dangerous diseases. These are the only reasons that prevent me from wanting you to be Queen of England.

Versailles 24 March 1712   In the Sanctum there is much talk of the past but not a word of the present, nor of the war or the peace, and never of the three Dauphins and the Dauphine, in order not to remind the King. As soon as he introduces the subject I quickly speak of something else, and pretend not to have heard him.

The French papers said that Queen Anne was determined at all costs to have you with her in England.[1] This wouldn't please me, for the reasons I have often told you. But what I should like would be for her to give you the pension that she herself enjoyed while she was still a princess; that would be only fair.

Versailles 27 March 1712   The doctors now admit that they didn't use the right treatment on M and Mme la Dauphine, but they say they weren't familiar with the disease.

[1] The papers were misinformed. There was nothing Queen Anne wanted less than visits from her Hanoverian relations, and her aversion did much to hearten Jacobite plotters in England and abroad.

Previously my son was popular with everyone, but since the Spanish troubles all Paris hates him, and they are never happier than when they can say something against him. The rumours aren't true, and even if they were I don't see what they have to do with the Parisians, but that's what they are like here. You can imagine that it was not pleasant for me to know that posters have been put up at the Palais-Royal: '*Voici où se font les loteries et où on trouve le plus fin poisson.*' *Les loteries* are meant to indicate that my son lives like Lot with his daughter.

The poets from the Pont Neuf consider it their duty to make up songs whenever a member of the royal house dies. It is funny to see them singing. They stand on benches, yell as loudly as they can, and whenever they mention the King or any other royalty they bow very low in mid-song.[1]

Marly 14 April 1712 Studying suits my son well enough and comes naturally to him, but when he tries to play the clown it makes one want to throw up, it suits him so ill. All the young people, even his daughter, make fun of him. Alas, my son's story is just like the one about the fairies who are invited to a christening. The first brings the child the gift of good looks, the second eloquence, the third brings talent in all the arts, the fourth endows him with physical grace in fencing, riding and dancing, the fifth gives him skill in the art of war, the sixth greater courage than anyone else, but the seventh fairy, whom they had forgotten to invite to the christening, says, 'I cannot take from the child what my sisters have given him, but for the rest of my life I will undo the effect of all the gifts he has been given. I will make him walk so badly that people will think he is a hunchback and lame, I will make his beard grow so black and make him pull such grimaces that his looks will be spoilt. I will give him a distaste for physical exercise, and make him so easily bored that he will take no pleasure in any of his arts, music, painting or drawing, and I will give him a love of solitude and a loathing for honest people. I will often bring him misfortune in war, and make him believe that debauchery suits him well, and make him find his best friends' advice distasteful. With these gifts all the good that my sisters have given him will be undone.' That is just what has happened, and this is why he would rather sit with his daughter and her chambermaids, listening to silly

---

[1] 'In France, every period is recorded in song', Liselotte had written previously. 'History is better learned from the songs than the history books.' She herself cherished a great volume of songs made up in Louis XIII's reign, a present from La Grande Mademoiselle.

jokes, than see worthwhile people or rule his own household as his position demands.

The King treats my son well, which gives me hope that the lies have made no impression on His Majesty.

It doesn't make any sense to me that Queen Anne should declare you her successor without granting you the pension that she herselt enjoyed. I hope it will arrive yet, for you do so much good everywhere that the pension would come in useful. I quite agree, '*Altesse Royale*' has become very vulgar now, much more common than 'Your Electoral Serene Highness'.

Marly 24 April 1712   I am writing this sitting in front of my window, where I can see the lovely *parterre* full of narcissi, tulips and *couronnes impériales*. This is bordered by a horseshoe of white, brown and red marble with great stone steps in the centre and more steps at each end, all decorated with statues and white marble flower-urns. Beyond the steps there is the hill with the cascading waterfall that is called '*la rivière*'. There are masses of white marble statues above and below. So you see, I have a lovely view, but it fails, unfortunately, to inspire me with agreeable thoughts. When I think that I shall never see you again, I can't help crying. Crying may not come to you as easily as it does to me, but, even so, you grieve inside, and that does more damage.

Versailles 21 May 1712   Although the old trollop is our worst enemy, I wish her a long life for the King's sake, because everything would be ten times worse if she were to die. He adores her so much that he couldn't live long without her, consequently I hope that she will live for a long time yet. Please don't reply to this letter.

As for the Duc de Berry, he might well not be quite so stupid if he hadn't been brought up in such ignorance; but, as it is, he knows nothing of the world, and is nevertheless very opinionated. He is much in love with his wife, who unfortunately doesn't return his sentiments. Although she behaves better than she used to, I'm afraid she is still a coquette, her natural tendency is too strong, and *bon chien de chasse de race*. Her mother, with all her solemn airs, has one affair after another, but to be truthful she manages them very well and would never cause a scandal. All Paris considers her a vestal virgin.

Versailles 29 May 1712   My knees hurt and I'm short of breath, but otherwise I am perfectly well and haven't any pain. My appetite is good, I sleep all too well, and when anything annoying happens I simply pay no attention to it, as when, for instance, my son spends no time with me, doesn't love me, gives his daughter anything at all but makes me wait over three years for what is due to me, doesn't visit me for even a quarter-of-an-hour during the day, but calls at nine o'clock in the evening and leaves at a quarter-to-ten.

Marly 8 June 1712 My son and I know all too well, unfortunately, who the people are who try to make him loathed and hated. It is a very special *cabale* at a Court that is more riddled by different *cabales* than ever. I will be more explicit at the first safe opportunity, and you will see that I am quite right to be alarmed. In the meantime I shall simply continue on my straight course and pretend to know nothing, except for warning my son as soon as I learn anything.

M du Maine, Mme la Duchesse and M le Duc d'Antin,[1] the most ambitious creatures on earth, have noticed that the King likes my son, and now they look for every opportunity to blacken his name. For the last year, since Monseigneur's death, they have drawn the old Maintenon into their *cabale*; it was she who told the King that my son had poisoned the last Dauphine and Dauphin. They thought the King would be so shocked that he would banish my son from Court at once, without even going into the matter. I know this because when the doctors came to tell the King that it was certain that these two personages had not swallowed any poison, he turned to Mme de Maintenon and said, '*Eh bien, Madame, eh bien, ne vous avais-je pas dit que ce que vous m'avez dit de mon neveu était faux?*' You perceive how right we were to think that the old woman hates us all.

Marly 19 June 1712 In accordance with my bad habits I slept for an hour after my meal, and now I am sitting in front of my beautiful window, where it is lovely and cool, between two of my birds, which are singing: a little redbreast and a canary. My parrot sits before me, my little dogs are playing round me, and immediately behind me stands Frau von Rathsamshausen, who is scratching a mosquito bite on my back.

Fontainebleau 20 July –712 I can easily explain how the King of Prussia comes to possess the collection of medals from Heidelberg. My late brother made the Elector of Brandenburg the executor of his will, and laid down that he should be given either the Julius Caesar tapestry

[1] All children of Mme de Montespan. The Maines were the leaders of the '*cabale*' anxious to see the succession of France in the hands of the King's oldest surviving grandson, Philip of Spain, even though, by accepting the crown of that country, he had ceased to be eligible for that of France.

or all the medals. I would have rather had the medals, as you can imagine, but Monsieur, who didn't care for them at all, said, '*Je vous baise les mains, les médailles ne seraient que pour votre divertissement, et je ne m'en soucie pas, mais j'ai besoin des tapisseries, et je veux celle de Jules César. Je suis maître de la communauté, c'est à moi de choisir, et je les veux.*' There wasn't much I could say then, and this is how my father's collection comes to be in Prussia.

Versailles 1 October 1712 The Duchesse de Berry is more impertinent than ever. She tried to put me out of countenance yesterday, but I told her what I thought of her.

She arrived all dressed up *en grand habit*, with more than fourteen *poinçons* of the most splendid diamonds in the world. All that was very fine, but on her face she wore twelve beauty-spots which were horribly unbecoming. When she came up to me I said, '*Madame, vous voilà à merveille*, but it seems to me that you have overdone the patches. It doesn't look very dignified for the first lady in the land to be covered in *mouches* like an actress.' She pulled a face and said that she knew very well I didn't care for patches. She, on the other hand, liked them very much and intended to please herself. 'Your mistake,' I said, 'is due to your extreme youth, because, beyond pleasing yourself, you ought to think of pleasing the King.' 'Oh,' she said, 'the King gets used to anything, and I have made up my mind to bother about nothing and worry about nobody.' I laughed and said, 'With these sentiments you'll go far. Listen while I tell you what I think, for it is for your own good. I do it because it is my duty as your grandmother, and besides, it's by order of the King.'

LUISE
Versailles 8 December 1712 I have been purged five times since Marly, which quite tires me out. As they absolutely promise to cure me completely if I follow their advice, I am obliged to do what they say, otherwise they would say that I'm killing myself through my stubbornness. I am better than I was because I can eat and drink again without choking or panting, which is more than I could do at Marly. I notice no improvement in walking, I am so weak and feeble that I can't walk the length of a room without panting, I am carried everywhere in a *chaise*.

SOPHIE
Versailles 10 December 1712 When you last saw your Liselotte jumping and running, she was young and light: now I am old and heavy and

Mme de Maintenon wearing religious habit, eighteenth-century French School.

Madame in old age, by Hyacinthe Rigaud.

greatly changed. You wouldn't know me now. My wrinkled eyes, my great pendulous cheeks, my snow-white hair, the hollow between my ears and my cheeks and my huge double-chin wouldn't remind you of Liselotte. I'm quite different from what I used to be: my long neck has grown quite short, my shoulders are broad and thick, and my legs are worse than thick because they're so swollen. So you see, you would never recognize me in this figure. When I open my mouth my teeth are also in a miserable state: one is broken, another one is black, the others are jagged—in short, my whole person is wretched.

Sometimes the King is kind enough to enquire after my health, of which I render him an account. I often speak of it in a way to make His Majesty laugh.

LUISE
Marly 15 January 1713 I must tell you that my doctor has ordered me to take coffee. I find it disgusting, and can't get used to the acrid, sooty taste.

A year later Liselotte wrote to Luise that she drinks coffee every day and that it agrees with her, but 'I shall never get used to it or come to like it'.

Versailles 30 April 1713 I shall neither gain nor lose by this peace, but one thing I shall enjoy is to see our Duchesse de Savoie become a queen, because I love her as though she were my own child. For another thing, there will be fewer lamentations, which were tedious, and for a third I hope that the posts will be faster. That is all, dear Luise, that I hope of the peace.

But once there is a general peace, it will be of long duration, you may take my word for it; on this side nothing is more longed for than a lasting peace.

By the terms of the peace treaty of Utrecht, Sicily came under the rule of Savoy, and Liselotte's step-grandchild was now known as the Queen of Sicily. The Duc d'Orléans and the Duc de Berry finally renounced their claims to the Spanish throne, and once again Philip of Spain renounced his claim to the throne of France.

Versailles 18 June 1713 I shall send my portrait to *ma tante* as soon as possible. Nothing has ever been more like than the way Rigaud has painted me. The little brown dog is still alive, cleverer than ever, and I love it with all my heart.

I can easily send you a present from the fair every year without ruining myself, and I'm glad to have found something to your liking this time. But, dearest Luise, didn't you inherit any jewellery from your mother? Here diamonds have become rare, but not coloured stones, specially when they are small.

> Liselotte is referring to the annual fair at Versailles, which, she points out, is not a town or even a village but only a spot, so that its fair is nothing but a country-fair. The sort of merchandise for sale, however, suggests that, rural or not, royalty was suitably catered for. Liselotte was the first to agree that *'les petits cadeaux entretiennent l'amitié'*.

SOPHIE

Marly 24 November 1713 My son and his daughter, who, as you know, used to love each other so much that it caused unpleasant talk, now begin to loathe each other like the devil. They quarrel constantly and, what is worse, the daughter is causing trouble between her father and her husband. The father went to Paris in despair. He keeps all this secret from me, but I hear about it all the same, because his wife tells me everything and I pretend to know nothing.

Versailles 7 January 1714 I have no doubt that your Prince Fritzchen[1] was absolutely delighted with the Christchild, because I still remember so well how I loved it, and how frightened I was of the seminarists, when they came carrying the star. But what made me realize it was only make-believe was that St Peter, who was to take me to where the Christchild had left my presents, gave me his hand, which was gloveless and calloused. I simply couldn't imagine that one could be scabby in Paradise, and I couldn't help laughing. Good Frau von Harling said quickly that the Christchild wouldn't leave presents for people who didn't believe in it, and it never did again from that time on.

LUISE

Versailles 22 March 1714 Thank you so much for sending the copy of the recipe for *sauerkraut* with pike, but as I don't like fish I should prefer it as it is usually eaten, without the fish. I shall translate it into French myself. Luckily I have a good stomach and can digest sauerkraut very well. To eat little at night is very healthy.

[1] Frederick, the son of George Augustus and Caroline, later Prince of Wales.

SOPHIE

Versailles 8 April 1714   I don't have a Calvin among my medals, and if it wouldn't rob your cabinet it would be very kind of you to send it to me. I have the popes, Dr Luther, Molinos,[1] M Arnaud,[2] M de Cambrai,[3] I collect everyone who has been extraordinary; I also have l'Abbé de la Trappe, but only in lead.

Marly 3 May 1714   The Duc de Berry is terribly and dangerously ill. On Sunday night, or rather Monday morning, just before four o'clock, he had an attack of fever and shivering, but he said nothing about it, and got up and dressed, for he wanted to go and see the King's doctor. But the shivering started again, and he couldn't hide it any longer, and his head ached so much that he had to go back to bed. The fever rose higher all the time, accompanied by vomiting. First he brought up some green matter, but then that was followed by pitch-black vomiting, and when the black matter was examined yesterday it was found to be congealed blood, which he excreted from above and below. The doctors weren't unduly worried: they thought the Duc de Berry was on the mend, because they believed they could stop the bleeding. We all went to Versailles to celebrate with Mme de Berry because her husband was out of danger, but in the night he had such a dreadful attack of vomiting that he couldn't keep anything down. I have just come from his room; he has just been bled for the eighth time. He looks frightful. He ate a plateful of jelly, which, by your leave, he sicked up again. He only has a little fever, but the congealed, black blood makes one tremble. I am dreadfully afraid that it will end badly. May God send us help—we need it.

The Duc de Berry died shortly afterwards from internal injuries sustained at a hunting accident of which he had not told a soul. He showed the greatest consideration for his grandfather on his death-bed, even refusing Extreme Unction until after the King's *coucher* in order to spare him the sad sight. In the end matters became too urgent for delay, the King himself went to fetch the Holy Sacrament, and everyone, except the Duchesse de Berry, who was pregnant, was present at the sad ritual. For a while Liselotte pities her granddaughter who, she says, is intelligent enough to realize that from the most fortunate being she is now changed to the most miserable, unless she bears a son, and 'she is firmly convinced she will only have a daughter'.

[1] Miguel Molinos, Spanish mystic.   [2] Antoine Arnaud, anti-Jesuit, Jansenist.
[3] Fénelon.

LUISE

Marly 10 May 1714   As I haven't yet answered your letter of April
17th I shall save it for the Sunday post, in so far as God spares my life
until then, which one never can tell. And even less now, after we have
seen the Duc de Berry die, only twenty-seven years old and apparently
big, fat and in the best of health and likely to live for a hundred years.
I am sure he would have, too, if he hadn't so carelessly killed himself.
But enough of this sadness. I think that, next to salvation, God's
greatest blessing is to let one die peacefully and without fear. I am more
afraid of the fear of death than of death itself.

SOPHIE

Marly 6 June 1714   The only good thing about the Princesse des Ursins
used to be her neck and her teeth, otherwise she painted herself too
much; it used to make her eyes look red and her skin too shiny, as if it
was covered with snot. To take rhubarb every day seems revolting to
me, and it won't rid her of the bitter gall she feels for my son. The
Princesse des Ursins governs the King of Spain as I do my Titti, except
that he obeys her even more faithfully than Titti does me.

Rambouillet 15 June 1714   It is a fact that the Princesse des Ursins has
more authority in Spain than the King himself, and he may easily find
himself in the position of his grandfather, Louis XIII, who asked one of
his courtiers, '*Est-il vrai que tu es chassé de la cour?*' and he answered,
'*Sire, j'espère que non, puisque vous n'en savez rien.*' That's how it goes
there, too. But I have made a mistake, it was the King of Spain's great-
grandfather. A thirty-year-old man is, after all, no longer a child to be
nursed by a woman.

If my son's portrait could talk it would speak sadly now, because he
grieves over his daughter's unhappiness.

Thank you for your kind wishes.[1] If one could lose a year each year,
one would become a child again in the end, but as long as you are alive
and well I shan't get tired of my life.

On June 8 the event which Liselotte had dreaded so much, the death of
her aunt Sophie, came to pass. The Electress was walking in the gardens
of Herrenhausen when she had a stroke and died immediately, '*sans
médecin ni prêtre*', as she had wished.

[1] Evidently Sophie had wished Liselotte many happy returns of her birthday in
May.

LUISE

Marly 1 July 1714   I can't remember, dear Luise, whether I wrote to tell you how I heard of the disaster, and that my confessor was asked to tell me about it. I was overcome by the sort of trembling that accompanies a high fever, and turned deadly pale, and it must have been a quarter-of-an-hour before I could cry, but I couldn't get my breath and felt as though I should choke to death. But then the tears came freely and lasted all day and night, then they dried and I choked until they flowed again, and it has been like that ever since. What is surprising is that I remain so healthy; I am not in the least ill. It must have been a stroke that caused our awful unhappiness. Oh God, how often *ma tante* wrote that she would prefer sudden death to dying in bed, with a parson on one side and a doctor on the other, neither of them able to help, and how she wished to avoid the performance. Alas, how right she was.

Oh Luise, how can I ever get over this? *Ma tante* was the only comfort I had in all my tribulations here. What is the point of living now? I am no use to anyone and a burden to myself. You are the only one left of all who were near and dear to me in Germany. Adieu, dear Luise.

Marly 10 July 1714   No words can describe what I suffer day and night, and in addition I have the torture of forcing myself to hide my grief because the King can't bear sad faces. Against my wish, I also have to join in the hunt again. Last time I cried bitterly because the Elector of Bavaria came to my *calèche* to condole in my loss. I simply couldn't contain myself, and broke down. It lasted all through the hunt. I could see quite well that I was being laughed at, but there was nothing I could do about it.

Marly 22 July 1714   Ah, dear Luise, if I had no other worries than that Mme de Berry prematurely gave birth to a daughter, I should be easily consoled. The child is in good hands, as it will most certainly have gone to heaven, and the mother is well. I don't consider her unfortunate to be without husband and children; her rank is higher than she could ever have wished, she is the first lady in France, her income is greater than mine by 250,000 francs a year. She is young and healthy, and so adored by her father and mother that she can do with them what she likes. She has everything in plenty, jewels, furniture, so I really can't see what her misfortune consists of. If she were Queen she would have to suffer more constraint without being any happier.

Marly 9 August 1714 Last Thursday and Friday my doctor gave me a purge which was so effective that I had to retire to my close-stool no less than thirty times. Perhaps you know, dear Luise, what it was that purged me so violently. It is a new medicine, but so *à la mode* that all Paris is using it now. It is a salt from England called here *du sel d'Epsom*. You dissolve it in water. The first day I was given three large beer-glasses full, and the next day two. The taste is not too bad—only bitter.

You will have seen in the gazettes that the King has made all his bastards *princes du sang*, so that they may legally inherit if the proper line should die out.

> The elevation of the Duc du Maine and the Comte de Toulouse infuri-ated the nobles of France, especially the dukes and peers over whom they now took precedence. There was an immediate petition to the King, followed by numerous others, for the reversal of this order, which was, however, not rescinded until some time after his death.

Versailles 23 August 1714 Dearest Luise, last Saturday I went to Paris. I went to the Palais-Royal to call on Mlle de Valois,[1] who no longer lives in the country, but in Paris in a convent built by the Queen Mother. I can never bear to spend any time there, because opposite the choir there is a chapel where the hearts of Monsieur, my eldest son, the Queen, the Dauphine, the three Dauphins and the Duc de Berry are kept, all of them enclosed in silver hearts shrouded in black veiling, and with a crown on the floor. This sight is quite unbearable to me; I should make myself ill with crying, and I take very good care never to enter this convent. Mlle de Valois, who is almost as tall as I am, stayed with me until five o'clock. Then I sent her back to her convent and went on to another one, the Ste Marie de Chaillot, where our Queen of England is spending the summer. There I heard for certain that Queen Anne of England is dead, and that a few hours after her death the Elector of Brunswick was proclaimed King of the three realms, England, Scotland and Ireland. How it will all end time alone will tell, as our dear Electress used to say.

Fontainebleau 6 September 1714 As soon as I get back to Versailles I shall do as the King of England desires, and burn all the letters from our dear Electress that contain family matters. So far I haven't been able to

[1] Charlotte Aglaë de Valois was the Duc d'Orléans' third daughter. She and her elder sister, Mlle d'Orléans, were boarded out to be educated by the nuns in Chelles. The convent to which Liselotte refers was the Val-de-Grâce, where the hearts of the dead Bourbons were laid to rest, though their bodies were in the crypt of Saint-Denis.

burn a single one, except for those that she herself asked me to destroy.

It is hard to believe that the English could ever be content with any king, let alone ours. I feel just as children do when they say '*J'aime papa et mama*'. I love our Elector, who has now become King, and the King of England here, and his mother, are dear to me too. I wish our Elector could have another kingdom, and our King of England his own, for I confess that I don't trust the English one iota, and fear that our Elector, who is now King, will meet with disaster. If his rule in England were as absolute as our King's here, I have no doubt that right and justice would reign, but there are altogether too many examples of the unfair way in which the English treat their kings. But my meal has arrived. Today I am eating earlier than usual because of the hunt.

> Liselotte had once written to her aunt that 'your letters are that part of my reliquary which I preserve with especial zeal', and the new King of England's request cannot have been a welcome one. He had arrived in England on September 29th.
>
> James III, 'our King of England here', unofficially spent a good deal of time in France, though officially he was now living in Lorraine.

Fontainebleau 16 September 1714 Fräulein von Rathsamshausen[1] should go to England now, for I see from the German gazettes that H.M. the King lists 'Defender of the Faith' among his titles, and that ought to make him stand by those who have left the Catholic faith for his own religion. I admit that this title surprised me. I am afraid the King of England will find more worry and trouble than pleasure in his regal condition, and will often say to himself, 'If only I were still Elector, and in Hanover.'

Fontainebleau 20 October 1714 This, alas, will be the last letter I shall write to you from dear Fontainebleau. We are leaving on Wednesday, and Monday will be the last time we shall hunt in this beautiful forest. There is nothing in Versailles or Marly to compare with it.

Another thing I like about this place is that all the halls and galleries look quite German. When you go into the Schweizersaal it looks just like an old German hall with niches and panelling and benches.[2]

---

[1] Leonore's daughter had eloped with a Protestant, and for this reason was not welcome in France.

[2] This similarity was accounted for by the fact that until Louis XIV revolutionized palace-design with the improvements at Versailles, and so created a new formula, most European palaces, Fontainebleau as well as Heidelberg, followed a traditional Renaissance pattern.

The air apparently agrees with me and so does the hunting, which helps to dissipate sad thoughts, and nothing is worse for me than to be sad.

I have given your compliments to the Electoral Prince,[1] and assured him of your respect. He didn't answer, and only bowed. I am not at all in favour with him. I think he is afraid that I might speak of religion, and try and persuade him to be converted. But the good man deceives himself. I am certainly no apostle, and want everyone to believe according to his own conscience. Perhaps he doesn't like me because I am an old woman, but that I can't do anything about, and it will get worse every day.

Versailles 3 November 1714 I've already read four pages of the newspaper without finding the place. I'll just have another look. There, I've found it, dear Luise. My speech when I presented the Electoral Prince has been very badly translated. For one thing, I never address the King as 'Sire', but as 'Monsieur'. No *enfant de France* calls the King 'Sire', that only starts with the *petits enfants*, such as my son, my daughter, etc. What I said to the King was simply, '*Monsieur, voici le prince électoral de Saxsen, qui souhaite que je le présente à Votre Majesté*'. The Prince stepped forward with a very high, noble expression and made his *compliments* without the least trace of shyness, and instantly won the approval of the King and the whole Court. If other reports that reach Germany from France are as inaccurate as the one of my presentation of the Prince, the reporters aren't worthy of their hire.

Versailles 18 November 1714 Later this evening I'm taking my granddaughter, Mlle de Valois, to the opera, and bringing her back here afterwards. This means that I must write to my daughter immediately after the hunt tomorrow, and shall have to hurry with this letter today.

The little Dauphin is teething and sometimes looks ill, but when he looks well he is a beautiful child. He has large, pitch-black eyes, a little round face, and a pretty mouth which, however, he keeps open rather too much.[2] He has a very well-shaped little nose and black hair, and

[1] Prince Friedrich August II of Saxony, later King of Poland. In 1712 he had been secretly converted to Catholicism, but his change of religion was not declared until 1717.

[2] The four-year-old Dauphin had apparently inherited this trait from his uncle, now King of Spain, of whom Liselotte had made the same observation. Unlike this staid man, however, he showed early signs of his ungovernable temper. Liselotte said that his entourage dreaded his tantrums so much that he was on the whole allowed to do as he liked, so that he was badly brought up and very spoilt, though 'a nice little boy'.

he is very well built, with straight legs and nice feet; in short, he is handsome rather than plain. He was always better looking than his brother, though not as lively and strong. Our Dauphin understands maps already, just like a grown-up. He is taught in play.

Is Duke Ernest Augustus to reign alone in Hanover in future? But you say that he, too, intends to cross the Channel, so Hanover will become a desert. It distresses me, because I care more for Hanover than for the whole of England.

I cannot understand, dear Luise, how you could make up your mind to cross the sea. Look after yourself, for God's sake.

Versailles 4 January 1715 I have met a good many Englishmen in my life, but they were not all alike. Some were extremely polite, others extremely coarse and impolite. I don't think it was very civil of the King of England not to send you a single word when he knew you were in London. Even if you were no relation of his, and only his mothers' *dame de ménage*, he should feel obliged to show you some courtesy, if only out of respect for his mother. But I think the good King cares little about those whom his mother loved. What can one say? Everyone to his own humour, and at fifty-four one no longer changes.

How is the opera in London? English, French or Italian? What makes me think it can't be French is that there is no French opera called *Armenius*. At the opera here, only people sitting in the stalls clap to show they are pleased, never those in the boxes. If I didn't have the convenience of having the opera close to my apartments, I should never set foot in it.

From what I hear of the air in London, I don't believe I could last there for twenty-four hours without falling ill. I'm told there is a constant smell of coal; I couldn't stand that, and the air is said to be quite thick, which wouldn't suit me either.

I hope with all my heart that you will settle your nieces to everyone's satisfaction. Your brother-in-law, dear Luise, would like to marry his daughters, like M Harpagnan, '*sans dot*', but no one welcomes that. Suitors tend to be as much in love with '*les beaux yeux de la cassette*' as with the beauty of the ladies.

Luise was spending some time in London to further the matrimonial plans of her motherless nieces. They were daughters of her sister (and Liselotte's half-sister) Caroline, Duchess of Schomberg and Leinster, the only Raugravine ever to marry. She had died in 1696. Her eldest daughter,

Frederika, became Viscountess Holderness later in the year, and the younger girl married a German kinsman, Count von Degenfeld-Schomberg, in 1717.

Versailles 10 January 1715 I confess that the King of England makes me quite impatient—to show so little consideration for the memory of his mother, and treat those whom she loved with disdain, though they are close relations! I come into that category. I can't think where he gets his haughtiness from; if I had been a Protestant, he wouldn't be King. I was nearer to the Crown than he, and it is only through my family, and that of his late mother, that he is King now.

I love hearing what goes on at foreign Courts; you would do me a real favour if you would tell me about the English Court.

There was no lack of news from other European Courts. The Queen of Spain had died in February, 1714. No time had been lost in providing the King with a new wife, as sexual abstinence—self-enforced during widowerhood owing to his extreme piety—made his entourage fear for his sanity. His second wife, Elisabeth Farnese of Parma, had been chosen by his new minister, Giulio Alberoni, whose influence was rapidly growing, and the Princesse des Ursins, both of whom hoped to govern the new Queen. The marriage by proxy had taken place in September 1714. Alberoni's hopes were well founded, but Mme des Ursins was to be disappointed in her ambitions even before the royal couple had celebrated their marriage in person.

Versailles 11 January 1715 The day before yesterday we heard that Mme des Ursins went to meet the Queen of Spain, as she was to be her *Hofmeisterin*. She was the true ruler of Spain. Her pride has caused her fall.

When she got to Xadraque, she only went halfway down the stairs to meet the Queen, and then found fault with everything, including her clothes and the fact that the Queen's journey had taken so long. She is supposed to have said that, if she were in the King's place, she would have sent the Queen straight back, or at least let her cool her heels there for three months or so, whereupon the Queen commanded three officers of her bodyguard to take this fool out of her sight and place her under arrest. Then she despatched a courier to the King, complaining about the lady, and he replied that she must do whatever she thought fit. So she put her into a coach with one maid and twelve guards, and packed her off to France at eleven o'clock that night.

I can't feel sorry for her because she always persecuted my son so abominably. It was she who convinced the King and the late Queen of Spain that my son wanted to dethrone them and had conspired against their lives and the Crown, which was so false that she couldn't produce any proof in spite of all her bribery. What annoys me now is that the wicked devil will come here: I'm sure she'll spread her poison against my son.

Versailles 12 March 1715 Regarding your niece, I am touched by your confidence in me, and must say that the marriage you yourself favour seems quite suitable to me, if the suitor is rich enough to enable them to live comfortably in the manner to which they are accustomed. For love fades with the passing of time, and if hard times come afterwards, and many children, who cannot be brought up in accordance with their station, then hatred grows for those who arranged the marriage, and instead of friends you will have bitter enemies. I have seen several cases, dear Luise, and I warn you.

Mme des Ursins duly arrived at the French Court, where, to Liselotte's disgust, she was welcomed with open arms and given a pension of 40,000 francs for political services rendered to the State.

Versailles 23 April 1715 How kind of the Princess of Wales to ask to be remembered. But give me your advice. What can I send her in return that might give her pleasure? Little things such as boxes, clocks and the like are nicer and better in England, and one can no longer send fashions, because the English have their own, which are followed here now.

I have heard such a strange story from England; I wonder if it is true? I heard that the Prince of Wales saw a play where some actress, supposed to be impersonating the late Queen Anne, pretended to get drunk, and flung herself into a chair. Then a milord climbed on to the stage and laid about the actors with his sword, and the Prince is supposed to have ordered his guards to shoot him down. The entire pit shouted that if a single shot was fired they would do away with the King's whole party, and the captain of the guards is supposed to have said to the Prince that shooting might be the thing in Hanover, but in England it just wasn't done.

People here say that the Prince is on very bad terms with his father, and that they won't speak to one another. The Princess of Wales is supposed to have received a sort of petition asking her to consider, just and God-fearing as she is known to be, that the only rightful heir to the kingdom is the one known as the Pretender, as he was King James II's son as surely as her husband was Count Königsmarck's.[1] How unspeakably insolent, if this really was said to the Princess! England is a mad country. There are a lot of stories about Lord Bolingbroke, but they would take too long to tell. People like the English are not to be found anywhere else in the world, specially if what I have written is true. I can hardly believe it. I have always heard that Kensington is a pleasant place. There are some views of it engraved on copper. We have them here. The Genoese envoy here has taken such a dislike to England that he says nothing would ever induce him to go back, and he would be sorry if even his portrait was found there.

Versailles 3 May 1715 I have my grandson, the Duc de Chartres, here, for whom I arranged a spectacle suitable for his age. Three dogs, three doves and a cat; a triumphal carriage with its passenger, a bitch called Adrienne. The big cat pulls the vehicle, one dove is the coachman, the two others are pages, and a dog acts the lackey and sits up behind. He is called Picard. When the lady alights, Picard carries her train. When she is dressed up, Adrienne walks on her hind legs. The cat's name is Castille, and she jumps through hoops. Picard can act the horse; he allows himself to be saddled and carries a doll on his back for a rider. Also, this dog, and this is what I like best, dances *les olivettes* through three hoops, very cleverly.

Versailles 10 May 1715 The old hatred will last as long as life itself, and the old drab will do everything she can think of to do me disservices and cause me chagrin. She has found a new reason now: I refused to receive her old bosom-friend, who was sent packing by the new Queen of Spain. The reason why I wouldn't see her is that my son asked me not to: she is his worst enemy, and accused him, quite openly, of being a poisoner. He not only proved his innocence but sent all the evidence to Parliament for safe-keeping.

I've thanked you already for the dear little engraving, and told you what I felt about it. But what are those peculiar headdresses that they've made the little princesses wear?[2] They look exactly like the folded

[1] A reference to the ancient scandal concerning the love-affair between the King's divorced wife and Philip von Königsmarck.

[2] The Princesses Anne, Amelia and Caroline, daughters of the Prince and Princess of Wales.

table-napkins which are produced at German Courts when company is expected.

Marly 14 May 1715 You can usually see from the calendar when there is to be an eclipse. Ours was only partial, not total as in England. The last one we had, nine years ago, was shorter, though darker, than this one, and was total in Spain, just as the last one was in England. A lot of people went over to England to see this eclipse. I am fairly *curieuse*, but no amount of curiosity would ever induce me to cross the sea. What I admire is the art of calculation by which we know the course of all the planets, and can foretell to the minute the eclipses of the sun and moon hundreds of years before they happen. A lot of people who looked straight at the sun have hurt their eyes, but there are smoked glasses made and we watch through those without any risk.

What lies are told everywhere! Our King is certainly not in the least childish, but is, thank God, in full possession of his faculties. I shall reach my second childhood before he reaches his; I am quite losing my memory and shall, no doubt, soon be playing with dolls again.

Marly 28 May 1715 I am sending you a lock of my hair and some of my brother's, which he sent me before his death. I hope you will be pleased to have it. Bracelets are worn only by people who make a point of showing off their pretty arms and hands. As I am not so endowed I never wear mine, but carry them in my pocket, in a case specially made for them.

Marly 26 June 1715 The King took us to inspect his regiment, which is encamped near here. We stayed from half-past two to six o'clock in the evening. It was certainly a sight worth seeing. They all have brand new uniforms, light-grey, with gold silk frogging and flame-coloured epaulettes. The officers wear gold braid instead of silk, bright red ribbon and white plumes. All the soldiers wear moustaches, which is very becoming. They are all tall, well-built fellows; every one of them might be an officer, they look so well. I know many of the young officers, because they used to come over to play with my grandson, the Duc de Chartres, only a very few years ago, and now they are grown men.

I much prefer the theatre to the opera. I often used to hear his Grace, our father, say that there were no better plays in the world than English ones. French opera singers are expensive merchandise, and a man may easily lose his money and his health at one and the same time.

Marly 18 July 1715   I had one of my son's daughters with me; she
had never followed the hunt before. She is the third of the surviving
ones—the first one died ages ago.[1] This one is called Mlle de Valois, a
girl of fourteen. When she was a child I thought she might grow into a
beauty, but I have been sadly disappointed in my hopes. She grew a
great hawk's-nose which ruined everything, yet she had the prettiest
little nose in the world; how children change! I can guess what
happened—she must have been allowed to take snuff, and that made
her nose grow.

If they had listened to me, not one of the children would have been
put into a convent, but the mother's ideas are different from mine. The
second girl is set on being a nun at all costs. It annoys me and delights
the mother.[2] But patience. I am sure that everyone who is mixed up in
this will be very sorry. I have nothing to reproach myself with, because
I have done my best to prevent it.

Marly 8 August 1715   As soon as I return to Versailles I shall order my
portrait, head and shoulders, to be copied from the Rigaud. He has
caught my likeness so perfectly that it is astonishing. You'll see, dear
Luise, how I have aged. Be sure to let me know if you want it oval or
rectangular—portraits can be either.

My daughter's letters give me pleasure, but they are never cheerful:
she is either ill or pregnant, or she has something else to complain of.

The Queen of Spain's[3] letters from Bayonne consist of nothing but
compliments and commissions, and often very tiresome commissions
at that. For example, she wants to make someone a bishop and someone else a captain of guards, then she wants an abbey for someone
else, and wants yet another one to have a pension. But if I tell you the
bad I must also tell you the good: through her niece, the Queen, she
did a great deal to help my son iron out his differences with the King of
Spain. She seems to be a good creature, only I wish she wouldn't use
so many babyish words which I'm not accustomed to, such as heart's-
mama and little-heart and little-treasure. I'll never get used to it as
long as I live, so I can't be very delighted with these letters either.

Mme d'Orléans would be pleased if all her daughters were to become
nuns. She isn't stupid enough to think that this would ease their path
to heaven—no, it's pure laziness. She is afraid that if her daughters
were with her she would have to look after their education, and
she admits herself that she doesn't wish to give herself that trouble.

[1] Also called Mlle de Valois.   [2] Louise Adelaide, Mlle de Chartres.
[3] Maria Anna of Neuburg, dowager Queen of Spain.

Versailles 15 August 1715   Alas, our King is not well. I am so worried that I am half-ill myself. I can't eat or sleep properly. God grant I may be wrong. But if what I fear should come to pass, it would be the greatest possible disaster that could happen to me. I can't tell you all the details, they are so terrible that I can't think of them without shivering. Don't tell anyone in England what I've said.

The King, whose health had been failing for the past year, was suffering from gangrene in the leg. His various symptoms had been observed by everyone but his physician, Fagon, who persisted in denying that the King's illness was serious. Fagon treated him by swaddling the affected limbs in feather pillows, and prescribed a diet which included pints of iced water and quantities of over-ripe figs, melons and mulberries. Saint-Simon remarked that such large amounts of fruit and water, un-relieved by alcohol, turned the King's blood gangrenous.

Versailles 20 August 1715   Mme de Maintenon hasn't been ill; she is perfectly well. I wish to God our King were as well as she is, I should have fewer worries than I unfortunately have. The King's illness frightens me so much that it makes my heart tremble.

Versailles 27 August 1715   Dearest Luise, I am in such grief that I hardly know what I am doing or saying, but I will try to answer your letter as best I can. But I must tell you first that yesterday we saw the saddest and most moving sight that we shall see in all our lives. Our dear King, prepared for death, after receiving the last sacrament and making his last wishes known, sent for the young Dauphin and gave him his blessing. Then he sent for the Duchesse de Berry, me, and all his other daughters and grandchildren. He bade me goodbye so tenderly that I am still surprised I didn't faint on the spot. He assured me that he had always loved me, and more than I ever knew, and that he was sorry he had sometimes caused me sorrow. He asked me to remember him now and then, which he believed I would, since he was convinced that I had always loved him. His dying wish was that the rest of my life might be happy. I threw myself on to my knees, took his hand and kissed it, and he embraced me. Then he spoke to the others and told them to be united with one another. Thinking that he was talking to me, I said that I should obey His Majesty in this, as in everything all my life. He turned, smiled and said, 'I didn't mean you, I know that you are too sensible to need this advice; I mean the other princesses.' You can imagine how I felt. The King's *fermeté* is quite indescribable; he gives all his orders as though he were only going on a journey. He has said adieu to all his people, and recommended them all to my son, whom he appointed Regent with such tenderness that it pierces the heart. I think I shall be the first of the royal family to follow the King when he dies. He is still alive, but grows weaker and weaker, and there is no hope left.

Why I think I shall be the first to follow the King is, for one thing, my great age, and for another, as soon as the King is dead the young King will be taken to Vincennes, and the rest of us must go to Paris, where the air doesn't agree with me. So there I shall be sitting in my grief, without fresh air, without exercise, and will surely fall ill. It is not true that Mme de Maintenon is dead, she is in perfect health, and doesn't leave the King's room, day or night. The King's constitution is so strong that I believe they could have saved him if only they had acted sooner.

Louis XIV died on September 1st. By the time Fagon realized that something was seriously amiss—and as late as 22 August four consultant physicians had applauded his wise treatment of the invalid—it was too late. Gangrene was spreading above the knee and nothing could be done. The King's post mortem showed all his organs to be in perfect health, and revealed that his bowels had a capacity twice as great as normal, which Saint-Simon took to explain his extraordinarily large appetite.

The King's successor was his five-year-old great-grandson, and Philippe d'Orléans was appointed Regent of France during the boy's minority. By a codicil to the King's will, however, his authority was severely curtailed, but Philippe promptly assembled the *parlement*, and emerged from its session on 7 September as Regent with full governing powers.

The Duc du Maine had been charged with the responsibility for the young King's safety and education. That clause, also, was modified, and du Maine was made responsible for the boy's education only. This move pleased all those who had found it hard to accept the bastard's elevation, but it infuriated du Maine's wife, chief of the Regent's enemies and a tireless plotter.

Versailles 6 September 1715   It is a very long time since I last wrote, but I couldn't help it. I was so overwhelmed by grief and sadness that it was impossible to write. I saved my poor streaming eyes for my daughter's letters on Fridays and Tuesdays, and you can imagine how many visitors I had to receive, and how many letters. Actually, I am upset both because of the King's death and also because I have to go to that accursed Paris, and for a whole year, too. But if I fall ill, I shall run away to St Cloud. My God, what torture I shall have to endure! But there is no point in complaining. I am an entirely spontaneous person, and if something touches me I have to experience it through and through, and until now it has done me no harm. But it is true that I was much comforted by the fact that all the people, the army and the *parlement* were on my son's side, and that his enemies, who deceived the King on his deathbed by plotting against my son, have seen him publicly acknowledged as Regent, and had to stop their intriguing. My son is so busy that he has no rest, day or night. I'm afraid he will make himself ill and, quite apart from this, such sad things are running through my mind, of which I cannot speak, that the consolation is far from complete. My son addressed the *parlement* himself, and I am told that he didn't speak badly.

Paris 10 September 1715 Yesterday our late King was taken to St Denis. The whole of the royal family has scattered like starlings. The young King went to Vincennes yesterday, Mme de Berry to St Cloud, my son's wife and I came here, and my son joined us after he had accompanied the young King to Vincennes. Where all the others have gone to, I don't know.

Paris 13 September 1715 The young King was taken to his first *lit de justice*[1] in the *parlement* yesterday. My son's Regency was registered there, it is safe and certain now. I only hope I may have a fever soon, because I have promised not to go away from here until I fall ill. Headaches don't count, because I am never without them in Paris, but with a fever I could go to our dear St Cloud. My son has more important things to think about than my comfort and pleasures. I think he is quite determined to obey the King's last orders and live peacefully with those around him. To show that he has no intention of governing solely according to his own whim he has already formed several councils, one for matters of state, one for religious affairs, one for foreign affairs and one for war, and he will only be able to act on their decisions.

I have quite made up my mind not to meddle in any of it, for between ourselves France, to her cost, has been ruled by women for all too long. I don't want people to be able to say this about my son on my account.

Paris 17 September 1715 The trade that my son has taken up is not easy.

[1] The occasions when the *parlement* met in the presence of the King.

Things are in such a wretched state that it will be a long time before they are in order again. I can see nothing but work and trouble ahead. And he has jealousy and animosity to contend with. More than forty handbills against him have been put up in the town, and the *ducs et pairs* have tried to antagonize the *parlement* against him too. But since my son is well-loved by the *parlement*, the people and the army, they didn't get far, and only had the humiliation of proving their ill-will.

Paris 24 September 1715   I see my son no more than once a day, and then for barely half-an-hour. People are now praising him to the skies because they all hope for favours. But since fifty ask him for what only one can have, he is left with forty-nine malcontents and as many enemies. My son works hard from six in the morning until midnight, and I fear he will make himself ill if he carries on like that.

Paris 27 September 1715   Although the Paris air has given me, since Tuesday evening, the worst cold and cough I've had for years—and such a headache, too, that I can scarcely keep my eyes open—I'll answer your letter of the 4th/15th[1] of this month, because writing to somebody one loves is a comfort.

Milord Stairs persuaded me to write to the Princess of Wales, and I did so last Thursday. Will you write to tell me whether my little note has pleased, and whether it was as agreeable to her Highness as Milord Stairs would have me believe?

I don't know whether my son will be King or not. That lies with the Almighty. But even if it should come about, he would only be able to act on the advice of his *conseil de conscience*, to which, as you may imagine, I haven't been elected. One thing, however, is certain: if he followed his own inclination, no man would be persecuted on account of his faith.

> Luise had asked Liselotte to intercede with her son on behalf of some Protestants who had been sent to the galleys for refusing to become Catholics.
>
> The Regent's lenient religious policy was much disliked by the old régime. There was a large anti-Orléans party which, in the event of the young King's death, wanted Philip V to be King of France instead of Orléans. The claims of the two men were equally good. For all that the King of Spain had renounced his rights to the succession more than

[1] England still followed the Julian calendar, and only adopted the Gregorian calendar in 1752.

once, he was supported in his pretensions in Spain as well as in France. This state of affairs made friendly relations between the two countries difficult to achieve, and caused the Regent to look for closer ties with England. To further these at every level Liselotte had been urged to correspond with the Princess of Wales.

She was also asked to deal with Leibniz, who was looking to the Regent for patronage. Conveying Philippe's refusal—though privately wishing that her son concentrated 'on the gowns of scholars rather than ladies' nightgowns'—she had written, 'The King was not studious, but he caused the arts and sciences to flourish. My son is the opposite, but it will be as it used to be in Heidelberg: electors who didn't drink built tuns; and those who drank did not build.'

LEIBNIZ

Paris 21 November 1715 I must have done as M Jourdain does in the play (*de la prose sans le savoir*), because I can't remember what I wrote that might deserve the least praise, unless I myself don't know what is praiseworthy. What I said of the great tun was a Heidelbergish notion.

My son is so beset by irritating affairs that I can only see him for a few minutes each day. He has given out all the academies, except for the one for the fine arts. He kept that for himself, so that he might refresh his spirit after his labours. If knowledge is the bread of heaven there must be many hungry souls, and I myself would, I fear, suffer the pangs of hunger, as no one could be less educated and more ignorant than I am.

CAROLINE OF WALES

Paris 15 December 1715 After the King's death I went to call on Mme de Maintenon in St Cyr. As soon as I entered her room she asked me, 'But Madame, what are you doing here?', and I answered that I had come to mingle my tears with those of the person whom the King had loved most. She said, 'Ah yes, he did love me, but he loved you very much, too.' I told her that he had done me the honour of assuring me that he had always felt friendly towards me, regardless of the fact that everything possible was done to make him hate me. By this, I wanted to show her that I know everything, but that I can forgive my enemies like a good Christian. If she has any good in her at all, she must feel pain at receiving kindness from one whom she has persecuted all her life.

Mme de Maintenon had retired to her rooms in St Cyr when the King had died. Her grief, said Madame, was on the wane. She was beginning to console herself with little parties, and had written to the King's doctor that she had rediscovered her stomach, which she had lost at Court, and was taking supper again.

LUISE

Paris 14 January 1716 I shall begin my letter to you today, otherwise I may be prevented from writing again, as I was last Friday, but that time the reason was a new one: my apartments nearly went up in flames. I had asked to be called at seven because I had an unbelievable number of letters to write that day, but awoke at half-past two to hear loud footsteps on the floor above. I tried to get back to sleep, but at three o'clock I saw my *valet de chambre* lighting my fire. I told him he must be dreaming, for it had only just struck three, but he said, 'I know, but Madame must please get up, the Opéra is on fire. Luckily the wind is carrying the blaze in the opposite direction, but if it changes the Palais-Royal will be in flames and Madame couldn't get out in time.'

You can imagine how I hurried into my clothes, dear Luise. When the fire had been put out, at seven, I went to the chapel to thank God for not having been burned to death, and then I went back to bed and slept till one.

Our little King in the Tuileries is in perfect health; he is very lively and won't keep still for an instant. To tell you the truth he is rather a naughty child, but they never say 'no' to him for fear of making him ill. If you ask me, if would be better for him not to be allowed to over-excite himself. However, everyone wants to be in a king's favour, no matter how young he may be.

So far it doesn't look as though the King of Spain will abide by his renunciation—God keep us from new wars. There are other people against my son as well,[1] but except for the clergy no one is openly against him, though everyone knows quite well who his enemies are.

Does Mme de Kielemansegg[2] now speak English as well as she does French? Few Germans write French as well as she does. Perhaps she has got so fat from drinking English beer?

Paris 21 January 1716 Dearest Luise, I don't know what the winter is like in England, but here the cold is greater than I have ever known in my life. We didn't get any letters from England all last week. Although

---

[1] The Jesuits were publicly preaching against the Regent. The rest of the pro-Spanish party was still lying low.

[2] Mme von Kielemansegg, known in England as the elephant, was one of George I's pair of ugly favourites whom he had brought over from Hanover. The other one, known as the beanpole, was Melusina von Schulenburg.

I am sorry about it I'm not surprised, since I was told that the Channel at Calais is frozen so far out to sea that when the English boat arrived it had to return to Dover. There was nowhere to land because of the ice. I regret this with all my heart, because I long to know what is happening now that the Pretender, as he is called, has arrived in Scotland, and if they are still being faithful to our King George.

Yesterday I received twenty-nine visiting German princes, counts and nobles. It reminded me of an old story. The year your brother, Carllutz, was here, I was on very bad terms with the Chevalier de Lorraine, and the rumour went round that I had sent for Carllutz to avenge me. A good many gentlemen of the Court, fine men, came to ask me to allow them to be the Raugrave's seconds. I laughed, and told them that I was not going to be the cause of any fighting. I don't know whether the Chevalier had heard anything or not, but once when Carllutz, I and several other Germans were together he came into the room, and when he saw us all he turned on his heel and ran as though he had seen the devil.

Paris 16 February 1716 I pity King George because he must remain with the English as a point of honour. His Majesty would be so much happier and so much more in absolute charge in Hanover, but one can't escape one's fate, and what God has predestined must come to pass. Those who side with the Pretender won't come into the open yet, for the thing isn't certain enough.

I am very sorry they have the plague in Celle; the Jews who brought it there deserve to be punished. I would write more, but the sandman is on my trail, so I'll say no more than that, asleep or awake, I love you with all my heart.

Paris 21 February 1716 Paris is an irritating place in every way, but with God's help I shan't have to remain here much longer. I've been here since the death of the King, but if God grants me life, as soon as it's green I shall go to St Cloud. There I shan't be pestered, or hear and see something new and peculiar every day. I must say one thing more before it chokes me: it was the Pope and the King of Spain who gave the money to the Pretender. The Pope gave three million livres, the King of Spain three times a hundred thousand. He didn't get a penny from my son.

CAROLINE OF WALES
Paris 25 February 1716 I won Monsieur over during the last three

years of his life. We even used to laugh together about his weaknesses.
He no longer listened to accusations and tales about me. He had confidence in me and always took my side, but before that I used to suffer
dreadfully. I was just beginning to be happy when the Almighty took
poor Monsieur from me, and I saw the work and trouble of thirty
years disappear in an instant.

Paris 13 March 1716 My son is neither handsome nor ugly. He used
to have a good figure, but now he's getting too fat for his height,
because he is small. He may no longer be handsome, but the women
still run after him out of pure self-interest because he pays them well.
This winter a funny thing happened. A young and pretty lady[1]
visited him in his room, and he presented her with a diamond worth
2,000 louis d'or and a box worth 200. The woman has a jealous husband,
but such was her cheek that she went to him and told him that she had
the chance to buy these things very cheaply from people who were in
need of money. He believed her and gave her what she asked for. She
took the money, thanked him from the bottom of her heart, and with
the golden box in her pocket and the ring on her finger went to an
elegant party. There she was asked where the ring had come from, and
the box? She answered 'M de Parabère.' He was present, and remarked
that one could hardly do less if one had a wife of quality who loved
no one but her husband. There was hearty laughter, for the other
people were not as simple-minded as the husband, and knew quite well
how the land lay.

Paris 19 March 1716 Once jealousy has taken root there is no getting
rid of it, one must take one's stand in time. My daughter hides her
feelings, but she often suffers secretly, and how could it be otherwise?
She loves her children beyond everything, and the creature[2] that the
Duke is so fond of, and this woman's husband, rob her of every penny
—they are ruining the Duc de Lorraine. He knows quite well that my
daughter knows everything, and I think he is grateful to her for not
plaguing him and for being so patient, because he lives on good terms
with her and she loves him so much that as long as he gives her a few
kind words she is content and happy.

[1] The Comtesse de Parabère, who had been the Regent's mistress since the previous
autumn.
[2] Mme de Craon, the Duc de Lorraine's mistress and the wife of his favourite,
whom he shortly afterwards made his *premier ministre*.

HERR VON HARLING[1]

Paris 5 April 1716 It is true that HRH the Princess of Wales does me the honour of writing very diligently. Her shortest letters are five sheets long, written on four sides; yesterday I received seven sheets, making twenty-eight pages, the previous one was thirty-five, and an earlier one was forty-three sheets. That takes up all my time, as you can imagine.

There is, thank God, not a word of truth in the rumour from Hanover: I saw the King on Monday and yesterday. On Monday there was a play, and the King was there, in the best of health, from beginning to end, and yesterday he ran to the dinner-table so fast that I couldn't keep up with him, because I no longer have my knight-of-the-rustling-leaves legs.

I assure you, I am far from wanting our young King's death. For my son himself it would be better if he stayed alive for many years to come. My son is, God be praised, still young enough to wait for a long while, and in the meantime, if the Lord grants us peace, the kingdom will recover. The young King is the rightful heir, and it is only proper that he should reign for a long time. And if I live to see the day when this King marries and has heirs, I shan't grumble. When a thing is just, I wouldn't say anything against it even if it were to my disadvantage.

CAROLINE OF WALES

St Cloud 3 July 1716 Mme de Montespan once went to a review. When she came to the German troops they shouted, 'King's whore, whore!' In the evening the King asked her how she had liked the review and she said, 'Perfectly beautiful, only I find the Germans too unsophisticated, the way they call a spade a spade, *parce que je me suis faite expliquer ce que signifiait leur cri.*'

LUISE

St Cloud 7 July 1716 It is a fortnight since I last wrote to you, and I was about to do so last Friday, but as I was finishing my letter to the Princess of Wales they came to fetch me because Mme d'Orléans was in labour. It was just eleven o'clock. It was half-past eleven before the carriage was ready, and we arrived at a quarter to one. When I came into the antechamber all was very still, and I was quietly told that she had been happily delivered almost an hour ago. But they said this with such sad faces that I could not doubt that Mme d'Orléans had a seventh daughter.[2]

---

[1] Widower of Liselotte's old governess.　　[2] Mlle de Chartres.

CAROLINE OF WALES

16 July 1716 My son has three bastards, two boys and one girl, but
he has legitimized only one of them, the one he had by the lady
who used to be with me.¹ He is called the Chevalier d'Orléans.²
The other one, now a lad of eighteen, is an abbot, for my son doesn't
want to have his bastards whom he hasn't recognized founding fam-
ilies.³ He was the son of La Florence. She was a beautiful girl, a dancer
at the opera; she is dead now. The girl is fourteen, she is the daughter
of the actress Desmares⁴ who is still on the stage.

LUISE

St Cloud 11 August 1716 The King never allowed any ceremony at
all at Marly. No ambassadors or envoys were permitted to come there,
there was no etiquette, and everything was higgledy-piggledy, *pêle-
mêle*. On the walks, the King made all the men keep their hats on, and
in the salon everyone, right down to the captain and the sub-lieutenants
of the guard, was allowed to sit down. It disgusted me so much that I
never wanted to stay there for long.

St Cloud 1 September 1716 You mustn't worry too much even if
I'm not always well. When you are over sixty, as I am, you can't hope
for constant good health; it must go downhill until at last you find
yourself below the ground.

My doctor is not at all a charlatan, and he doesn't much care for
medicines; but my people, who are full of self-interest and afraid that
they might lose their *charges* through my death, give him no peace.
Don't grieve before the time comes, dear Luise. I doubt whether
taking the waters would agree with me; that means going for walks,
and I can't walk any more.

I'm no use for company any more either, I have become too broody.
Only our dear Electress could cheer me up, but unhappily she
is no more. I can't get over her death, and the King's, too, still

¹ Mlle de Séry, Comtesse d'Argenton. Liselotte had written to Sophie on 21 July
1701, 'My son is charming to me; he has a good heart, but he is only "Saluting the
fence round the garden", as he is in love with one of my ladies whose name is Séry.'

² Jean-Philippe, born 1702, who was made legitimate in 1706, and died Grand
Prieur de France.

³ The Abbé Charles de St Albin, who appears in Liselotte's letters every now and
then. He died, Archbishop of Cambrai, in 1764.

⁴ The lady whose face was used for the picture of Antigone that the future Regent
was painting for the Electress in 1699. See letter of 26 July of that year.

lies heavy on my heart. By the moon, it is a year today since his death. Tomorrow we come out of mourning. All his children, except for the Princess de Conti, have long since ceased to mourn him in their hearts.

I have a description of England in two volumes with fine engravings. Hampton Court is shown too, and I agree that it is beautiful.[1] It used only to be a bishop's house. I can't understand how one can prefer another country, however beautiful, to one's fatherland. But I imagine the Prince thinks he is obliged to say so, to make himself popular with the English.

CAROLINE OF WALES

St Cloud 10 November 1716 When my son asked Mme de Maintenon, quite gently, why she was slandering him, when she must know in her own conscience that what she was saying was wicked, she answered, 'I repeated the rumours because I believed them.' My son said, 'No, you couldn't have believed them, since you knew the contrary to be true.' So she said, with such insolence that I had to admire my son's patience, 'Isn't it true that the Dauphine died?', and my son said, 'Couldn't she have died without my help? Was she immortal?' She said, 'I was in such despair about her death that I picked on the person they said was behind it.' My son said, 'But you know, from the report given to the King, that I had nothing to do with it, and that Mme la Dauphine wasn't poisoned at all.' 'It is true,' she said, 'and I will say no more about it.'

LUISE

St Cloud 19 November 1716 If it should turn out to be dropsy,[2] I couldn't cure myself by eating chocolate, as my father did. My stomach can't take it. If I only eat a tiny piece, it hurts and feels heavy.

Thank God our dear Princess arrived safely at St James's. The journey worried me greatly, because she had suffered from bleeding and such pains, and is so close to the event. I hope you will tell me of her happy delivery by the first post. HRH wrote to me that she will give you that commission.

I should feel little gratitude if people dressed up for my birthday, because I don't care about clothes and have never in my life paid any attention to what people are wearing. If someone put on my own

[1] Luise had taken a house at Hampton Court, where the Prince and Princess of Wales were staying.

[2] Liselotte to Luise, 6 November 1716: 'My legs are so swollen that my doctor fears it may be dropsy, all the more so as my mother died of it.'

clothes and appeared in them before me, I shouldn't notice. I never notice how people are dressed unless they wear something ridiculous.

Paris 1 December 1716 I was very shocked that our dear Princess of Wales had such an unhappy lying-in, and cried bitterly, but God be praised that she is still alive and is out of danger. Please, dear Luise, be my ambassadress with the English Regent. Tell the Prince of Wales that no one in the world shared more closely in his grief, and in the happiness that his wife was saved.

> Liselotte was not correct in referring to the Prince of Wales as Regent. He had been made 'Guardian and Lieutenant of the Realm' during his father's absence in Hanover, as the term Regent carried the implication of too much power.
> Caroline of Wales had been delivered of a dead son on November 8th, after four harrowing days of labour during which her doctor had been prevented from attending her, for reasons of modesty, despite a petition from the Cabinet. This petition had so infuriated her German midwife that she refused to touch her patient, and resumed her ministrations only just in time to save her.

Paris 11 December 1716 I am sending you a small reward in return for the good news of the Princess's health: an insignificant little golden box with a little diamond ring set with four tiny but genuine green diamonds. I hope you will like it, and that green diamonds are still rare in England. Write and tell me if they are common or not.

For God's sake, dear Luise, don't start using spectacles. Have a little patience, sight improves. I have had that experience and now read more easily than I did ten years ago.

> Liselotte hated, apparently, all such artificial aids. Some weeks later, reminding Luise that she was her junior by ten years, she warned her off false teeth. 'Nothing makes the breath stink worse, therefore give up the thought, dearest Luise.'

Paris 15 December 1716 To think that the Princess is already exposing herself on Sunday to the danger of smelling strong scents! I shan't rest until I hear how it has gone. If I hadn't been able to stand perfumes I should have been dead long ago. Every time I was lying in Monsieur came to visit me, wearing perfumed Spanish gloves.

Liselotte's health continued to trouble her. She suffered from painfully swollen legs, and was unable to sleep. Then the opposite happened and she was unable to stay awake, and complained of shortness of breath. 'If I walk the length of two rooms, I snort like a dancing-bear,' she wrote to Luise. She was continually purged and bled. On one occasion during the blood-letting she moved her arm too soon and lost many more ounces of blood than had been intended. This made her weaker than ever before. Altogether, the cures exhausted her almost more than the disease, now officially diagnosed as dropsy.

Paris 30 April 1717   Slowly my disease is leaving me, but I look at the beautiful weather with wistful eyes: I am weak and can't enjoy it properly. The Princess of Wales says that the English climate is making you look thin and ill. I wish you were at home and not in danger of catching consumption.

Paris 14 May 1717   Dearest Luise, I had a grand visit today from my hero, the Tsar. I found him rather likeable, that is, what we used to call likeable long ago, with no affectations and without *façon*. He is very intelligent. Although he speaks broken German, he makes himself understood quite well. He is polite with everyone, and is making himself very popular.

I received him in a strange get-up. I can't wear a bodice yet and appeared, straight from my bed, in my nightdress, camisole, dressing-gown and a belt.

I'm given hope that my wound will be quite healed in four days' time, but they don't want me to wear stays even then, so I shall creep about like this for a few days longer.

Madame was not the only lady to receive Peter I in *déshabillé*. The other was Mme de Maintenon, who had taken to her bed on hearing that he was visiting St Cyr, where she lived in her retirement. When the Tsar entered all the curtains in her room were closed, except for one half-drawn bed-curtain. The Tsar drew them back one after another, the window curtains first, the bed-curtains second, but the visit cannot be counted a success as he only took a long hard look at her, and departed without a single word having been exchanged.

CAROLINE OF WALES
St Cloud 11 June 1717   I was very pleased indeed when Monsieur made *lit à part* immediately after the birth of my daughter, because the

business of having babies was not at all to my liking. So when he proposed it I answered, 'Yes, Monsieur, with all my heart, provided you don't hate me and continue to be fond of me.' He promised that, and we were both very pleased with each other.

LUISE

St Cloud 17 October 1717 The King contracted enormous debts because he didn't want to give up any of his royal splendour. So he was forced to borrow money, in which his ministers were only too eager to help him. Because whenever the King borrowed a penny they and their creatures got a pistole, and by their thieving tricks made the King and the kingdom poor, and themselves good and rich. My son works day and night to put things to rights, but he gets little thanks, and has many enemies who twist everything he does. He has so little interest in money that he never even takes what comes to him by right of the Regency, although he can hardly afford to go without because of his many children.

Among the people the young King has about him, who are far from well disposed towards my son, there is one who though he may be his brother-in-law and looks as though he had swallowed all the saints, is a false hypocrite and the wickedest man in the world. In the King's time, whenever he flattered anyone and had a good word to say to them, it was certain that he had done something nasty. He made his own mother leave the Court to please his old governess the Maintenon, and he was so afraid she might turn up again one day that he had her furniture thrown out of the window. You can easily imagine what such a man is capable of; I fear him like the devil on my son's account, and don't think my son is careful enough so far as he is concerned.

St Cloud 24 October 1717 In France and England the dukes and milords are so extremely arrogant that, if they had their way, they would consider themselves grander than the princes of the blood, though most of them don't even belong to the nobility. I once put one of these dukes finely in his place. He was standing in front of the Prince of Zweibrücken, and I said loudly, 'How is it that M de Saint-Simon is jostling the *Prince de Deux-Ponts?* Is he about to ask him to take one of his sons for a page?' Everyone laughed so much, he was obliged to leave.

St Cloud 13 November 1717 The little King has a pretty figure and plenty of intelligence, but he is an ill-natured child who only loves his old governess and no one else in the world. He takes a dislike to people without reason, and loves making cutting remarks. I am not at all in his good books, but I take no notice, as by the time he is on the throne I shall no longer be in the world, and shan't be dependent on his whims.

Paris 27 November 1717 Saint Cloud is a summer residence. Many of the rooms where my people are lodged in have no fireplaces, which makes them unbearable in winter. I should kill most of them off, and I couldn't be so cruel; as soon as I see any suffering I feel pity. The other thing that brings me to Paris is that the Parisians are fond of me and like me to come and spend the winter here, so it is only right that I should have come. Although I don't have much space in my lodgings I have a good warm room and closet, and I should be considered most eccentric if I didn't return to town for the winter like everyone else. As in everything else in life, it is one's duty to do the sensible rather than the pleasant thing.

'One is so constantly pestered in this disagreeable Paris,' says Liselotte, 'that I am far from lighthearted, besides being really worried about my son.' The Regent's old eye injury—Liselotte believed it to have been caused on the tennis court some eighteen months ago, but it was commonly attributed to a blow from a lady's fan—was giving him endless trouble. The treatment prescribed by his doctors only made it worse, but it began to get a little better when he tried 'a black powder given to him by a curé, a German'.

Paris 28 November 1717 As soon as I was dressed I went to the chapel to say my prayers, and then on to my son, who can now see a little better with his bad eye. He had been unable to distinguish colours, but now he can recognize red, because while I was there Cardinal de Polignac arrived in his red robes, and he saw that at once, so there is an improvement.

But what worries me is that my son, who practised great restraint while he was taking his medicines, will now resume his usual entertainments, and the debauched ladies will run after him and invite him to their suppers and make him lead his disorderly life, and ruin his eyesight or lose it altogether.

St Cloud 2 December 1717 I'm glad my letters arrive so regularly now. M de Torcy is no friend of mine, and if he could harm me in any way I'm sure he wouldn't let the opportunity pass. But I'm not worried:

my son knows me too well, and knows also how much I love him, and it would be difficult to set us at odds.

The fact that the letters are sealed doesn't mean a thing; they have a compound of quicksilver and other things which, when you press it on the seal, takes an exact impression. When they have it ready for use they break off the sealing-wax, noting if it is black or red. Then they read the letters and seal them neatly, and no one can see that they have ever been opened. My son can make this amalgam (that is what it is called).

Paris 2 December 1717 Fires often break out in Paris, and people get burned to death. The orange trees weren't burned, for they hadn't yet been placed in the Orangerie.[1] My daughter imagines she will arrive here on the tenth of February, but I don't believe it yet. I can see that her husband is looking forward to it too; but there is his mistress and her husband, who is the Duke's favourite, and these two will have the shirt off his back and won't let this trip take place. They would rather put the money in their own pockets. Where self-interest reigns, one can't count on anything. I should be pleased to see my daughter, but I know from long experience that the things one looks forward to most turn out the worst. Sixteen years ago, when the Court of Lorraine was here, my daughter fell ill with smallpox three days afterwards. God knows what will happen this time. My daughter can't have an arm-chair in my presence, nor can my son and his wife, so the Duc de Lorraine can't have one either, but for the rest we shall dispense with ceremony.

Paris 9 December 1717 Certainly I have never seen anyone—I don't say princely, but noble—brought up as badly as these children here.[2] They have the same governess as I had for my daughter, who is, thank God, not as ill brought-up. I tackled the governess once and asked her why she didn't educate my grandchildren as she did my daughter, and she said, 'With Mademoiselle you used to back me up, but when I complain about these children the mother laughs at me and so do they. When I realized this I let things take their course.' Since I didn't make the marriage, I have no part in the children's education either.

[1] During a fire in the Orangerie the watchman, who had put his lantern on the straw protecting the plants before he dropped off to sleep, had been burned to death. Liselotte's letter serves to reassure Luise about the fate of the costly trees.
[2] Liselotte's Orléans grandchildren.

Paris 19 December 1717 We had hoped that my son's eye would get better, as the black powder had such a good effect, but it is just the same, although my son used the powder again. But the man who supplied it doesn't doubt his remedy yet; he says that, in his experience, once there has been the slightest improvement the complete cure follows without fail. But it takes time, and for the first two months no improvement is noticeable, so we must be content with the hope, and pray to God that it will go as the village curé says. It is quite true that if my son's mistresses really cared for him they would care for his health and well-being, but I can see, dearest Luise, that you don't know Frenchwomen. Nothing counts except their debauches and their greed, and money comes above everything; they don't care an iota for anyone. There is another thing, too, which I cannot understand; my son is never jealous, and doesn't mind if his servants sleep with his mistresses. That seems quite revolting, and clearly shows that he doesn't really love them.

The young King visits me a few times each year, much, I expect, against his will and inclination. He doesn't care for me, and I imagine that is because I told him once or twice that it is unbecoming to a great king like him to be *mutin* and *opiniâtre*.

It seems there is trouble between the King of England and the Prince of Wales. How like the English to come between father and son.

The cause of the breakdown of even superficially civil relations between George I and his son had occurred during the christening of the new baby Prince, born to the Prince and Princess of Wales in November, when there had been a bitter altercation over who should be godfather. The Prince was banished from St James's. The Princess was allowed to stay until she had recovered sufficiently from the birth to be moved, but she did not avail herself of this permission and followed her husband. The three little Princesses and the baby Prince had to stay behind.

Paris 23 December 1717 I am so sorry for our dear Princess of Wales that I shed tears for her yesterday. It is so pitiful, the way the Countess of Bückeburg described her departure from St James's. The poor Princess went into one faint after another when her weeping little Princesses said goodbye.

The entire province of Brittany is on the point of rebellion, and troops had to be sent there. My son is to be pitied. He is a tormented soul.

The troubles in Brittany stemmed from unpopular taxes. Resisting the royal commission sent from Paris to collect the money, the nobles of the province appealed for help to the King of Spain 'as the lawful Regent of France'. Spanish intervention helped to keep the province in unrest for a long time and was, in part, responsible for the hostilities between France and Spain which were soon to break out.

Paris 13 February 1718   We hope to have my daughter and her husband here next Friday, or a week today at the latest. I am very pleased indeed, but God grant that her visit may take its course without any trouble. I am frightened that the bad company with which my daughter will have to mix will do their best to besmirch her reputation. If I allowed that to happen, the outcome might be very unhappy, because the Duc de Lorraine is not so indifferent to his honour as the men here; he wouldn't think that any gossip concerning my daughter was a laughing matter. If I warned her I should be considered a spoilsport, and bad-tempered as well. No one would thank me for it, not to speak of even more unpleasant consequences, so you see it won't be an un-diluted pleasure.

Paris 17 February 1718   I should like it to be fine tomorrow because I want to drive out to meet my daughter and bring her here, but it looks like rain, so my daughter may have a wet reception after all.

Liselotte's daughter and her party arrived on February 18th. Young Liselotte, who was quite beside herself with joy, had apparently not altered at all. Her husband, on the other hand, was hardly recognizable; he had become brick-red, and even fatter than the Regent. Mme de Craon, also of the party, retired to her sickbed soon after her arrival, and there was a great deal of worry as to the nature of her disease. Madame feared smallpox, and since neither the Regent nor the Duke himself, who she knew was unlikely to abstain from nocturnal visits to his mistress, had ever had the illness, she foresaw nothing but disaster. However, Mme de Craon reappeared a few days later, fully recovered, and Liselotte was free to worry about other matters.

Paris 24 February 1718   My God, how I pity our poor dear Princess of Wales! I heard from England yesterday that her last-born little prince died of catarrh on the chest. She saw him at Kensington just before the end. I wish she hadn't seen him, for it will be even more painful for her now. God grant that this Prince's death may extinguish all the

The Regent, Philippe d'Orléans, with the portrait of Mme de Parabère, by Nicolas de Largillière.

Madame's daughter-in-law, Mme d'Orléans, eighteenth-century French School.

flames kindled at his christening! But alas, there is no sign of that yet. God forgive me, but I think the King of England doesn't believe that the Prince of Wales is his son, because if he did he couldn't possibly treat him as he does.

Paris 10 March 1718 Before you receive this letter, my Lorraine children will have left. They intend to go tomorrow week—that is, the Duke does; my daughter would very much like to stay longer. The Duke wanted to go tomorrow, but I asked for this extra week. My daughter is, thank God, so steadfast in her morals that she can mix with anyone at all without risk of harm. But the way young people behave nowadays makes one's hair stand on end. A daughter who shamelessly procures pretty chambermaids for her father, so that he will turn a blind eye to her own debauches! A mother who lets matters take their course to further her own ends![1] In short, everything you see and hear is horrible and frightful.

Paris 13 March 1718 Never have there been such women as there are now. They behave as though their salvation consisted in sleeping with men; those who have some intention of marrying are still the most honest of the lot. The things you see and hear every day are quite indescribable, and about the highest in the land, too. Such manners were not usual in my daughter's day. She is in a perpetual state of amazement, unable to contain herself, and her astonishment often makes me laugh. Above all she can't get used to the sights at the Opera, where ladies with great names lie publicly in the laps of men who are said not to hate them. 'Madame, Madame!' she cries, and I say, '*Que voulez-vous que j'y fasse, ma fille? Ce sont les manières du temps.*' '*Mais elles sont vilaines,*' says my daughter, and that is true.

Paris 24 March 1718 I cannot eat, and my stomach is full of wind which plagues me at night. But I believe that with a little patience it will improve. But what is not very healthy for my spleen is my daughter's departure; they have arranged to leave next Monday. The present that Mme de Berry gave my daughter is very *galant*. She gave her a *commode*; a commode is a large table with large drawers, and the top is very fine, with gilt ornaments. In these drawers were all sorts of *à la mode* stuff: shawls, *coiffures*, *andriennes*, ribbons, stockings, everything that's *à la mode*, certainly worth a thousand pistoles, and very pretty gloves, fans and . . .

[1] Liselotte alludes to the current rumours about the widowed Duchesse de Berry, the Regent, and the complacent, lazy Duchesse d'Orléans.

24 March, half-past two o'clock. I was in too much of a hurry to continue this morning. My son gave his sister an elegant present, too, a *nécessaire*, that is, a rectangular box containing porcelain cups and everything that is needed for taking chocolate, coffee and tea. The cups are white, with a raised design in gold and enamel, and there is a drawer with an Indian tray. Under this tray there is a little blue cushion with all kinds of gold objects underneath, needlecase, thimble, corkscrew-case, two golden boxes and some more things, all made of pure gold and finely worked.

Paris 31 March 1718 My daughter hasn't left yet, thank God, but it will happen soon. You are right when you say that in such cases it is best to look for distraction and not talk about it, and to find something else to fill the mind, and that is what I shall do. But everything went off very well, thank God, and my Lorraine children were pleased with me and I with them.

But now, to return to your letter. There is not a word of truth in the story that the King of England gave the Princess of Wales a present of lace. Unfortunately, everything is still in a very bad way. I think I told you last Sunday of the fine gesture of the Prince of Wales, who would have nothing to do with the people who wanted to make him the leader of their party. If that doesn't move the King, nothing will.

Historians are liars, too. In the history of my grandfather, the King of Bohemia, they say that my grandmother, the Queen of Bohemia, was so ambitious that she gave her husband no peace until he became king; there's not a word of truth in the story. The Prince of Orange, the King's uncle, started the whole thing, the Queen knew nothing of it and in those days thought only of plays, ballets and reading romances.

Our King, in his history, is made to withdraw from Holland out of generosity, for the sake of peace. The real reason was that Mme de Montespan had returned to Versailles after she had had her baby, and wanted to see him again.

Now, if lies like this are told about things which happened under our very noses, how can one believe what is said about things that happened long ago and far away? So I think that history (except for the holy scriptures) is as untrue as the romances, the only difference being that these are longer and are more amusingly written.

Paris, Easterday, 17 April 1718 You will have seen from my last letter that my daughter and her husband left here ten days ago. It was hard on both sides. Yesterday I had a letter from her; she reached Lunéville safely.[1] She sent me the measurements of her eldest son, he is eleven to-morrow week and is just as tall as my grandson, the Duc de Chartres, who will be fifteen on August 4th. My Lorraine children are all strong, the mother is strong and healthy too, and not such a lazy dawdler as Mme d'Orléans. Such laziness has never been seen before. She has had a couch made to lie on when she plays cards. We all laugh at her, but it doesn't help. She plays lying down, eats lying down, reads lying down, in short most of her life is spent lying down, and that can't be healthy; in fact, she is almost always indisposed; one day she complains of her head, the next day of her stomach, there's almost always something wrong. That can't make for healthy children, although the three eldest daughters are strong and well. The first and the third are big and stout, they are like trees, especially Mlle de Valois. But enough of my grand-children. My daughter's departure didn't affect my health, I am very well now, and shall thank your good wishes and prayers for this.

St Cloud 1 May 1718   My son isn't rich enough to marry his daughters off well; moreover, who wants to see all those illborn children take precedence over their own? I'm quite of the old school—*mésalliances* are horrible to me, and I've noticed that they are never successful. My son's marriage has spoilt my life and soured my cheerful temper.

St Cloud 8 May 1718   I am writing to you with a sad and heavy heart, because the good, pious, virtuous Queen of England died yesterday morning at seven o'clock at St Germain. She is bound to be in heaven; she never kept a penny for herself, she gave everything to the poor, she used to support entire families. She never spoke ill of anyone, and if someone tried to tell her some gossip she used to say, 'If it's something unpleasant about anyone, please don't tell me, I don't like stories that attack the reputation.' She bore her misfortunes with the greatest patience in the world, and this not from simplicity, for she had great intelligence. She was polite and pleasant, although not beautiful, always cheerful, laughed and joked in a well-mannered way, and always praised our Princess of Wales. I was very fond of this Queen, and her death grieves me.

She died of a disease of the chest. This was accompanied by a fever with two *redoublements* a day, and it carried the Queen off within a week.

[1] The party had had a carriage accident at Bar, but no one was hurt except Mme Craon, who suffered from concussion and complained, according to Liselotte, 'in the way mistresses have, in order to make their lovers more attentive'.

I used to send a page over to St Germain, to find out from the doctor who sat up with her what had happened during the night. The page whom I sent yesterday came back whitefaced and upset, and said, '*Madame, la reine est morte ce matin.*' You can imagine the shock. Still, I had a feeling it might happen, because I had said to the Rotzenhäuserin, who was showing me a fan of taffeta patterns to help her choose a dress, 'Don't be in too much of a hurry, let us see first how the Queen's illness turns out. I'm afraid we may suddenly hear that she is dead.' I had hardly finished speaking when the page came in.

St Cloud 29 May 1718 As it was my birthday yesterday (the 28th new-style, 17th old-style, when I was born), by way of a little cele-bration I went to Paris at eleven o'clock to see my children. I started with the King, who is, thank God, in perfect health, and then I went to the Palais-Royal and visited Mme d'Orléans. My son came to see me there, but he was too busy to eat with us, and Mme d'Orléans too lazy, so I ate only with my ladies and three of my granddaughters. We had some splendid music during the meal, not because of my birthday but simply by chance, because one of the King's musicians wanted to show my son what he could do. Then I went to the Carmelites to thank them, because they had given me a present. Since knotting is now the fashion, they had made me a knotted bag. Tell me if you knot too, dear Luise. Mme d'Orléans does nothing else, day or night, at the play, wherever she may be, she is perpetually knotting.

Now for your letter, dear Luise. I never drive past Chaillot without shuddering when I think of the virtuous and pleasant Queen of England lying dead up there in the nuns' choir. It will be a long time before I get that out of my mind. The page who brought me the news so bluntly is a new boy, not yet three months with me, and he didn't know how fond I was of the Queen. He thought he was supposed to report it as it was said to him. The Queen was perfectly content to die. She thanked God for her deliverance from this life. I agree with you, dear Luise, that she is more likely to become a saint than her husband, but I think he must be in heaven too, he suffered with such patience in this world. The Queen had great fortitude, and genuine royal qualities: nobility, generosity, politeness and a very agreeable mind. She used to tease me about my passion for the theatre, but admitted that she had been just the same. She never complained, and used to laugh about the time when she couldn't go out any more because all her horses had died and she had no money to buy new ones. She laughed at her royal condition, how magnificent it was, and how all the splendour of the world was only vanity. She said it all so naturally and without complaint. I lost a pleasant companion in Her Majesty.

St Cloud 9 June 1718 Dearest Luise, today I got up a whole hour later than usual, because I went to bed an hour late last night. I didn't get back from Paris till ten. I had gone there at half-past ten in the morning to take part in a long, very boring ceremony, the laying of the foundation stone for a church to be built in the grounds of a convent called L'Abbaye au Bois. I was quite embarrassed, because they greeted me with cymbals, trumpets, flutes, fifes and gun-salutes. I had to go down a long street to where the ceremony was to take place, surrounded by all that noise. You can imagine the crowds that had collected. Before I set off on my march I heard mass in the convent, with beautiful music. Where the stone was to be laid, priests sang three psalms and said some prayers in Latin, of which I didn't understand a word. There was a raised place, entirely covered with carpets, with an arm-chair on it and a canopy, where I had to sit. They brought me the stone. It had my name written on it and my medal set in the centre. Then they threw some mortar on the stone, which I had to spread, then they placed a second stone on top. After this I had to give my blessing, which made me laugh—it's powerful stuff, my blessing. After that I sent the first gentleman of my household, M de Mortagne, to the site to put the stone in position for me, as I really couldn't climb up and down the steps, as you can imagine, dear Luise. The ceremony lasted a good hour and a half, because after the stone was laid, accompanied by the din of cymbals, trumpets, drums, oboes and fifes, as well as cannon-fire, they sang a Te Deum to music, which lasted for ever.

St Cloud 30 June 1718 It is neither strange nor wonderful that I should love you. Didn't we have the same father, whom I loved better than my own life? It isn't your fault that you aren't my mother's daughter, and you make up for the misfortune of your birth by your many virtues.

Hailstorms have flattened seven villages in Lorraine. It is absurd to imagine that there are men and women hiding in the clouds, who throw down hailstones to devastate everything on earth. In Paris people don't believe in witches, and you don't hear them talked about at all. In Rouen, where people do believe in them, you hear of them all the time.

It is nothing new for a husband to have a mistress; you won't find one in ten thousand who loves no one but his wife. They deserve praise if they simply live on good terms with their wives and treat them kindly.

Mme Châteauthiers[1] says that if you want to put anyone off marriage, you only have to hear me talking on the subject; the Rotzenhäuserin replies that I was never really married and have no idea what true marriage is. To be in love with a man and to be loved in return alters things and makes all the difference. Then I accuse her of being fond of lying with men; she gets furious and I laugh at her.

HERR VON HARLING
St Cloud 3 July 1718   Thank goodness I still have a good German stomach and a sound digestion. In the evenings I always eat a little salad, which surprises the French. They all ruin their digestions by overeating noon and night. I think it is a real proof of love to bring up children strictly. As soon as you reach the age of reason you recognize why it was done, and are grateful to those who acted for your good with such affection. All children have a tendency to evil, and therefore have to be held in check.

CAROLINE OF WALES
St Cloud 5 July 1718   When I think of burning, shivers go down my back, because I know how they carried on in the poor Palatinate for more than three months. Whenever I tried to get to sleep I used to see all Heidelberg in flames, and that made me start up so that I almost fell ill.

LUISE
St Cloud 19 June 1718   Knotting is more *à la mode* than ever, and for a good reason. When ladies who aren't entitled to a tabouret do needlework, they are allowed to sit in the presence of Mme de Berry and myself, and knotting counts as needlework, so when ladies come to call they knot. I am enclosing a set. The little bag hangs from the arm, and the shuttle, which is called *la navette* here, is put inside, together with the cottons or silks, when one has finished. Let me know if this is how it is done in Germany and England, or if it is done differently. In case you are tired of knotting and it is no longer done in Germany, it could be a little present for your niece. But if you think it is too insignificant, or that people might laugh at you, you can do whatever you like with it.

St Cloud 14 July 1718   If you were here, I should make you sit down in my closet even without knotting. Carllutz didn't have a *tabouret*

[1] One of Liselotte's *dames d'honneur*, and a lifelong friend.

either, but every evening I made a pile of five or six cushions by my dressing-table and we used to chat until one or two o'clock in the morning.

It is only too true that my son has trouble with the *parlement*. He told me that they were meddling in affairs which were none of their business, and as long as he held the royal authority he would keep it intact, and return it to the King on his majority in the same state as he had received it, and not allow any inroads to be made on it. My son's sister-in-law and her husband are his worst enemies; they are at the bottom of all this. If he had listened to me he wouldn't be related to them, and could act without fear of seeing tears at home. My son must certainly try to find some means of paying off the King's debts. The people are no worse off than they were in the King's day, but there is no way of easing their lot, and my son's enemies take advantage of this misfortune in order to incite the people against him. There is not a word of truth in the story that he is putting money into his own pocket.

HERR VON HARLING
St Cloud 28 July 1718   I must hurry because my meal has been served. I only want to say that I haven't received any sausages. To show how much they like them here, they once guzzled up a whole case that our dear Electress had sent.[1] Nobody is surprised at my liking these foods. I have made smoked ham fashionable too, and many other German dishes, such as sweet-and-sour cabbage, salad with *Speck*, red cabbage and venison, which was very rarely eaten here. All this I have made *à la mode*. And pancakes with buckling, too—I taught our good late King to eat this, he loved it.

LUISE
St Cloud 4 August 1718   Apropos of conspiracy, my son told me at the play yesterday that the Tsar bribed one of the Tsarevitch's[2] mistresses to hand over a letter which said that he had plans to assassinate his father. The Tsar called the great Council together, all the bishops and councillors of state. When they were assembled he called for his son, embraced him, and said, 'Is it possible that you want to have me murdered, after I have spared your life?' The Tsarevitch denied everything. Then the Tsar handed the letter to the Council and said, 'I can't

[1] Liselotte had written to the Electress to say that not only had the sausages not reached her, but a crate of Rhine wine from Lorraine had gone astray at the same time. 'No doubt they needed the hock to wash down the sausages.'
[2] Peter the Great's son, Alexej.

sit in judgement over my own son, you do it, only treat him fairly and kindly', and left. The Council unanimously pronounced the death sentence. When the Tsarevitch heard this, he was so shocked that it was thought he had had a stroke, but he was only speechless for a few hours. As soon as he had regained his speech he asked to see his father for the last time. He came and the Tsarevitch confessed everything, asked, in tears, for his father's pardon, lived for two more days, and died repentant. Between ourselves, they must have poisoned him to forestall the disgrace of seeing him in the hands of the knackers.

The fate of the Tsarevitch greatly shocked Liselotte, in spite of her loathing of all *cabales*. There was no lack of *cabales* in France; at Sceaux the Duchesse du Maine was busily plotting against the Regent, and was issuing a great deal of anti-Orléans propaganda. She had also embarked on a correspondence with Cardinal Alberoni, Philip V's powerful minister.

The letters that passed between the Duchess and the Cardinal, by way of the Spanish embassy in Paris, dealt with a plot to kidnap the Regent and plans for a general civil war, after which the King of Spain would be called to assume the Regency of France. This plot was not the only problem the Regent had to face: the *parlement* was being more obstructive than ever, and the nobles, who had never come to terms with the elevation of the bastards, were ceaselessly urging him to downrank them once and for all.

St Cloud 27 August 1718   Dearest Luise, I am writing today so as not to miss the post, because tomorrow I go to Paris, which is in an uproar. My son made the King hold a *lit de justice*. He called for the entire *parlement* and solemnly advised them not to interfere in the government, but only to concern themselves with their own business, which is to execute lawsuits and pronounce justice. Since it was known for certain that M le Duc du Maine and his wife had caused the *parlement* to rebel against the King and my son, he was relieved of the control of the King's education, which would pass to M le Duc,[1] as well as of his rank as *prince du sang*. His younger brother, on the other hand, would be confirmed in all his titles for his lifetime, because he has always behaved faithfully and loyally. The people in the *parlement* and the Duchesse du Maine are so wicked and so desperate that I am mortally afraid that they will assassinate my son. Because, even before all this happened, Mme du Maine was heard to say at table, in public, '*On dit que je révolte le*

[1] Louis Henri de Condé.

parlement contre le duc d'Orléans, mais je le méprise trop pour prendre une si noble vengeance de lui, je saurai bien m'en venger autrement, autrement.' You can see from this what sort of a creature she is, and that I am right to be afraid for my son. The people are such devils here, there is no pleasure in living like this.

> Liselotte said that when the Council members had been summoned they walked through the Tuileries wearing their red robes in order to stir up the populace, but the only cries heard were, 'Where are the red lobsters going?'

HERR VON HARLING
St Cloud 21 September 1718   As far as M and Mme du Maine are concerned, there are so many rumours of new conspiracies every day that it makes one's hair stand on end. I don't think the devil in hell could be worse than the old Maintenon, her Duc du Maine and his wife, who says loudly that her husband, brother-in-law and sons were nothing but cowards. She, a mere woman, would demand an audience with the Regent expressly to thrust a dagger into his heart. There you see, M Harling, the meekness of this lady's spirit, and how much there is to fear from people like that, especially when they have such a large following. For their *cabale* is very strong; it consists of more than ten people, the richest and greatest of the Court. And, what is worse, the richest, all of whom support the Spanish party and consequently the Duc and Duchesse du Maine, want to have the King of Spain here. My son is too clever for them, they want someone they can rule according to their own ideas, and the King of Spain would be quite suitable for that. So they will leave no stone unturned until they see him here, and for this reason my son's life is in danger. If disaster should strike, I beg the Almighty to take me first.

LUISE
St Cloud 28 September 1718   It isn't idle flattery when I say I wish you were with me in my closet—I really mean it. You are funny when you say that you aren't clever at thinking of diversions or nice to look at. Do you think I only need Venuses and *Belle Hélène* faces round me, and that I, at my age, am surrounded by nothing but dancing, leaping persons?

St Cloud 29 September 1718   All Frenchmen love Paris above everything. I am fond of the Parisians, but I don't like Paris; everything there is unpleasant. The kind of life they lead there, and everything one hears and sees, is unbearable. It is quite true that women have their veins painted blue now, to make people believe their skin is so transparent that the veins show through. Another thing that is true is that there are fewer beautiful people now than there used to be. I think they ruin their looks with all their paint.

HERR VON HARLING
St Cloud 20 October 1718 The Spanish ambassador, the Prince de Cellamare, is very clever—he's a wily character. The Duchesse du Maine totally forgets that her husband is only a bastard who is forced to deny his mother, because if it were proved that his mother, the Montespan, was a married woman he wouldn't be recognized as the King's son, but, according to law, would pass as the son of M de Montespan. She has convinced herself that the Duc du Maine is the King's rightful son, and that he suffers the greatest injustice in the world by having my son given preference over him.

CAROLINE OF WALES
St Cloud 4 November 1718 The reason why Mme la Dauphine[1] was always surrounded by wild young people, almost all of them relations or connections of the old Drab, was that they all tried to amuse and entertain her for fear that boredom might lead her to look elsewhere for company.

Afterwards she liked to have young men in her rooms, to amuse the King, who enjoyed seeing them tear about. They only allowed the King to see their innocent amusements; everything else was kept from him and he only learned of it after her death.

It was a sort of pleasantry that Mme la Dauphine called the old Drab '*ma tante*'. All the maids of honour used to call their mistress, the Maréchale de la Motte, 'mama', but if the Dauphine had called the Drab 'mama' it would have been taken as a declaration of the King's marriage. So they left it at '*ma tante*'.

HERR VON HARLING
St Cloud 17 November 1718 How Alberoni made his fortune had nothing to do with merit. It is rather a dirty story, but since it is quite funny, and I hope will make M Harling laugh, I shall tell it here.

When M Vendôme commanded the army in Italy, the Duc de Parme sent the Bishop of Parma to treat with him. M Vendôme had

---

[1] The late Duchesse de Bourgogne.

many good points, but, as with most people, they were mixed up with bad points, and the Duc de Vendôme had two great faults, his debauches with men, and his disgusting and shameless dirtiness. In all his life in the army he never gave an audience except from his close-stool. So he made no more *façon* with this Bishop than with other high officers, and sent for him. The Bishop arrived with a large retinue, many clergymen, and they all ceremoniously entered the room, where they found M de Vendôme on his beautiful throne. The Bishop was given a chair for his talks with M de Vendôme. When he saw that M de Vendôme's face was covered with a mass of scabs he said, 'It seems to me, monsieur, that you are very hot. The climate in this country can't agree with you.' M de Vendôme answers, 'It's much worse on my body than on my face—look', gets up, and confronts the Bishop with his naked posterior. The Bishop rises and says, 'Monsieur, I see that I am not the proper person to negotiate with you, our manners are too different, but I shall send you one of my *aumôniers*, who will be just your *fait*', and sent him Alberoni. He was once in the room when M de Vendôme was about to wipe his bottom, ran up to him, fell on his knees and exclaimed, '*Ah, quel cul d'ange!*', and M de Vendôme was so charmed that he kept him with him and made him his favourite. Alberoni betrayed his master, the Duc de Parme, to M de Vendôme, and afterwards, when Vendôme was in Spain, he betrayed him to the Princesse des Ursins, and the Princesse des Ursins to the Queen of Spain. This is how that honest man made his fortune.

CAROLINE OF WALES
Paris 9 December 1718 My son had to have the Spanish ambassador, Prince de Cellamare, arrested. Letters which he had written were found on a courier, the Abbé Portocarrero, who has also been arrested, revealing a plot against the King and my son. The ambassador was arrested by two Councillors of State.

HERR VON HARLING
Paris 15 December 1718 I was so shocked and confused by the dreadful treachery against my son which has been uncovered that I was incapable of writing. The Almighty revealed the affair in the strangest way. My son had been asked to arrest an English bankrupt who was travelling through France to Spain. This bankrupt had with him a Spanish abbé, a nephew of the Cardinal de Portocarrero, who had recently died, and he was so ill at ease that they became suspicious, and thought the fellow must have something on him. They searched him and found a

package from the Spanish ambassador, Prince Cellamare.[1] To add to the misfortune the abbé's valet, who was travelling more slowly, met the regular mail. When he asked what news there was, he learned that an Englishman and a Spanish abbé had been arrested at Poitiers. He immediately put his horse round and galloped back to Paris, went straight to the ambassador and warned him that his parcel had been found. The ambassador lost no time in burning all his papers, and he had time to speak to all his couriers. So I feel that not everything has been discovered.

Paris 22 December 1718 How happy are those who have nothing worse to fear than thieves, for thieves are more easily dealt with than people who conspire against their fatherland and plan to assassinate their rightful masters. Such a thing leaves one in fear and trembling. It is now known that my whole family was to have been assassinated, except for me personally, because I am, quite undeservedly, loved by the people, and it was thought that the people would revolt against them if they did me any harm. As though I shouldn't be harmed if my son and his children were killed!

LUISE
Paris 29 December 1718 Dearest Luise, I meant to write two hours ago but I couldn't, I had such a shock that my hand still trembles. My son came and told me that he has had to arrest his brother-in-law, the Duc du Maine, and his wife, because they are the ringleaders of this abominable Spanish conspiracy. All is discovered, proof has been found in the Spanish ambassador's own handwriting, and the prisoners have confessed everything, and it is all too true—the Duc du Maine is at the head of the conspiracy. My son was forced to arrest him, his wife and all his people.

HERR VON HARLING
Paris 5 January 1719 One of the prisoners in the Bastille has confessed everything already, and two noblemen admitted receiving money from the Duc du Maine to instigate revolts in the provinces. When he heard this my son, in the King's name, had the Duchesse du Maine arrested by the captain of the King's guard, because she is a *princesse du sang*, but her husband, who is not a *prince du sang*, was arrested by a lieutenant of the lifeguards. Cardinal de Polignac has been exiled to one of his abbeys. He was Mme du Maine's lover, and she drew him

[1] The package was discovered under the floor boards of the coach.

into the plot. Formerly, in the King's lifetime, this Cardinal and my son were the best of friends, until the Cardinal fell in love with Mme du Maine when he saw her performing in the theatricals at Sceaux. You can imagine how much the arrest of the Duc du Maine and his wife has grieved Mme d'Orléans and the Comte de Toulouse—who is a very honest man, and never in his life allowed himself to be involved in his brother's schemes—as well as Mme la Princesse and her daughter, the Princesse de Conti. It breaks one's heart. The Duc du Maine thought that nothing could ever be proved against him or his wife, because they never wrote a single word in their own hand, and had everything written by one of the ladies and a chambermaid. But Alberoni's letter speaks clearly enough.

LUISE

Paris 5 January 1719   Last week I told you how it came out that the Duc and Duchesse du Maine were behind the conspiracy. Since then we have found out something else that points to the Duc du Maine. A letter to him from Cardinal Alberoni has been found, containing these words: '*Dès que la guerre sera déclarée, mettez le feu à toutes vos mines.*' Nothing could be clearer, they are wicked and damnable people.

The two of them are two little devils, led by two old witches and supported by two archfiends. The Duc and Duchesse have written to all and sundry whitewashing themselves and blackening my son's name. You can't imagine what libels they have spread against my son in the provinces, and abroad too. My son's enemies have such a large following among all sorts of people that I am hard put to it not to be afraid. My poor son has no time to be ill, and he had to rush to the quinquina bottle.

Paris 8 January 1719   Dearest Luise, once again we have bad news. The entire palace of Lunéville was burnt down, with all the furniture, on the third of this month at 5 o'clock in the morning.[1] A hut caught fire and the people in the house, wanting to keep quiet about it, started digging trenches underneath and thought they had scotched the flames. But the wind carried the fire to a nearby timber yard, the wood caught instantly, and the fire spread to the ballroom, from the ballroom to the roof, and in an hour everything was burnt down. The *garde-meuble* was the first thing to go. They tried to save the archives and papers, but a hundred people were burnt to death in the attempt. The palace

---

[1] The château of Lunéville, restored after the fire, is some twenty miles outside Nancy. Liselotte suspected that it had been deliberately burnt down at the instigation of Mme de Maintenon, in revenge for the treatment of the Duc du Maine.

chapel, too, which was newly built and is said to have been very beautiful, is in ashes. The loss is reckoned at fifteen or twenty million. The children were saved, and carried out wrapped in blankets with only their shirts on their backs. My daughter, who had nothing to cover her legs, intended to have herself carried out in a *chaise*, but her porters were trembling too much to be able to carry her, and my poor daughter was forced to walk through the snow in the garden with bare feet, and the snow lay two foot deep.

HERR VON HARLING
Paris 26 January 1719 My son's enemies, who are very numerous at Court, don't spread their lies about him because they love the Duchesse du Maine but because they hate him. This is all the more ungrateful because he has done more for the courtiers since he has been Regent than the King did in his entire reign. But when there is a Regency everyone who isn't Regent is discontented.

The fiendishness of the Duc and Duchesse du Maine is indescribable. Nothing would surprise me about him, as his mother was the most frivolous, unchristian and villainous person in the world. But what is so amazing is that his wife, who had the most virtuous mother, is still worse.

My son's wife is to be pitied. She held the mistaken opinion that her brother suffered an injustice by not being made Regent, and having her husband given preference over him and the princes of the royal line. She refused to see that it is a shameful thing to be a bastard, and that she has been elevated by her marriage. It often makes me so impatient that I have to leave the room rather than be forced to talk about it.

PS. Now comes a request: to send me a packet of red cabbage seed, which is not to be found anywhere in France. I want to grow them at St Cloud, for if I should see the year out I hope they will cure my cough, since nothing is better for my chest.

LUISE
Paris 6 February 1719 It isn't surprising that you are getting no letters from England at the moment, seeing what atrocious winds and storms we are having now. There was a storm here a week or ten days ago that did quite incredible things. It stripped the lead off a church steeple and carried it across the river to another village, it lifted two great, heavy church doors off their hinges and stood them up against a wall a hundred paces away, it turned the weathercock upside down on the steeple of St Germain-les-Auxerrois, and split a tree, sharpened the

end and planted it upright in the ground twenty paces away as though it was growing there.

Paris 26 February 1719   I wanted to find out from my son if it was true that his wife was trying to persuade him to go out at night, down to the masks at the ball.[1] He admitted it, and added that when he told her he wasn't going, for my sake, she answered that her daughter, the Berry, was frightening me on purpose so as to have him to herself, and that he was injuring his reputation by showing that he feared for his life. I beg you, dear Luise, tell me if the living devil in hell can be more evil than this creature. I have always regarded this marriage as an atrocity, and you can imagine how pleasant it is for me to see this sort of treachery now.

My confessor is doing his very best to convince me that nothing in the least wrong is going on between the Duc de Lorraine and Mme de Craon, and that he is never alone with her. I laughed in his face and said, '*Mon père*, tell that to your monks in the cloister, who know nothing of the world. And if you think you are white-washing the Jesuits, who are their confessors, you deceive yourself, because all the world knows that they tolerate double adultery.'[2] Père Lignières was silent, and he hasn't mentioned the matter since.

CAROLINE OF WALES
Paris 21 March 1719   The Craon used to be my daughter's maid of honour, and that was when the Duke fell in love with her. Craon was in disgrace at the time, for he had cheated dreadfully at gambling and was to be thrown out for a rogue. But as he was a clever fellow he soon noticed that his master had fallen in love with Mlle de Ligneville, though the Duke was keeping it a close secret. At this time my daughter's *dame d'atour* died, and the Duke knew how to turn events to make her the new *dame d'atour*. Craon is rich, the *dame* is hard up, and he proposes to marry her. The Duke was glad to give her to someone who would play up to him in this affair, so she became Mme Craon and afterwards my daughter's *dame d'atour*. Then the old *dame d'honneur* died, and my daughter thought she was doing the Duke a great favour, and Craon too, by appointing her as *dame d'honneur*, and that's what brought her into *déshonneur*.

---

[1] Public balls at the Opera—when the wearing of masks was the only condition of admission—had been held since 1716.
[2] Liselotte was referring to Louis XIV and Mme de Montespan.

HERR VON HARLING

Paris 30 March 1719   M Rigaud, who is the best portrait-painter now, will start Harling's portrait tomorrow. He didn't want to begin until the days got longer, because he paints very slowly and needs a lot of time. But there is no one like him for painting a likeness, he caught both the late King and me so very well.

We often have news, but it is rarely good. Yesterday the young Duc de Richelieu was taken to the Bastille because some letters had been intercepted which proved that he has had dealings with Alberoni. This young person is the *coqueluche* of all Paris, with women of every condition running after him like (by your leave) bitches on heat. It was a scandal to see. He had an amusing idea once: he had all his mistresses painted in the habits of the various religious orders; he is said to have a great many of the portraits. Everyone considers him so charming, but I never found the little toad charming at all.[1] The little devil—I always call him 'the goblin' because he looks just like a poltergeist—is being sent to the Bastille for the third time. When he emerged for the second time he said, 'See that you keep my apartment clean, I shall be back.'

LUISE

Paris 16 April 1719   In spring and summer Schwetzingen was nicer to live in than Heidelberg; there were better walks in the Ketscher wood. If it is still in existence, you will find plenty of excellent strawberries there soon. In the little wood between Schwetzingen and Heidelberg they used to be very good too, but the best bilberries are in Heidelberg by the hill. There are none to be found around Paris. I have them sent from Normandy, but they are smaller, sourer and drier than those in the Palatinate.

PS.[2] I heard this morning that the old Maintenon croaked yesterday evening between 4 and 5 o'clock. It would have been a great good fortune if this had happened thirty-odd years ago.

HERR VON HARLING

Paris 20 April 1719   Last Saturday night we lost a pious soul at St Cyr, the old Maintenon. A thunderstorm was the cause of her death. It

---

[1] Louis Fernand Armand du Plesssis, Duc de Richelieu, had been engaged in a good many love affairs above his station. Now he was having an affair with Liselotte's least favourite grandchild, Mlle de Valois, who was utterly infatuated with him.

[2] This was written on the outside of the letter, which was ready for posting.

Marie Louise Elizabeth fille de Philippe Duc d'Orleans et de Françoise Marie de Bourbon, est née le 20 aoust 1695 et à Epousé Charles duc de Berry le 6 juillet 1710.

Madame's eldest granddaughter, Mme de Berry. Engraving by Desrochers.

Louis XV enters Paris, September 1715, accompanied by the Regent, M. le Duc and Mme de Ventadour.

made the measles from which she was suffering turn inwards, and she died of them just as if she had been a young person. She had taken four years off her age, she said she was only eighty-two, really she was eighty-six. If she had died twenty years ago it would have given me great pleasure, but now I'm neither sad nor glad.

I must say, I wish the little goblin, damn him, would get his just deserts—he really is too impertinent. To show that he doesn't mind about his imprisonment, he sent for his flute and his bass viol, and for a draughts-board with which to amuse himself. He is spreading the rumour all over Paris that my son had him put into prison for making *doux yeux* at Mlle de Valois. My son's patience with this insolent fellow is driving me wild. Harling was supposed to give M Rigaud a third sitting today, but he was in no condition to sit still, having eaten too well of a good sucking-pig. He couldn't even go out with me yesterday.

St Cloud 6 May 1719   I'm beginning my letter today because I may be too weak tomorrow. In an hour's time M Teray is going to bleed me, by way of precaution. It is a *partie de plaisir* which I am holding with my horses; they are being bled today as well.

St Cloud 7 May 1719   I don't think your nephew will be able to write to you today, because blood-letting is the height of fashion at St Cloud. Yesterday it was Frau von Rathsamhausen's turn and mine, today it's Harling's and Wendt's—there will be much German blood spilt at St Cloud. From me they drew the most beautiful blood in the world, just like chicken's blood.

St Cloud 11 May 1719   Mme de Berry has had a hard time since she's been at Meudon. She's had a continuous fever for the past fortnight. It's gone now, but it left her so weak that she has to learn to walk again like a little child, and must be held up by the arm.

It is not so astonishing that the Maintenon died as that she died like a young person. If people can recognize one another in the next world, where all is equal and no differences of rank exist, the lady will have to choose between Louis XIV and the crippled Scarron. If the King has learned there what was concealed from him in this world, he will gladly return her to Scarron.

At the end of March Mme de Berry had discreetly given birth to a daughter. The father was her favourite, M de Riom, whose attentions she shared with her female favourite, Mlle de Mouchy. Liselotte learned

o

of this affair only after her granddaughter, who claimed to have married
Riom previously, was dead. The child lived to become a nun.

CAROLINE OF WALES
St Cloud 12 May 1719   When the Maintenon was told she was going
to die she is supposed to have said, '*Mourir, c'est la moindre évènement
de ma vie.*'

LUISE
St Cloud 13 May 1719   You ask what has made me so irritable. I
can't give you the details, but it was the maddening flirtation between
Mlle de Valois and that dreadful Duc de Richelieu, who has passed
round all her letters to him, because he only cares for her out of vanity.
All the young people at Court have seen the letters in which she
arranged their assignations. Her mother would have liked me to have
her back here with me, but I've refused point-blank. No one deceives
me more than once.¹ But they won't take no for an answer, and you can
imagine how much that infuriates me. I really loathe the creature, and
can hardly bear to look at her, which I can't avoid if I want to prevent
even more gossip. The sight of that stupid girl makes me quite sick.

St Cloud 4 June 1719   Yesterday, in Paris, a man of eighty died; may
God forgive him for the harm he did me during the thirty years I
lived with Monsieur! It was the Marquis d'Effiat, who used to be
Master of the Horse and Master of the Hounds to Monsieur, and later
to my son. He bequeathed a beautiful house and an estate worth a
hundred thousand francs to my son, who, however, didn't want to
accept it and gave it to the heirs. He was enormously rich, and kept
chests full of gold in his rooms, so that when a fire broke out there
recently six men couldn't shift them because they were so heavy. He
leaves no children, and his heirs are overjoyed.

St Cloud 8 June 1719   Writing is my favourite occupation, because
I don't like needlework; to my mind there is nothing more tedious
in the world than putting in a needle and pulling it out again.
    You did make me laugh, dear Luise, when you said that my letters
do you as much good as 'balsam on your head'. It is to be hoped at

¹ On a previous occasion, when Mlle de Valois had visited Liselotte at St Cloud, she
had conducted her Richelieu *affaire* there. Liselotte found out, and promptly packed
her granddaughter back home.

least that this balsam won't flow from your head into your beard, as it did with Aaron.[1]

Ma tante, the Abbess of Maubuisson, never liked being waited on. She said, 'I have left the world in order not to see any Courts', tucked up her habit, and walked all over her convent and her garden by herself. She used to laugh at herself and everything else, and was very amusing. She had our father's, the late Elector's, voice, resembled him about the eyes and mouth, had many of his mannerisms, and knew how to make herself feared and obeyed.

St Cloud 11 June 1719 I see from your letter of the second that the King of England reached Hanover safely. I may say *'je reconnais mon sang'* from the aversion he has to all ceremonies, for they are unbearable to me. But it can't have displeased the King that the peasants and townspeople followed him all the way to Herrenhausen with their good wishes, because that is proof of the great affection they have for the Elector.

CAROLINE OF WALES
St Cloud 13 June 1719 In my opinion the Duchesse de la Vallière always loved the King; the Montespan out of ambition, the Soubise out of self-interest, and the Maintenon out of both. The Fontanges loved him with all her heart, but like a *heroine de roman*—she was frightfully romantic. Ludre loved him too, but he soon had enough of that *amour*. I couldn't put my hand in the fire for Mme de Monaco and swear that she never slept with the King. Lauzun went out of favour for the first time during the period when the King was in love with her. Lauzun had an *affaire réglée* with this woman, but in secret. He had forbidden her to make eyes at the King, but once, when she was sitting on the floor and entertaining the King, Lauzun was in the room as captain of the guard. He was so overcome by jealousy that he couldn't contain himself. He came up as though to pass by Mme de Monaco, and stamped on her hand so dreadfully hard that he almost crushed it. The King, who first learnt of the affair through this, grew angry, Lauzun answered back, and that was how he was sent to the Bastille for the first time.

Mme de Freimes once said to Monsieur, *'Vous ne déshonorez pas les dames qui vous hantent, mais elles vous déshonorent.'* He was blamed, too, for allowing himself to be ravished by Mme de Monaco—she made him sleep with her against his will. I knew very well that he had nothing to

[1] Psalm 133, 2.

do with the Grancey, but I couldn't bear the way this woman made money out of my whole household, and that no one ever bought an appointment in our house without paying this Grancey her *pot de vin*, nor that she was insolent to me and always made trouble between me and the late Monsieur. I often gave her a good piece of my mind, and people who knew no better took that for jealousy. The Chevalier de Lorraine became her *amant déclaré* as soon as he returned from Rome, he and d'Effiat made Monsieur keep her; beyond that he didn't care for her at all. But he got so tired of her eternal begging that he would have thrown her out if he hadn't died first. He got very tired of the Chevalier de Lorraine too, because he saw that his attachment was only self-interest. During the last three years Monsieur wouldn't hear a word said against me, he declared that he wouldn't stand for it.

LUISE

St Cloud 22 June 1719   The doctors now say that the pain in Mme de Berry's feet isn't caused by gout, but they don't know what does cause it. In the meantime the poor creature is suffering quite dreadfully, it is pitiable. She is growing thin and weak, and I'm beginning to be afraid. I hadn't seen her for a couple of days, and found her very changed. Her life last year was extremely disorderly, and I told her that she would come to regret it. She wouldn't listen and now she is sorry, but it's too late. She used to come here three or four times a week to bathe in running water, staying in the water for four hours, stuff herself with ham, sausages, salads, cakes, pastries and fruit until eight o'clock in the evening, sit down to a meal at 10 o'clock and gorge herself until one in the morning, walk about until four, breakfast on cheese, milk and cake, and then go to bed. How can that be healthy?

> Mme de Berry died on July 20th. The post mortem showed her liver to be diseased and her stomach ulcerated. The Regent was distraught with grief, but 'He does not want to weep and tries to be strong', says Liselotte. Mme de Berry's body was laid to rest without a funeral oration because, according to Liselotte, they had such difficulties in composing one that they thought it better to do without.

St Cloud 10 August 1719   I never thought the late Duchesse de Berry would recover from her illness, she had such a poor pulse throughout. But that was not surprising: her favourite killed her as surely as if she had cut her throat. Whenever she was there to look after her she brought her all sorts of things to eat and drink, pâté, salad, melon, figs, plums and iced beer, which transformed the *fièvre lente* into a *fièvre continue* with two *redoublements* each day, and that killed her. This favourite, who is called Mouchy—she is the daughter of a woman who was under-governess to Mme de Berry—ran away three hours before her Princess's death. Otherwise they would have stoned her. Mme de Berry's maids were just waiting to despatch her quickly after her mistress. She didn't care tuppence about her Princess's death. On the day she was taken to St Denis, Mouchy visited one of her good friends and ate, drank and made merry. That is the greatest ingratitude. Mme de Berry did more for her than she deserved. My son was so offended that he banished her from Paris.

My Harling thinks his portrait will have arrived by now. It is well done, by the same man who painted my portrait, M Rigaud. He paints well but he speaks very badly, because he stammers so dreadfully that it takes a quarter-of-an-hour before a word comes out. He should always communicate by singing, for when he sings he doesn't stutter.

St Cloud 24 August 1719 Dearest Luise, I went to Paris yesterday, and thought I had come to the fires of hell. I have never known such heat in all my born days, the very air you breathed was fiery. If it continues, man and beast will die of heat. Oxen on their way to Paris from the country drop dead because there is no water in the villages they pass through.

Anyone who has only one son and loves him is torn with anxiety, especially in this country, where there are so many fiendish people and so few good ones. But what I say to my son, and what I whistle into the wind, is all one—he never follows my advice. His damned godless flatterers swarm round and change his mind. They are a bad lot, and profess not to believe in God or his word, they are debauched, blaspheming fellows. Under the pretext that if he doesn't relax after his arduous work he won't be able to endure it, they make him lead an insane life. In France everything that is not eating, drinking and whoring is considered tedious.[1]

St Cloud 27 August 1719 Everywhere you go you hear people complaining about two things: the heat and the damnable bedbugs, which plague me all night long. The Princess of Wales says in her letter

---

[1] The Regent's 'roués' used to gather each evening for what contemporary gossip described as orgies. No servants were admitted to the feast, and a set of silver cooking utensils was said to have been employed by the Regent in person.

that all London is suffering, too, and the Queen of Sicily writes that her bed was overrun.

Mme de Berry inherited her late husband's entire appanage, and this, together with a pension of 660,000 francs a year, now reverts to the King. My son, as her heir, has been left with all her debts. Over and above her people's wages, which she hadn't paid for three or four years, my son has to pay out another 400,000 francs which is owing. It's sheer robbery. Her servants seem to be completely reconciled to losing her.

You aren't the only one, dear Luise, to make mistakes in French: Frenchwomen themselves spell dreadfully. I think I know more French orthography than German by now. Our dear Princess of Wales spells very badly too, but then, she taught herself to write, so it's no wonder.

The Spaniards are altogether unlucky this year, and Alberoni will have to consider making peace after all.[1] Also, my son has had the good fortune to find an Englishman called M Law. The French, however, true to their habit of altering all names, call him Las. He is very clever in financial affairs, and my son has great hopes of paying off all the King's debts before the end of this year. It was no mean sum, because it amounted to two hundred thousand millions. I tell my son that he and his M Law have found the philosopher's stone. Half the King's debts are paid already, so if Alberoni doesn't make peace the young King will have money enough for making war.

John Law, a Scot, had founded his Paris banking house in 1716 and the *compagnie d'Occident*, better known as the Mississippi Company, shortly afterwards. Through Orléans' support his banknotes, tied to Mississippi stock, had become legal tender, and his bank in the Rue Quincampoix the *banque royale*.

Law's financial manœuvres were creating a boom, Mississippi shares were soaring and all France was in a fever of speculation.

St Cloud 3 September 1719   Last Friday my son came to me and made me rich. He said that he thought my income was too small, and increased it by 150,000 francs. As I have, thank God, no debts, it comes very *a propos* to put me *à l'aise*, as they say here, for the time that I have left.

The Mouchy must have been the most unworthy favourite that ever was, the way she used to deceive and rob her princess. She was of low birth, too; her maternal grandfather used to be Monsieur's barber. The mother was not much use either, for after she was widowed she kept

[1] France had been at war with Spain since January.

house for a married man. As they say, and taken all together, that's all rotten eggs and rancid butter.

What was strange was that this Mouchy robbed her own *amant*, the Comte de Riom. Mme de Berry had given him a fortune in jewels and ready money. He put it all in a box and left the box at Meudon, and now his beloved Mouchy has taken it away with her. I think that's amusing. One could say, as our late father did in a similar case, '*Accordez-vous, canailles.*'

St Cloud 17 September 1719 We arrived at Chelles at half-past nine. My grandson, the Duc de Chartres, was there before us. My son arrived a quarter-of-an-hour later, and after another quarter-of-an-hour Mlle de Valois appeared. Mme la Duchesse d'Orléans had arranged to have herself bled on purpose, so that she wouldn't have to attend. She and the Abbess are not the best of friends.[1] And even if they had been friends, the mother's natural idleness would have prevented her from coming—it would have meant getting up too early in order to drive down to Chelles. A little after ten we went into the church. The Abbess's *prie-Dieu* was of violet-coloured velvet, embroidered all over with golden *fleurs de lis*. The King's musicians were in the tribune; they sang a motet. The Cardinal de Noailles[2] said Mass. The altar at Chelles is beautiful, all black and white marble, and there are four great pillars which support white marble statues of former abbesses. One of them is so like our Abbess that it might have been modelled after her, but it was made a long time ago and she's only twenty-one.

After the Te Deum we went back to the convent. I ate with my son and my grandson, the Duc de Chartres. Half-an-hour later our Abbess went to eat in her hall, with her sister Mlle de Valois and twelve abbesses, at a table with forty *couverts*. It was a pretty sight, the black nuns surrounding the colourful tables, which my son's people had arranged so that they looked very magnificent and attractive.

St Cloud 1 October 1719 It happened very *a propos* that my son in-creased my pension, because I was very ill-provided for after Monsieur's death. It wasn't my son's fault but the old Drab's, who intrigued against me and got my son's people to make these arrangements, pretending it was the King's express wish. There wasn't a word of truth in this, and the proof was that, when the King came to realize that I couldn't

[1] The Regent's daughter, Louise Adelaide, Mlle de Chartres, now Soeur Bâtilde, had been appointed Abbess of Chelles on September 14th.
[2] Archbishop of Paris.

manage, he at once increased my pension by 40,000 francs. That made the old whore almost burst with fury. But something that made me laugh at the time was that the Duc and Duchesse du Maine asked my steward how I could manage, with so little, to live according to my station and yet stay out of debt. Lagarde—that was my old stward's name—said, 'It is because Madame is not extravagant, and avoids foolish expense.' That settled that fine pair. All their enormous debts came from their nocturnal *fêtes* at Sceaux, which used to last well into the following day, with fireworks, plays, masques and new little operas; we used to call them the *nuits blanches*. If my son hadn't lost his daughter, and if the King hadn't inherited vast sums from her, I shouldn't have accepted this increased pension, because I should not like it to be said that my son was feathering his family's nest at the King's expense.

CAROLINE OF WALES

St Cloud 8 October 1719   It is quite untrue that our Queen ever gave birth to a blackamoor. Monsieur, who was present at the birth, said the little princess was ugly, but not black. Nevertheless, it is impossible to get the idea out of people's heads that the child is still alive. But it is quite certain that the ugly child died, for the whole Court saw it die.

LUISE

St Cloud 26 October 1719   Good M Law was quite ill a few days ago, he was worried and persecuted so much. He is not given a minute's peace day or night, and that made him ill. No, I don't think any nation in the world is more grasping than the French. They drive one mad and absolutely furious with their begging. Everything they write and say makes me so extremely impatient that I charge about like a wild boar. No one could be cleverer than M Law. But I wouldn't change places with him for all the world: he is being tormented like a soul in hell.

Liselotte was shocked—and amused—at the behaviour of French society in its quest for riches, and the spectacle of avaricious duchesses kissing Law's hands. She darkly wondered what other parts of his anatomy were kissed by persons of less exalted rank. Princesses raised sham fire alarms in his courtyard, to beg for shares when he came rushing from his house. A dowager Mrs Malaprop implored him to give her *une conception*, and, though he knew very well that she meant *une concession*, he replied with a straight face that he would willingly do so, and only feared she had left it a little late.

Ladies at the Opera were surprised to find themselves seated next to their own cooks, splendidly bedecked with diamonds. Coachmen were employing coachmen of their own, and M Chirac, the royal physician, frightened a patient almost to death by murmuring, while feeling her pulse, 'It's falling, it's falling.' He had some difficulty in persuading the invalid that her pulse was good and strong, and that it was his Mississippi stock which had temporarily dropped.

Liselotte was soon to complain that she was getting as sick of tales of millions as though she had eaten them, as she put it, 'by the spoonful'. But in the meantime she entertained her relations with further anecdotes.

St Cloud 23 November 1719   A lady whom M Law didn't wish to see thought up an astonishing way to speak to him—she ordered her coachman to turn her carriage over in front of M Law's door, calling out, '*Cocher, versez donc!*' At first he refused, but then he obeyed his mistress's command and overturned the coach in front of M Law's front door, so that he couldn't go in or out. He rushed up to her in a fright, thinking she might have broken her neck or her legs, but as he approached the lady told him she had done it on purpose to talk to him. All this, perhaps, was not so bad, but what six other ladies of quality did, out of pure self-interest, was beyond insolence. They waylaid M Law in his own courtyard and surrounded him. They wouldn't let him go, until at last he said, '*Mesdames, je vous demande mille pardons, mais si vous ne me laissez pas aller il faut que je crève, car j'ai une nécessité de pisser qu'il m'est impossible de tenir davantage.*' The ladies replied, '*Hé bien, Monsieur, pissez, pourvu que vous nous écoutiez.*' He did, and they stayed there. Isn't it horrible? He almost died of laughing.

St Cloud 26 November 1719   However did the wild pigs get fat this year? We've had no acorns at all. The Bois de Boulogne is full of oak trees, and I had a good look at a lot of the trees, but I didn't find a single acorn. I made our Grand Duchess eat a Martinmas-goose, filled with chestnuts and large raisins, but in fact this is not what I relish most.

My son sent me 400 shares for my household. But although that makes 2 million in all, they only stretched to those who are *en quartier* and *ordinaire*. All the others, including many who are not in my service at all, have asked for some, which made me very impatient.

CAROLINE OF WALES
Paris 5 December 1719   I hear that the bridegroom has fallen in love with Mlle de Valois, that is, with her portrait. I find her beautiful rather than attractive. She has beautiful eyes, skin and colouring. Her

mouth is not bad, her teeth are healthy and white but not very even, one upper tooth looks ugly when she laughs, and her hawk's beak of a nose spoils everything, to my taste. She is very tall, not badly made, her body is a little too short and thick, her head is sunk between her shoulders and she has very long legs. One can see why she never wanted to learn dancing—she walks like a woman of eighty and shows *mauvaise grâce* in all she does. She has black eyes and hair. Thus the bride, and if only she were as good inside as she is on the outside, she might be passable enough.

> Liselotte's granddaughter, Mlle de Valois, still in love with the Duc de Richelieu, had reluctantly obeyed her father and become engaged to the Duc de Modène. In return her father had released Richelieu from the Bastille.

Paris 12 December 1719   M Law isn't the only one who is buying fine jewels and estates. M le Duc is growing as rich as Croesus, and so is everyone else who owns shares.

Paris 15 December 1719   As a rule the King didn't want anyone except the royal family at his table. There were so many *princesses du sang* that far too big a table would have been needed. When we were all together the table was quite full. The King sat by himself at a long table. In the centre, to his right, sat M le Dauphin and M le Duc de Bourgogne. Below, on the left, were the Dauphine and the Duc de Berry. At one *retour* were Monsieur and I, at the other my son and his wife. The other places were only for the *gentilhommes servants*, who served the King and us. When they wait on the King they don't stand behind the chair, but in front of him on the other side of the table. They wait on us too. When the *princesses du sang* or other ladies ate with the King, they were not served by *gentilhommes servants* but by officers of the King's household, who used to wait from behind the chairs like pages. Pages used to wait at the royal table only on journeys, and never on the royal family.

HERR VON HARLING
Paris 21 December 1719   I had only been here a week when I had to pay heavily for having come. I suddenly had such a dreadful cough that I couldn't leave my room for sixteen days, and four times they thought I was done for.

I hope that spring will be pleasanter. I couldn't have stayed in St Cloud, as for one thing it would have looked so strange for me not to return to Paris when all the world comes into town from the country; for another, people would have thought that my son and I had quarrelled; and for a third, I had to be present at the nuptials of my granddaughter, Mlle de Valois.

I can say nothing about M Law's bank—I don't understand anything about it. It is all Greek to me. The late King's debts are supposed to be paid off, but I can't say how or when.

Paris 14 January 1720   So little has M Law's credit fallen that he was made *Contrôleur Général des Finances* three days ago. Perhaps the gossips who spread rumours that his bank has closed are hoping for just this, as it is supposed to cause great jealousy.

The talk of my son's injustice to the Duchesse du Maine will soon stop, because he read out in Council her letter and confession. He is too good, rather than the contrary, because he forgave her everything, although she meant to deprive him of the Regency and bring the King of Spain over in his stead. It can certainly be said that my son is not a revengeful man, because if he had wanted to revenge himself he had ample opportunity.

Paris 28 January 1720   The Paris air is worse than ever, and when you don't see the dead being carried through the streets you meet the Holy Sacraments being carried to the sick. What is more, they are all infectious diseases—measles, smallpox and purple fever.

Five or six young gentlemen who were to have danced in the King's ballet with His Majesty are ill, and I'm worried about the young King because he mixed with all these children. The ballet, said to be very pretty, is to be performed next week.

LUISE
Paris 28 January 1720   Since I am so often ill, M Teray is purging me with the green juice of watercress, sorrel and *chicorée*. (I have forgotten what that is in German—*Wegerich*, if I'm not mistaken. I'll just look it up in the German *Botanicum*. Ah, here we are. It is *Wegwart, Wegweiss, Wegling, Sonnenwend, Sonnenwirbel, Sonnenkraut, Sonnenbrand*.) There are enough names for you, so take your choice, but it makes a green drink, which has to be taken lukewarm; incredibly bitter and revolting. This year we have enough ice to fill all the ice-pits and ice-houses. I often take iced drinks and they do me no harm, but I don't take them as

cold as others do. I think the weather here must be bad for strokes, because every day you hear of them. The Princess says it's the same in England. Many blame coffee, others tobacco, because before these were *à la mode* you didn't hear so much about strokes as you do now.

Alberoni goes no further than Genoa, where all that bad lot is assembling.[1] The Princesse des Ursins is there too. It is a pity Mme du Maine can't join them as well. I think I told you that Alberoni wrote to my son to beg his pardon and offering to betray Spain. Isn't he a fine fellow? He also declares that the libels against my son that were published in his name had all originated in Paris.

At the moment there are so many coaches and such crowds in Paris that when I came back from a visit to Mme la Princesse and Mme la Duchesse it took me three-quarters of an hour to get from the Pont Neuf to the Palais-Royal because of the traffic!

Paris 4 February 1720 It is true that Paris and Heidelberg are under the same sign, and in the same constellation too: Virgo. But my son's former doctor, who was a German, a learned man called Homberg, may have discovered what makes these places so different. He said that one day, while he was out for a walk, and was wondering why the air of Heidelberg was so pure and the Paris air so foul, he came to a place where a paving stone was being taken up. Underneath he saw some pitch-black soil, more than a foot deep. He put some of it in a piece of paper, carried it home and analysed it. He discovered that it consisted of nitre and saltpeter, and deduced that this acridity, drawn up by the force of the sun, accounted for the bad, acrid air. This nitre comes from the many thousands of people who piss in the street. I found M Homberg's reasoning very enlightening.

Paris 11 February 1720 I shan't write this afternoon, because the entire wedding-assembly is to take place in my house, as I am the bride's grandmother and the first lady at Court. Afterwards I shall take my children and grandchildren to the King in the Tuileries, where the reading and signing of the marriage contract will take place. Then there will be the betrothal, which is certain to be conducted by Cardinal de Rohan, and tomorrow the nuptial mass in the King's chapel.

Paris is no longer quite so full; the high cost of living has driven many people away. Today all dealings in gold and silver have been forbidden.

---

[1] Alberoni had been exiled from Spain in December, and peace negotiations between Spain and the Quadruple Alliance began. The war, effectively over by the summer of 1719, ended on 17 February 1720.

Louis d'Or and thalers are no longer legal tender, only banknotes and twenty sous pieces. I won't allow anyone to talk to me about millions and shares and premiums and subscriptions. I don't understand it, and it bores me too much. Of all the people I know in France, only my son and Mme Châteauthiers are absolutely disinterested. Everyone else, with not a single exception, is quite ridiculously full of self-interest, especially the princes and princesses of the blood. They got into a fight with the clerks at the bank, and did all sorts of other scandalous things. Money rules the world, it is true, but I can't think of another place on earth where it rules people more than it does here.

> Mlle de Valois was married by proxy to the Duke of Modena. After the wedding ceremony she entered the coach which was supposed to be taking her to Modena, but in fact travelled no further than the Palais-Royal. She made every possible attempt to delay her departure, and even went so far as to visit her sister in Chelles when that establishment was in quarantine for the measles. She duly caught the disease, and was unfit to travel for some weeks.

HERR VON HARLING

Paris 10 March 1720   The Princesse de Modène departs tomorrow. If that creature is ever happy it will be an agreeable surprise to me, because I am certain of the contrary. She has a strange madcap mind, which will cost her dear, because it won't do anywhere, especially in Italy.

Paris 31 March 1720   I think the devil must have been set loose this year, with all this murdering. Not a night passes without people being found murdered for their *billets des banques*. People of high quality are dabbling in this ugly and dreadful trade, amongst others that young, good-looking Comte de Hoorne of Flanders. The Comte was only twenty-three, M de Mortagne, my *chevalier d'honneur*, who had presented him to me about three weeks ago, died in his bed last Monday, and on Tuesday the Comte died on the wheel. It makes one sad. All France begged for mercy for the Comte, but my son said that for such an abominable deed an example had to be made, which duly happened, to the great satisfaction of the *peuple*, who cried '*Notre Régent est juste!*' Yesterday they found four newly killed bodies in a well in the rue Quincampoix, and a week ago two fellows were burned whose curses were so frightful and blasphemous that the registrar was sick.

Now that paper had taken the place of gold, bank messengers carried much larger sums than before. The Comte de Hoorne, broken on the wheel after he had 'thoroughly repented, so that he made a good, beautiful and pious end', had ambushed a *commis* in an attempt to re-coup the fortune that he had lost gambling. He was condemned to death by special parliamentary decree. Liselotte's 'all France' who came to plead refers to the Comte's princely relations—he was connected with almost every noble family of Flanders, France and Lorraine. They came to Paris to plead, not for his life, but for a more aristocratic form of execution. The Regent refused their petition, declaring that the shame lay in the crime, not in the form of punishment.

LUISE

Paris 31 March 1720 Every day there are new stories about the banknotes. It annoys me very much not to see gold any more; for forty-eight years I've carried gold in my pocket, and now there are only silver pieces. They are worth thirty sol now, but each month their value becomes less. It is certain that M Law is heartily loathed. My son told me something today in the carriage that moved me to tears. He said, 'The people say something which has touched my heart.' I said what, and he replied that when Comte Hoorne was executed they said, 'If anyone injures our Regent personally, he pardons everything and punishes no one, but if anyone injures one of us he takes it seriously and ensures that justice is done, as can be seen in the case of Comte Hoorne.'

M Law's good intentions are shown by the fact that he has bought estates and put all his money into this country, so he must intend to stay here.

Paris 7 April 1720 My son comes first with me, I am not one of those mothers who love their grandchildren more than their own children. I love my two children best. My son is the best man in the world. Mme du Maine visited him yesterday, and he received her so politely and well. Yesterday Mme la Princesse asked me to receive the Duchesse du Maine too. I replied that since my son, whom she had so grossly insulted, had seen and forgiven her, I should have to agree to see her as well, so I imagine she'll come stalking along one of these days. I can't decline, but God knows it won't be a pleasant visit.

I have never been able to endure hot rooms. When my apartments in Heidelberg became overheated I couldn't stand it, and opened all the windows. Here there is no such danger, but our chapel is an oven. We inherit this from our father the Elector, not being able to bear heat. In my day they used to burn more turf than wood in the fire-places in Heidelberg. I don't know if that is still the case—do tell me.

Paris 11 April 1720   Impossible for the clergy to govern me; I think too little of them. The Elector used to say, 'Things will go ill with the world until we have got rid of three kinds of charlatans—clergymen, doctors and lawyers.'

St Cloud 21 April 1720   Since our Queen used to drive out with eight horses, I have never had fewer. It was the late Duc de la Feuillade who started it. It is necessary here, because our carriages are very heavy; it is not a question of rank, for anyone who wishes to can drive with eight. As I say, I must have had eight horses in front of my coach for forty years now, but for the *calèche* I usually have only six. It amused me, dear Luise, that you thought I drove out with eight because I was the first lady. I'm not as proud as all that, but I look to my dignity as is proper.

HERR VON HARLING
St Cloud 5 May 1720   There is a little less murdering in Paris now, but there are fights instead. A few days ago eight people were left for dead. And the perpetual gambling, which leads to the keeping of bad company, seduces most of the young people of quality. The third thing that ruins them is that they pride themselves on having no religion and being independent of the world. They abandon the Lord and the Lord abandons them, so it's not surprising that they fall into every sinful vice. They would do well to say every day the little prayer that Frau von Harling made me say: Lord, do not forsake me, and I will not forsake you.

Our Princesse de Modène will have a sad day soon when she arrives in Genoa, where she will leave the French ladies and the royal house and be handed over to the Italians. God be with her; she will need His help. Few women in France are brought up to look to the things that matter, and not to get attached to trivialities; they are taught to judge whether a coiffure is becoming rather than what virtues are suitable to make a princess respected by the world.

St Cloud 16 May 1720   The good news of the reconciliation between the Prince and Princess of Wales and the King of England delighted me to the bottom of my heart.[1] No doubt there is rejoicing in Hanover too, and I send my compliments on the occasion to Prince Frederick.

[1] This had taken place in April.

CAROLINE OF WALES
St Cloud 31 May 1720 My son has had to remove Law, who used to be idolized by the people, from office. He needs protection, his life is not safe, and it is frightful to see how afraid the man is.

HERR VON HARLING
St Cloud 9 June 1720 Yesterday the *premier président* and the three highest presidents of the *parlement* came to my son to hold council with him and the Chancellor about all the affairs of the bank and the mint, but what they decided I won't write, as I have neither sense nor memory enough to explain it well. It will soon be made public.

I am beginning my walks again. Yesterday I walked in an avenue at Madrid with Mlle de Chausseraye and didn't get too tired. Her house, a gift from the late King, is small and neat. There is a little wood with several avenues, a little *parterre*, a large kitchen-garden. She keeps bees, doves and beautiful cows, so there is much to amuse me, because I love all animals, and everything that is rural pleases me more than the finest palaces or anything to be found in cities, except when Baron[1] acts in a play, which is what I like best in Paris. He played *Le Misanthrope* last Wednesday; there can be no better acting in the world, and he had a triumph. My weakness and tiredness have made me less bad-tempered than this muddle about the banknotes. To my mind it is better to be a French peasant than a French regent—at least one is sure of one's life and has fewer enemies.

At the end of May Law had issued an edict that all notes were to be halved in value, and could only be encashed in monthly instalments. The immediate rush on the bank caused much damage to life and limb and did nothing to stabilize the economy. The edict was withdrawn soon afterwards, but the Mississippi bubble had burst, and crowds of hungry people beleaguered the bank in the rue Quincampoix, trying to cash their notes.

CAROLINE OF WALES
St Cloud 21 June 1720 In France we no longer have two penny pieces to rub together, but we have (by your leave, and in good Palatine language) paper arse-wipers in plenty.[2]

[1] The most celebrated actor of his day. Liselotte much admired him for 'not declaiming, posturing or grimacing'.
[2] Liselotte particularly specifies paper, as she had been astonished to find, when she came to France, that cloth, not paper, was used at Court.

HERR VON HARLING

St Cloud 4 July 1720   I find as much diversion as I can in innocent amusements, do not meddle in anything, and wish only to have peace and quiet for the rest of my life. I went to Paris yesterday, to eat with my grandchildren. Afterwards I received a great many visitors and then I went to the theatre, where Baron and the Desmares were acting. The Desmares has a daughter by my son. He has not legitimized her but he is very fond of her. He married her off to a man of quality, the Marquis de Ségur, who used to be a page to the late King. When this lady is in our box the Desmares can't stop gazing at her, and one often sees tears of emotion in her eyes. Baron is just six months older than I am; he will be sixty-nine in November, but he seems much younger on the stage.

Of the *billets de banque* I will say nothing; they are my aversion. My son leads a dreadful life and is, like Moses, a tortured soul.

LUISE

St Cloud 11 July 1720   It is a rare thing for me to see much of my son, but I did see him for a moment last Sunday evening and Monday morning. I never talk about affairs of state, nor do I ever advise him. It would be difficult to give good advice on matters which one does not understand. But, so far as I can gather from rumours, things are going very badly indeed. I wish Law to the devil, with his art and his *Système*.

St Cloud 18 July 1720   I went to the Carmelites as usual and found Mme de Lude there. We were having a peaceful time together, when Mme de Châteauthiers came in and said, 'Madame, you must hear what is going on. The courtyard of the Palais-Royal is full of people, they have brought with them the bodies of people crushed to death at the bank. Law has been forced to hide in the Palais-Royal, and his carriage has been smashed into a thousand pieces. They forced his doors at six o'clock this morning.' You may imagine how I felt, but I couldn't show my emotion, because in such cases one must not appear frightened. I went on to the King as usual, but had to make a great effort to control myself. There was such a crowd in the rue St Honoré that we couldn't move for half-an-hour. I heard the people grumble, but only about Law. I didn't hear a word against my son.

CAROLINE OF WALES

St Cloud 6 August 1720   The King didn't like city-life. He was convinced that the townspeople of Paris had no love for him, and that His Majesty was not safe there. And the Maintenon could keep a better hold on him at Versailles. She herself was certainly in Paris, where she was dreadfully disliked. Whenever she went there the people called out threats after her. In the end she didn't dare drive about in her own coach.

LUISE

St Cloud 8 August 1720   Crossing the sea is a beastly thing, when you consider that you might land in India as easily as in England. Monsieur used to make us laugh with his tale of how once when he was in Dunkirk, on a very fine day, he felt like a little expedition on the sea. In the boat he sat next to the pilot, who seemed so sad that Monsieur asked him what was wrong. 'Sad memories,' the pilot replied. 'It is just a year to the day, in lovely weather like this, that I took my wife and children out for a turn on the water, and a storm blew up and carried us straight to India. My wife and children died there.' Monsieur, upon hearing this, said, *'Ramenez-moi au plus vite à bord!'*

St Cloud 10 August 1720   It's true, Luise, it's true, I'm fairly popular, but I don't know why, for I do the people neither good nor harm. You can never rely on the love of people, though—they're too fickle. I must confess I never liked M Law's system, and always wished that my son hadn't adopted it. I never understood anything about it. I was shocked when gold was done away with. It seemed like fraud to me, if I am to be truthful.

St Cloud 18 August 1720   I have never in my life seen an Englishman or a Scot appear so foolish and terrified as M Law does now. Wealth breeds fear, and no one likes to abandon his belongings, but I believe there must be times when he wishes himself in Louisiana or Mississippi. I thank you for your good wishes for my son. Even in the King's time he had many enemies; all those who sided with the King of Spain and wanted to bring him here are his arch-enemies, and that includes all the Maintenon's creatures at the old Court. Therefore Law doesn't add to my son's enemies at Court, but he certainly does in the *parlement*[1] and among the people.

Not only did I once see the set of draughts belonging to Charles V, but I also saw his crystal chessmen. They were very beautiful. He must have played all sorts of games. All these things come from Spain.

---

[1] The *parlement* had been exiled to Pontoise, because its members refused to pass certain measures designed to restore the credit of the Mississippi company. It returned to Paris only after Law had left France.

HERR VON HARLING
St Cloud 12 September 1720   I went to Paris to a party yesterday, which has become an annual event for me, at the Duchesse de Lude's, who used to be the *dame d'honneur* of Mme la Dauphine (the last one) and is my good friend. She gave us a magnificent feast, four hot courses and a dish of fruit and *confitures*, but as I eat no *confitures* so far as I was concerned it was a feast for the eyes only. After we had played Hoca for a few hours I went to the King, and then to the Palais-Royal, and after I had seen my son and his wife I went to the play with my four grandchildren.

Alberoni has stolen 198 bottles of *vin de champagne* from the King of Spain. They were sent for his Majesty, but he only gave him two, as well as a piece of cheese, sold all the rest and pocketed the money. According to his accounts the war cost 28 millions, but when they checked the figures they found that the war had cost only one, and he had put 27 millions into his own pocket. For that alone he deserves the gallows.

LUISE
St Cloud 14 September 1720   It is incredible how prices have risen; what used to cost thirty francs costs a hundred now. I ask nothing of the King, nor of my son, and less still of M Law, but I like to be paid regularly so that my servants don't suffer. Up till now, thank God, I have never owed anyone anything, neither the tradespeople nor anyone else, and I should be very sorry to find myself in debt. M Law's little daughter cannot fail to marry well. He is going to give her three millions apart from the trousseau, and if a duke or prince were to press him I think he'd let another little million fly.

HERR VON HARLING
St Cloud 22 September 1720   I quite agree, the *vieux langage* is much more expressive than the French we speak now. They tried to put *Don Quixote* into modern French, but it wasn't a success.

The gazettes and newspapers are full of lies. Anyone who wants to injure someone else writes on a scrap of paper what he would like to have published, wraps it round a thaler and addresses it *au gazetier d'Hollande*, and it is certain that the contents will appear in the Dutch papers. Although I have never gone in for this practice, I've often seen other people do it.

CAROLINE OF WALES
St Cloud 18 October 1720   Monsieur once made me laugh so much. He always brought a much be-medalled rosary to bed with him, and before

he went to sleep he told his beads. When that was over I heard a great rattling of medals, as though he was moving them about under the blanket. I said, '*Dieu me le pardonne, mais je soupçonne que vous faites promener vos reliques et images de la Vierge dans un pays qui lui est inconnu.*' Monsieur answered, '*Taisez-vous, dormez, vous ne savez que vous dites.*' I got up quietly, put the nightlight so that it shone into the bed, took hold of Monsieur's arm, laughed and said, '*Pour le coup, vous ne sauriez plus me nier.*' He laughed as well. '*Vous qui avez été Huguenotte, vous ne saviez pas le pouvoir des reliques et des images de la Sainte Vierge,*' he said. '*Elles guarantissent de tout mal les parties qu'on en frotte.*' I replied, '*Je vous demande pardon, Monsieur, mais vous ne me persuadez point que c'est honorer la Vierge que de promener son image sur les parties destinées à ôter la virginité.*' Monsieur had to laugh, and said, '*Je vous prie, ne le dites à personne.*'

HERR VON HARLING
St Cloud 31 October 1720   King François I walks in the *galerie d'Ulysse* at Fontainebleau in a green velvet dressing-gown, with his mistress covered in diamonds. I often walked in this gallery at night, but the good François I never did me the honour of showing himself to me. Perhaps he didn't think my prayers powerful enough to help him out of purgatory, and he may not have been so very wrong.

The cursed plague won't stop at Provence;[1] the disease is spreading further and further afield, and I am afraid that greed and avarice will finally bring it right into Paris. Since everything is extremely expensive in Paris now, and cheap in Marseilles and Toulon, there is reason to fear that the tradespeople may import the plague into Paris, because coffee, for example, costs five sols in Marseilles and sells at thirty livres in Paris, and other goods in proportion.

I have been told that never before have so many people in Paris gone mad and lost their reason as they have done this year. They speak of nothing but M Law and the Mississippi. In England it's no better: six gentlemen, ruined by the Southsea, have drowned themselves.

LUISE
St Cloud 2 November 1720   The *pommade divine* has quite cured me.[2] Mme d'Orléans is cured too, but I was better a week before she was. She is always happy to have an excuse for idling in bed. I don't think there

---

[1] The plague had broken out in Marseilles in June, and at the time of this letter there had been at least 70,000 deaths in Provence.
[2] Liselotte's knees were troubling her again.

is a lazier creature in the world. She admits it herself, and laughs about it. I don't often eat grapes, only some muscatels in the morning, because they help me to keep regular; in the afternoon, at table, I eat none, only an apple which they call *pomme de Calville* here. Since *Bacharacher* is not drunk until it is seven or eight years old, I don't imagine I shall taste much of this year's vintage. God knows where I shall be in eight years' time, and for the joy I take in living now, dear Luise, it wouldn't distress me to know that I shouldn't see them out.

I hope to be able to send you something from the fair soon. Everything is getting cheaper again, and we are beginning to see gold once more, but it stands very high still—a louis d'Or is 54 francs. But it will fall month by month, and there is hope that in time everything will be as it was. God grant it! Because I am as tired of the Mississippi bank and shares as if I had eaten them by the spoonful, and shall thank God when I hear no more of them.

I have already thanked you for the Tsar as well as for Prince Eugene,[1] but do so once more with pleasure. How Prince Eugene must have changed to have a long pointed nose now—he never had that in his youth.

St Cloud 21 November 1720 Did the grapes they sent you from the Palatinate come from Schrussheim? They are usually very good, and I like them better than those from the other side. I don't think grapes from Heidelberg can be bad for one. I still remember the enormous amount of grapes I ate in the vineyards of Schrussheim: I was so full that I could hardly walk, but it did me no harm and made me eat my dinner all the better.

St Cloud 23 November 1720 Today it snowed for the first time this season, but the snow melted at once. It must be cold in Germany now, and in the Palatinate. I have no desire, nowadays, to be back there: I should be in tears day and night if I were. I mustn't remember the old times too much, either, for it soon makes me pensive and sad. Everyone I used to know in my youth is still quite clearly in my mind. I could paint our entire Court of those days, young and old.

CAROLINE OF WALES
St Cloud 26 November 1720 *Ma tante*, our dear Electress, didn't visit the Princess Royal,[2] but the Queen of Bohemia[3] did, and took me with her.

[1] That is, for medals depicting these two personages.

[2] Mary Stuart, widow of William II of Orange.

[3] Elizabeth Stuart, widow of the Winter King, during the time Sophia and Liselotte stayed with her at The Hague.

Ma tante said to me, 'Take care, Lisette, don't get lost as you usually do, so that no one can find you, but stay close to the Queen and don't keep her waiting for you.' I said, 'Oh, *ma tante*, you'll see, I'll be so good.' I had often played with the son,[1] whom I found with his mother, only I didn't know it was his mother, so after I had gazed at her for a long time I looked round for someone to tell me who this woman was. There was no one except the Prince of Orange, so I went up to him and said, '*Dites-moi, je vous prie, qui est cette femme qui a un si furieux nez?*' He laughed and replied, '*C'est la Princesse Royale, ma mère.*' I was so shocked that I was struck dumb, and to comfort me Mlle Hyde[2] took me and the Prince into the Princess's bedchamber, where we played all sorts of games. I had asked to be called when the Queen was ready to leave; we were just rolling about on a Turkish carpet when the summons came. I jumped up and ran into the audience-chamber, but the Queen had already reached the anteroom. I quickly pulled the Princess Royal back by her skirt, and, making her a pretty curtsey, walked in front of her, following the Queen to the carriage. Everyone laughed, I didn't know why. When we arrived home the Queen went to *ma tante*, and sitting on her bed, laughing so that she almost choked, said, '*Lisette a fait un beau voyage*', and told her what I had done. Our dear Electress laughed even harder than the Queen, called me, and said, 'Lisette, you have done well, you have revenged us on the proud princess.'

LUISE

St Cloud 5 December 1720   The plague, which seemed to have finished in Marseilles, has started again, worse than ever. It is supposed to be frightful in Poland, too, and has broken out in Silesia. I'm convinced that it will soon spread all over Europe. But it doesn't frighten me as, whatever happens to me, it will be by God's divine providence. If I die of the plague I shan't die of anything else. It wouldn't surprise me if they got the plague in Saxony, because the King of Poland and his people are bound to carry it from Poland.

Paris 19 December 1720   John Law has gone to one of the estates that he bought, six miles from here. He is supposed to make up his accounts there; we hear that it is uphill work. I'm sure he'll bolt in the end,

---

[1] William of Orange.

[2] Anne Hyde was lady in waiting to the Princess of Orange before her marriage to James Stuart (later James II).

with the help of M le Duc, who, incognito, has already visited him twice.[1]

I've never been able to learn how to cut quills, which I much regret because only one of my people can cut them to my taste. Luckily he is much younger than I am, so I hope to keep him until the end. He used to be my *valet de chambre*, but then he bought the appointment of the *porte-manteau*.

CAROLINE OF WALES

Paris 27 December 1720 When he took his leave John Law said to my son, 'Monseigneur, I have made great mistakes. I have made them because I am human, but you will find neither malice nor treachery in my conduct.' His wife doesn't want to leave Paris until all his debts are paid.

LUISE

Paris 19 April 1721 It is in the Pope's interest to maintain the Constitution, so it is hard to believe that the quarrelling will not begin again.

I speak of the Pope in French-Catholic and not German-Catholic terms. He is not considered infallible in France; the entire Sorbonne has declared against it. When the Pope isn't reasonable he is not obeyed in France, and people are free to talk about it as they please. We have no inquisition in France. To refer to him as 'Holy Father' is only a manner of speaking, and means no more than simply to call him 'the Pope'. No one thinks of him as holy. Still, he is a great ruler. A Bishop of Noyon I used to know never called him anything but 'Monsieur de Rome'; he often made me laugh.

I had no love for the late Pope,[2] but, purely for the sake of truth, I must tell you that it is absolutely untrue to say he was in love with the Pretender's wife.[3] For one thing he was a man of seventy-three, and, for another, he suffered from such a dreadful rupture that his belly and intestines were held in by a silver plate. This is no condition for being in love, as you can easily imagine. No wonder, though, that he was interested in this Princess, for he officiated at her baptism and marriage, and he thought that if the Pretender could regain the English throne the

---

[1] A few weeks after retiring to Guéremande John Law left France altogether. He took with him only a small part of his personal fortune and died, a poor man, in Venice in 1729.

[2] Clement XI had died on March 19th.

[3] Maria Clementine Sobieska, who had married James (III) in 1719.

whole country would once again be in his own power and the priests'.
So, you see, he was quite right to interest himself in this Princess and
her husband. A seventy-three-year-old *galant* with a silver plate is a very
shocking *galanterie*! No French cardinal can lay claim to the papacy
unless he was born in Italy. Alberoni has a greater chance of becoming
Pope than any of them.

St Cloud 26 April 1721   M Teray knows his business, and inspires
confidence. I do as I'm told, but I am absolutely convinced that our hours
are numbered, and that we can't exceed the limit. So long as I am meant
to be alive the doctors will find every possible cure, but once the fatal
hour comes which the Almighty has ordained for taking me out of this
life, they will be quite powerless. I view the prospect with indifference.
I know that I was born only to die, and await the time without impatience or fear, and pray to God to let me have a peaceful end. Nothing
you read in the Bible about the time before the Flood, or Sodom and
Gomorrah, comes anywhere near the life people lead in Paris. Of nine
young people of quality who dined with my grandson, the Duc de
Chartres,[1] a few days ago, seven had the French *malaise*. Isn't that disgusting?

HERR VON HARLING
St Cloud 11 May 1721   It suits me to be out of Paris. My health is much
improved. When I open my window the air here is scented like a
bouquet of flowers, very different from Paris, where you smell nothing
but emptied close-stools and chamberpots, which have not an agreeable
perfume.

LUISE
St Cloud 24 May 1721   Next Wednesday is my birthday, according to
the new calendar. The weather is most unspring-like today; there is a
cold north wind—just like November. I thank you with all my heart
for your good wishes, dear Luise, for my birthday. There is no danger
that I shall change my way of life. I am just as the old French proverb
says: '*Je suis comme le camelot, mon pli est pris.*' But I did enjoy myself a
little after all, for I found a new medal for my cabinet, a Nero. I have
collected 957 medals since I began ten years ago, and if God gives me a
few years longer I hope to reach a thousand and leave my son one of
the rarest and finest *medaillier* in all Europe after the King's, because my
medals are all in extremely good condition.

[1] Louis was not yet eighteen.

St Cloud 24 July 1721   When I was young I was never ill, thanks to hunting, which after God helped to keep me well for many years. Exercise is good for the health; I hunted on horseback for thirty years, and in *calèches* for ten. As long as Monsieur was alive I used to ride. Since the King's death I have said goodbye to everything to do with hunting, but I have had three serious illnesses since then, which makes me believe that hunting kept me in good health in my younger days.

Holland, to my way of thinking, is a pleasant country. Amsterdam is worth seeing too. Utrecht is still dear to me, I had such an enjoyable time there. One thing is certain; anyone who has seen Holland will find Germany dirty, but to find Germany clean and pleasant one only has to see France. Nothing could be more stinking and pig-like than Paris.

While I was in Heidelberg I never read any romances, but I've made up for it in the time I've spent here;[1] there isn't one I haven't read. Even *Amadis*[2] (but I only got to the seventeenth volume, and there are twenty-four) and *le roman des romans, Théagène et Clariclée*. At Fontainebleau this story is painted in the King's *Cabinet d'Oval*, and very interesting it is. Apropos of Fontainebleau, if one isn't used to hunting one can turn fine somersaults there, but I didn't have as many falls there as I had around here. I think it must be because I loved the place so much. Nothing bad or disappointing ever happened to me there; on the contrary, I have had more enjoyment there than in any other place in France.

St Cloud 7 August 1721   Yesterday I called on the King, who had been ill. I was surprised to see him running gaily towards me; he had been bled from the arm and foot, had taken an emetic, and had had another general purge the day before. The people are quite foolish with joy, they troop round in groups with drums and fifes, and shout *Vive le roi* so loudly that you can't hear yourself speak. *Te Deum Laudamus* was sung in all the churches, my son went to the one at Notre Dame. In the evening at eight, when I left town, the whole place was illuminated by fireworks and Chinese lanterns.

[1] Liselotte's father had forbidden his children to read romances, because he felt that such practices might turn his sons into adventurers and his daughters into whores.

[2] *Amadis de Gaulle*, by a number of writers. The first four volumes, by the Portuguese Vasco de Lobeira, were regarded as a masterpiece by Cervantes, who based the character of Don Quixote on the hero of this work. *Théagène et Clariclée* is by Héliodore.

HERR VON HARLING

Paris 17 September 1721 First, our big news: last Sunday a courier from Spain brought letters to the young King and my son. The King of Spain wants to send the Infanta, his daughter, to be educated here. The Duchesse de Ventadour is to bring her up; she will go and fetch her in the spring. The little Infanta will be four on March 31st, so our young King will have to wait another eight years before His Majesty is a married man. What a lot of water will flow under the bridge before this marriage is concluded! In the meantime it will make for peace between the two crowns.

> Plans to link the Spanish and the French branches of the Bourbon family had formed part of the Franco-Spanish peace treaty, signed in the spring of 1721.

LUISE

St Cloud 25 September 1721 Today we are all in *grand habit*, because I have to attend a ceremony at three o'clock this afternoon: the reception of that damned Cardinal Dubois, who has been sent his biretta by the Pope.[1] I shall have to greet him, and ask him to sit down and entertain him for a while, none of which will be easy, but trouble and irritation are my daily bread. But behold our Cardinal stalking in, and I must stop writing. . . . The Cardinal has begged me to forget the past, and has made the most beautiful speech imaginable. He is very clever, that's certain, and if he were as good as he is intelligent there would be little left to be desired. But there is devilish little good about him, and that's the rub.

HERR VON HARLING

St Cloud 2 October 1721 I must go to Paris this morning to join with my son and his wife in celebrating the happy news that we received last Monday: a courier arrived from the King of Spain asking for the hand of my granddaughter for his eldest son, the Prince of the Asturias. They will be a very young couple, because the Prince was fourteen on 25 August and Mlle de Montpensier will be twelve on 11 December. I should think it all very fine if only it didn't bring with it so many visits and compliments that one hardly knows where to turn, but as the proverb says, '*Il faut avoir les charges avec les bénéfices.*'

---

[1] Dubois, who had become Archbishop of Cambrai in 1720, had now been made a cardinal.

Our young bride has no name yet. Although she has been baptized, the ritual of naming hasn't taken place. The King and I will hold this ceremony. Before Mlle de Montpensier embarks on her journey, she will be furnished with three sacraments: christening, communion and confirmation—that can't often happen.

I am quite well now, thank God, but at my age I can't expect to be really strong, although I can walk for a good hour still.

The plague has now reached Avignon, through the avarice of a legate. In order to make a profit (being avaricious, like all Roman clerics), he imported cheap goods from places infected with the plague, sold them dear, and thereby brought the plague into the town. He deserves to die of it.

LUISE

St Cloud 6 November 1721   I went to bed early last night. I counted nine o'clock after I had got into bed, went to sleep soon after, woke up at half-past four, and rang to have my fire made up and the room put to rights. In the meantime I said my morning prayers, and just after half-past five I got up. I dressed, put on a good pair of beaver stockings and my cloth petticoat, and over this a long, good, padded dressing-gown which I fastened with a large, wide belt. When that was done I had two lights lit and sat down at my table. Now you know, dear Luise, my morning's work as well as I do myself. I write until half-past ten, then I send for my honey-water and wash myself as clean as I can, rub my painful knees and thighs with *eau vulnéraire*, which my doctors recommend, ring, and have all my women come in. Then I sit down at my dressing table and everybody, men and women, enters while my hair is being done. When I am coiffed all the men, except for my doctors, surgeons and apothecaries, leave the room, and I put on my shoes, stockings and *caleçons*[1] and wash my hands. While this is taking place the ladies have arrived to attend on me and pass me the things I need for washing my hands and hand me my chemise. Then the doctor-crew leaves the room and my tailor comes in with my dress. I put this on as soon as I have put on my chemise. When I am laced up all the men come back in, for my *manteau* is so constructed that I am fully dressed as soon as the laces are tied. All my underskirts are tied to the bodice with tabs, and my *manteau* is sewn on to it. I find this very convenient. When I am dressed, usually at a quarter to twelve, I go to chapel. Mass lasts twenty minutes at most, and immediately afterwards Junker

---

[1] *Caleçons*, or drawers, were only worn by the most old-fashioned and straight-laced women of the old regime.

Wendt, the first steward, comes in and calls me to dinner. Our meal takes a good hour. Every Monday, Wednesday and Saturday I drive to Chausseraye at Madrid at half-past one, but when I have any business in Paris I go to the Carmelites on Wednesdays or Saturdays. We hear Mass there and then go on to the King, from there to the Palais-Royal to Mme la Duchesse d'Orléans, where my son usually joins us, and I go in to dinner with my ladies and his children. My son rarely eats dinner because his brain doesn't work after he has been eating and drinking. Afterwards, at about three o'clock, I drive out to pay calls. Then I go back to the Palais-Royal. On Wednesdays I go to the French and on Saturdays to the Italian Comedy, and when that is over I return to my carriage and come back here, and so to bed, as the bride said. On Thursdays and Sundays I drive about the garden, before church during this season and after church in summer. I never go out on Fridays and Tuesdays, for on these two days I have too much to write to Lorraine and England. On Sunday, Wednesday and Saturday mornings I read the Bible. Now you know my whole life, dear Luise, just as though you were here.

HERR VON HARLING
St Cloud 20 November 1721 Last Sunday the marriage contract between the Prince of the Asturias and Mlle de Montpensier was signed in the King's apartments. Afterwards he came to our box at the Opera and then, after supper, attended the ball. I came back here after the Opera and didn't stay for the ball. This made all Paris say that I had had a stroke and was as dead as a doornail, but that they had kept it quiet in order to go on with the ball. That made me laugh.

LUISE
St Cloud 22 November 1721 M le Cardinal Dubois is to make great changes in the post office, and to repair all the harm done by Torcy's avarice and self-interest. For example, the post to Lorraine: to save a courier he had the mail thrown into the first chaise that was going to Nancy, so that anyone who was interested enough could read all the letters. He did a number of things like that, when he was in charge of the post. He is a real hypocrite, because under the pretext of prayers and piety he does all the harm he can, and his greatest pleasure is to do someone an injury. I'm glad he's no longer in charge of the post. Although the little cardinal is not much better than that horrible Torcy, he will know how to hide his meanness better and not be so obvious about it, because he likes to be praised.

If only the King were still alive! Then I had more joy and pleasure in one day than I have had in the six years of my son's Regency. For one thing, we had a proper Court then, and not this middle-class existence which I can't get accustomed to, because I was born and bred at Court. While the King was alive my son used to be with me for days at a time: now I hardly see him for an hour a month. In Paris, where we share an antechamber, I often go for three days without seeing him at all. What is more, his Regency causes me more worry and anxiety than joy and consolation. It has made me uneasy for many years, worried that he may be assassinated, because of the horrible hatred that has been stirred up against him. Now he no longer restrains himself in his *galanteries*, but runs about for nights on end, which he couldn't have done in the King's lifetime, and his health is always in danger. I used to love the King with all my heart, for he was truly agreeable company. I really used to enjoy chatting and laughing with him, because he loved it when one talked freely, and the other princesses, with the exception of Mme la Duchesse,[1] could never bring themselves to do that. We went out hunting three times a week, in the mornings or after dinner. I never had to spend the night in that dreadful Paris, and only went there for the Opera, because we had plays enough at Court. The evenings were spent with various people, and during the day one could be by oneself as much as one liked—in short, my life was not half so boring as it is now. What is the use of independence when I no longer have anything enjoyable to do? Nevertheless I could bear the tedium, since I have renounced all pleasure and no longer care for it. But to live in secret fear without showing a sign of it makes for black moods. I love my son with all my heart, and he lives on such good terms with me that I have nothing to complain of. But the more content I am with him the sadder it makes me never to see him, and to have such good reason to be in fear for him. Still, I admit that it is a great thing to rule over a kingdom.

Mlle de Montpensier, now the Princess of the Asturias—Liselotte calls her 'our little Spanish fly'—set out for her new home immediately after her wedding by proxy.

LUISE
St Cloud 6 December 1721   You couldn't call Mlle de Montpensier ugly; she has a smooth skin and pretty eyes. The nose might pass if it weren't

[1] Louise-Françoise de Condé.

so narrow, and her mouth is very small. But with all this she is the most unpleasant child I have ever seen, so far as her manners are concerned: the way she talks and eats and drinks makes one lose one's temper just to look at her. I assure you I shed no tears at saying adieu, and nor did she. Spain has a stepdaughter, a stepgranddaughter and now a granddaughter of mine for past and future queens. My favourite of all was the stepdaughter, whom I loved like a sister—she couldn't have been my daughter, for she was only nine years younger than I was. I was still very young for my age when I arrived, and we used to play and tear about together. We often made so much noise, when we played with the late Carllutz and the little Prince of Eisenach, that it must have been quite unbearable. There was an old lady here, Mme de Freimes, whom we used to plague abominably. She hated loud bangs, and we used to throw *pétards* into her skirts, which drove her to despair. She used to run after us and try to hit us—it was the greatest fun.

Paris 20 December 1721 I much prefer wearing the *grand habit* to the *manteau*, which I have to wear now that I am ill, else I should be laughed at. One looks too much like a chambermaid in the *manteau*. The wide skirts which are worn everywhere are my aversion, they look insolent, as though one had come straight out of bed. The *manteau* as I wear it is nothing new, Mme la Dauphine[1] used to wear one. The fashion of the beastly skirts first dates from Mme de Montespan. She used to wear them when she was pregnant, so as to hide her condition. After the King's death Mme d'Orléans revived them again.

Paris 25 December 1721 I told you in my last letter how the fashion of loose skirts came from Mme de Montespan, who invented it to disguise her large belly when she was pregnant. But it was little use, for everybody always knew, and whenever she appeared in this skirt it was like a signal.

St Cloud 5 February 1722 Dearest Luise, I begin writing today with a great glassful of green juice inside me. I took one yesterday too, which purged me thoroughly. I don't think it is quite done with yet, I still feel something walking about in my guts. There, it's been dispatched . . .

Now I come to your dear letter of January 20th. I don't know if you ever heard our father the Elector repeat what M Grillon said to him when he put him into prison at Vincennes:[2] '*Tenez, voici votre*

[1] Maria Anna of Bavaria.
[2] Charles Louis had been Richelieu's prisoner at Vincennes from 1639 until 1640.

logement. Prenez-y patience en enrageant.' I always remember that when I hear of people being forced to be patient.

HERR VON HARLING

Paris 1 March 1722   I'm as cross as a bedbug because of to-morrow's tedious events. For six hours I have to sit in a coach with the royal child, *la reine future*, as she is called, who will be in tears because she is surrounded by unfamiliar faces. Arches of honour have been erected all over Paris, and at every one there will be an address, which is also my aversion. My health is now quite perfect, but to-morrow may well see a change, for boredom is most unhealthy for an old knight-of-the-rustling-leaves.

> On January 10th the Infanta of Spain had been exhanged for Mlle de Montpensier, at a ceremony on the Ile de Faisans, near Bidassoa, on the border between Spain and France. As the Spanish travellers neared Paris Liselotte, a member of the welcoming party because of her position as first lady of France, met them at Berry.

Paris 5 March 1722   First I must tell you a little about our small Infanta, whom we escorted into Paris last Monday. The entry was magnificent: all the way from Berry to Paris there were such crowds as I have never seen before in my life. What I liked best was that there was not a window empty on the whole route, from the gates of Paris right up to the Louvre; every one was hung with tapestries and crowded with people in their best clothes. It was a marvellous spectacle. What I liked less was that we went the whole way at a walking-pace, and it took a good seven hours without food or drink—that doesn't suit a rustling-leaves-knight. I can't admire the little Infanta's patience enough, for the poor baby was in that coach for seven hours without crying or getting ill-tempered. She must be the best child in the world, a really good child. This is what she called out to the officer of the bodyguard, '*Ah, ne battez ces pauvres gens qui me veulent voir.*' She only began learning French after Bordeaux. It frightens me, for children who are so clever often die young. God preserve us from that.

LUISE

Paris 26 March 1722   I don't enjoy walking in the Tuileries any more, there are too many people. Since the King's death, and in the course of our bourgeois life in Paris, I have become shy of people. I can well believe that to make a habit of going to bed late, as in the King's day, when I never went before one o'clock in the morning, wouldn't do. Actually, it was worse still, because I used to write until four or five o'clock, and that, to tell the truth, isn't good for anyone's health and makes you feel sleepy and stupid all the next day. But I don't do that any more. At the latest I go to bed at 11 o'clock. I don't get on too badly with the King. I played a prank on his governors yesterday which rather amused me. The King had colic the day before yesterday, and yesterday I gravely went up to him and put a little piece of paper into his hand. Maréchal de Villeroy asked me in a pompous voice, '*Quel billet donnez-vous au roi?*' I answered, equally seriously, 'A remedy for the colic.' The Maréchal: 'Only the King's physician may prescribe for the King.' I answered, '*Pour celui-ci je suis sure que M Dodart l'approuvera. Il est même écrit en vers et en chansons.*' The King grew embarrassed, read it secretly and began to laugh. The Maréchal said, '*Peut-on le voir?*' I said, '*Oui, il n'y a point de secret*', and he found the following words:

> *Vous qui dans le mésentère*
> *Avez des vents impétueux*
> *Ils sont dangereux*
> *Et pour vous en défaire*
> *Pétez*
> *Pétez, vous ne sauriez mieux faire*
> *Pétez*
> *Trop heureux, trop heureux de vous défaire d'eux*
> *A ces malheureux pour donner la liberté tout entière*
> *Pétez*
> *Pétez, vous ne sauriez mieux faire*
> *Pétez*
> *Trop heureux*
> *De vous délivrer d'eux.*

Everyone laughed so hard that I was almost sorry to have played the joke. The Maréchal de Villeroy was quite put out of countenance.

The ancient Maréchal de Villeroy was famous for preventing every-body and anybody from privately communicating with the King; the Regent himself had the greatest difficulty in arranging for an audience *à deux*.

St Cloud 11 June 1722 I must confess that I worried a great deal about the Princess of Wales and the two Princesses. I am not so brave, and if my children were quite well I couldn't possibly steel myself to make them ill, even though it was for their own good. When I had smallpox I was so ill that if the pain had lasted even half-an-hour longer I should have died of pain. But the inoculation is supposed to be quite different, because the pain is supposed to be less severe, and to last for a much shorter time, and it is believed that the smallpox will never come back. That must be what made the Princess do it. God grant that she may find that this is so and that the dear little Princesses are protected for the rest of their lives from this horrible disease. My doctor doesn't think this remedy is safe, he says he doesn't understand it.

Two of the Princess's daughters, Amelia and Caroline, had just been inoculated against smallpox, with a serum that Lady Mary Wortley Montagu had brought from the East—almost a hundred years before Jenner began to vaccinate.

St Cloud 13 June 1722 We left the dinner table a good hour ago. To aid my digestion I went to see my new canaries being fed. I have thirty newly hatched birds from my six old pairs, each one more beautiful than the last. But there, they have come to announce my carriage, but I'll just finish this page. I haven't got my strength back yet, I can't walk the length of a room without puffing as though I had run down a hare. Gold-powder I've got, but hyacinth-pills I simply can't get down. When I had smallpox they gave me some, but I almost died of them. How can you possibly swallow the disgusting things, dear Luise? I have made up my mind never to touch them again as long as I live, they are worse than any disease. *Ma tante* once sent me two golden boxes filled with gold-powder, but I didn't take it. To tell you the truth I don't like taking things, whatever they may be.

HERR VON HARLING
St Cloud 4 July 1722 My visit to Versailles[1] made my heart so heavy that I hardly knew where to turn. Because, although I love the young King and his dear bride and *Infantchen* with all my heart, I must confess that I can't get used to seeing nothing but children everywhere, and nowhere the great King whom I loved so much. This sadness made me so dreadfully tired, because I haven't got back my strength yet.

[1] In June the King had moved from the Louvre to Versailles.

St Cloud 23 July 1722   This year there is no getting to rights when one has been ill. Four days ago, when I began taking this vermouth-wine, I was much better and thought I had got over the worst, but the day before yesterday all my *vapeurs, langueurs* and aches returned.

St Cloud 29 July 1722   Our young King has nothing in him of his great-grandfather but resembles Mme la Dauphine, his late mother, as one drop of water resembles another, only he is much better looking than she was. His mouth and colouring are prettier, and his teeth are much better. When the old Maréchal, his governor, is not with him he talks quite cheerfully and nicely, but as soon as his governor is there he becomes dumb and not a word can be got out of him.

LUISE

St Cloud 5 September 1722   Thank you for your good wishes for the marriage of our Mlle de Beaujolais.[1] Her little Prince is a year younger than she is, and when she arrives in Spain her husband will be seven and she will be eight, so their joint ages will be fifteen. She is amusing to look at, and is now trying to act the grown up; she always makes me laugh. But I feel so sorry for her youngest sister,[2] she has become so sad since she knows that they have to part. I have never seen children love each other so much as these two.

The maps of Mannheim and Schwetzingen will give me much pleasure, but also a sigh or two, in so far as they will remind me of the good old days. But the Elector Palatine[3] is really too humble to suggest lying at my poor swollen feet!

St Cloud 17 September 1722   They have almost killed me with their remedies, as they call them. First that damned blood-letting, which made me lose so much blood; then the *jus*, which purged me so violently that it affected my gall bladder, and in the end gave me a fine attack of jaundice. The whole affair reminded me of *Le Médicin Malgré Lui*, when he asks his patient, '*Mangez-vous bien, allez-vous bien?*', and when the answer is in the affirmative says, '*Eh bien, je vous donnerai quelque chose qui vous ôtera tout cela.*'

[1] Mlle de Beaujolais, another of the Regent's daughters, was now betrothed to Don Carlos of Spain, younger brother of the Prince of the Asturias.
[2] Mlle de Chartres, the Regent's youngest daughter, aged 6.
[3] A distant relation of Liselotte.

HERR VON HARLING

St Cloud 19 Stepember 1722 Short of dying, no one could be worse than I was during my horrible jaundice, which was caused by endless purgings. They tried to treat me like a Frenchwoman, and never considered that French jokes like bleeding and purging aren't fit for a German knight-of-the-rustling-leaves. Now I have sworn off all this, and am much better.

St Cloud 26 Stepember 1722 I hope I shall be able to travel to Rheims, to give my daughter the pleasure of showing me all her children. This is the only reason that will take me to Rheims; I am not at all curious to see the *Sacre*,[1] all my curiosity has deserted me. If it were not for my daughter I should certainly not be going to Rheims. The whole trip won't take more than three weeks in all, four days there, four days back and the rest of the time in Rheims. The King will set off on the 16th, and take seven days on the journey. He will arrive on the 22nd, the *Sacre* and the Coronation will take place on the 25th, on the 26th my grandson and the Comte de Charolais will receive the Cordon Bleu, on the 28th the King goes to St Marceau, there to touch the *entrailles*, saying *Le roi te touche et Dieu te guérit*. I think that is well said, and the safest thing.

St Cloud 1 October 1722 Although I'm better than I was, I can't boast of any great good health. But I have firmly decided to give my daughter the pleasure of seeing me in Rheims, and also hope that the change of air will do more good than any medicine. It's all one whether I die in St Cloud, Villers-Cotterets or Rheims. Yesterday in Paris I saw the crown that will be used for the King's coronation. There can't be anything more splendid, more beautiful and more magnificent in the world. The great Sancy[2] and his friends made a *fleur de lis*, and above it, between two rows of beautiful pearls, are great rubies, emeralds and topazes. Everything is so beautifully set that it cannot be described. But now I must go and dress.

St Cloud 3 October 1722 There has been no change in my condition since I wrote to you two days ago. It must go as God wills. I am preparing for my journey to Rheims, and what will become of it 'time will

[1] The anointing of the King, whose coronation was to take place in Rheims cathedral in October.

[2] The famous diamond, pear-shaped and weighing $53\frac{1}{2}$ carat, was named after one of its early owners.

tell'. I enclose a letter from your nephew and assure you that, whatever condition I may be in, I shall always be his and your true friend.

LUISE

St Cloud 5 November 1722   It was impossible to answer your letters today, not only because I was so tired but because of the continuous bustle and ceremonial, and also because of the doings of my children who were with me all the time, as well as an incredible number of other people, princes, gentlemen, counts and bishops and archbishops and cardinals. I don't believe it would be possible to see or imagine anything more beautiful in the whole wide world than the King's coronation. I've been promised the official description of it by Saturday. If God gives me health and life until the day after to-morrow I'll send you a report of it, dear Luise. My daughter was quite astonished when she saw me, because she had thought that my illness was only an excuse. But when she saw me in Rheims she had such a shock that she burst into tears. I was very sorry. She has fine children, although I'm afraid the eldest will be a giant; although he's only fifteen, he is six foot tall.[1] The other four are neither big nor small for their age. The youngest, Prince Carl, is what His Grace our late father used to call 'a peculiar sort of saint'; he never closes his mouth and is always gay, argues continuously with his sisters, and is very amusing. The handsomest of the three boys, to my mind, is the middle one.[2] Of the girls the youngest one may be the prettiest, but the elder one is so well-made that one couldn't call her plain.

St Cloud 19 November 1722   I think I've already told you that during the past eight days I have been purged eighty times, which has made me so weak that I don't know if they will be able to pull me through again.

St Cloud 26 November 1722   I've never felt so weak in all my life. No wonder, when with my delicate digestion I have had to take their medicine every morning and evening since last Sunday. I feel as if they are dragging my soul out of my body. I should look forward to my journey to the next world if only it could be accomplished quickly and without pain. To tell you the truth, this illness makes me tired of life.

[1] He died when he was sixteen.

[2] Franz Stephan (Emperor 1745–65, husband of Maria Theresa and father of Marie Antoinette).

St Cloud 3 December 1722 Dearest Luise, what I have to say of my health today will not, I think, please you. I get worse every day and the end may well be near, but I am, praise be to God, prepared for whatever may come. God may know if I shall get over this, and time will tell, but I've never been worse than I am now. The weather here is not unpleasant, there was some rain today, though only a little. I don't think the weather can have any effect on me now. Time, dear Luise, will soon show what is to become of all this. Should God take me to him, you must find comfort in the knowledge that I die without pain or regret, and willingly leave the world in the hope that my Redeemer will stay by me to the end. In this belief I live and die, dear Luise; for the rest it must go as God ordains. A lot of people here complain of coughs and cold; my illness is more serious, and gets worse daily.

There, they are bringing me another dear letter from you of November 21st, but I can't answer it now, I am far too ill. If, if God keeps me alive until the day after tomorrow, I will answer it, but for now I will only say that I shall love you with all my heart until the very end.

Elisabeth Charlotte

This is Liselotte's last letter. She died in the night of 8 December 1722. Just before her death she said to one of her ladies, who was about to kiss her hand at the final leave-taking, 'You may kiss me properly; I am going to the land where all are equal.'

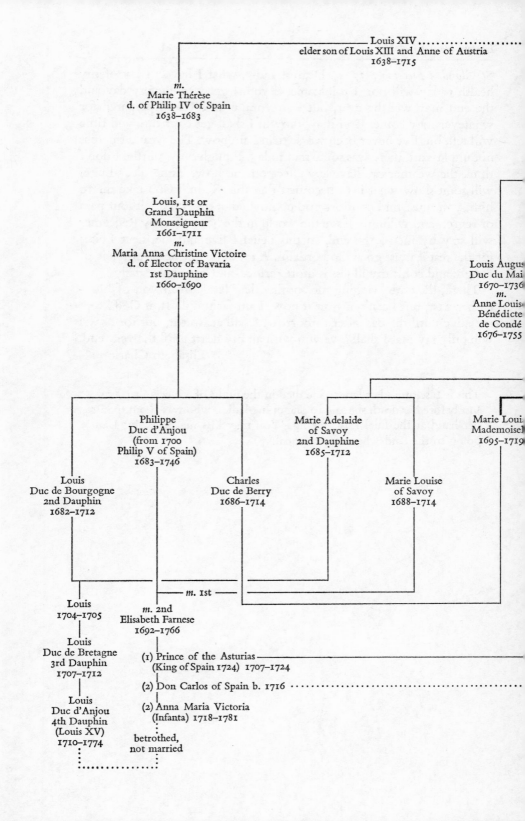

Louis XIV . . . .
elder son of Louis XIII and Anne of Austria
1638–1715

m.
Marie Thérèse
d. of Philip IV of Spain
1638–1683

Louis, 1st or
Grand Dauphin
Monseigneur
1661–1711
m.
Maria Anna Christine Victoire
d. of Elector of Bavaria
1st Dauphine
1660–1690

Louis Augus
Duc du Mai
1670–1736
m.
Anne Louise
Bénédicte
de Condé
1676–1755

Philippe
Duc d'Anjou
(from 1700
Philip V of Spain)
1683–1746

Marie Adelaide
of Savoy
2nd Dauphine
1685–1712

Marie Louis
Mademoisel
1695–1719

Louis
Duc de Bourgogne
2nd Dauphin
1682–1712

Charles
Duc de Berry
1686–1714

Marie Louise
of Savoy
1688–1714

Louis
1704–1705

— m. 1st —

m. 2nd
Elisabeth Farnese
1692–1766

Louis
Duc de Bretagne
3rd Dauphin
1707–1712

(1) Prince of the Asturias —————————
(King of Spain 1724) 1707–1724

(2) Don Carlos of Spain b. 1716 . . . .

Louis
Duc d'Anjou
4th Dauphin
(Louis XV)
1710–1774

(2) Anna Maria Victoria
(Infanta) 1718–1781

betrothed,
not married

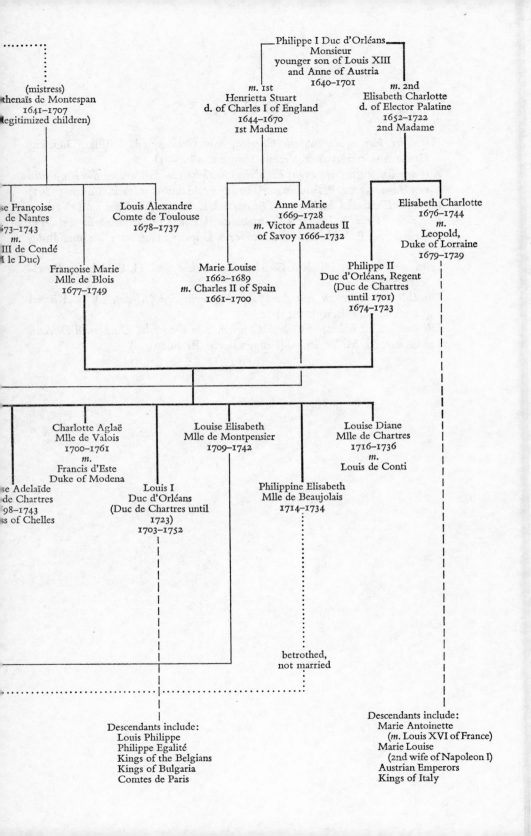

Philippe I Duc d'Orléans
Monsieur
younger son of Louis XIII
and Anne of Austria
1640–1701

m. 1st
Henrietta Stuart
d. of Charles I of England
1644–1670
1st Madame

m. 2nd
Elisabeth Charlotte
d. of Elector Palatine
1652–1722
2nd Madame

(mistress)
thenaïs de Montespan
1641–1707
legitimized children)

se Françoise
de Nantes
73–1743
m.
III de Condé
1 le Duc)

Louis Alexandre
Comte de Toulouse
1678–1737

Anne Marie
1669–1728
m. Victor Amadeus II
of Savoy 1666–1732

Elisabeth Charlotte
1676–1744
m.
Leopold,
Duke of Lorraine
1679–1729

Françoise Marie
Mlle de Blois
1677–1749

Marie Louise
1662–1689
m. Charles II of Spain
1661–1700

Philippe II
Duc d'Orléans, Regent
(Duc de Chartres
until 1701)
1674–1723

Charlotte Aglaë
Mlle de Valois
1700–1761
m.
Francis d'Este
Duke of Modena

Louise Elisabeth
Mlle de Montpensier
1709–1742

Louise Diane
Mlle de Chartres
1716–1736
m.
Louis de Conti

se Adelaïde
de Chartres
98–1743
ss of Chelles

Louis I
Duc d'Orléans
(Duc de Chartres until
1723)
1703–1752

Philippine Elisabeth
Mlle de Beaujolais
1714–1734

betrothed,
not married

Descendants include:
Louis Philippe
Philippe Egalité
Kings of the Belgians
Kings of Bulgaria
Comtes de Paris

Descendants include:
Marie Antoinette
(*m.* Louis XVI of France)
Marie Louise
(2nd wife of Napoleon I)
Austrian Emperors
Kings of Italy

SOURCES

Briefe der Herzogin Elisabeth Charlotte von Orléans, ed. William Ludwig Holland (Litterarischer Verein Stuttgart 1867–81)

Aus den Briefen der Herzogin Elisabeth Charlotte von Orléans an die Kurfürstin von Hannover, ed. E. Bodemann (Hannover, Hahn'sche Buchhandlung 1891)

Briefe der Elisabeth Charlotte von Orléans, ed. L. Geiger (W. Spemann 1893)

Briefe der Herzogin Elisabeth Charlotte an ihre frühere Hofmeisterin und deren Gemahl, ed. E. Bodemann (Hannover & Leipzig, Hahn'sche Buchhandlung 1895)

Briefe der Herzogin Elisabeth Charlotte von Orleans, ed. H. F. Helmolt (Insel-Verlag 1908)

Die Briefe der Liselotte von der Pfalz, Herzogin von Orleans, ed. C. Künzel (Langewiesche-Brandt 1911)

Die Briefe der Liselotte: Elisabeth Charlotte von der Pfalz, Duchesse d'Orléans, Madame, ed. M. Westphal (Langewiesche-Brandt 1958)

BOOKS USED

Arkell, R. L. *Caroline of Ansbach* (Oxford University Press 1939)

Boehn, M.v. *Modes and Manners* (Harrap 1935)

Baker, L. M. *The Letters of Elizabeth, Queen of Bohemia* (Bodley Head 1953)

Cronin, Vincent. *Louis XIV* (Collins 1964)

Erlanger, Philippe. *Le Régent* (Gallimard 1938)

Geerds, R. *Memoiren und Briefe der Kurfürstin Sophie von Hannover* (Lange-wiesche-Brandt 1913)

Girard, L. (Ed.) *Collection d'Histoire XVI, XVII, XIII\<sup\>e\</sup\> Siècle* (Bordas 1962)

Henderson, E. F. *A Lady of the Old Regime* (Bell & Sons, 1909)

Henderson, N. *Prince Eugen of Savoy* (Weidenfeld and Nicolson 1964)

Knoop, M. *Madame, Liselotte von der Pfalz, Ein Lebensbild* (K. F. Koehler 1956)

   Kurfürstin Sophie von Hannover (August Lax 1964)

Lalloué, Christiane. *Princesse Palatine, Une Princesse Allemande à la Cour de Louis XIV* (Union Général d'Editions 1962)

Lewis W. H. *The Sunset of the Splendid Century* (Eyre & Spottiswoode 1955)

   Louis XIV (Andre Deutsch 1959)

   The Scandalous Regent (Andre Deutsch 1961)

Mitford, Nancy. *The Sun King* (Hamish Hamilton 1966)

Oman, Carola. *Elizabeth of Bohemia* (Hodder & Stoughton 1938)

   Mary of Modena (Hodder & Stoughton, 1962)

Quennell, P. *Caroline of England* (Collins 1939)

Sackville-West, V. *Daughter of France* (Michael Joseph 1959)

Steegmuller, F. *La Grande Mademoiselle* (Hamish Hamilton 1955)

Saint-Simon, Duc de. *Memoirs* (Various editions)

Sévigné, Marquise de. *Letters* (Various editions)

Wolf, John B. *Louis XIV* (Victor Gollancz 1968)

Ziegler, Ginette. *The Court of Versailles* (Allen & Unwin 1966)

Larousse Universelle, Librarie Larousse, Paris

Brockhaus Konversations-Lexikon, Leipzig/FA Brockhaus

HISTORICAL EVENTS

Calendar of historical events 1672–1722 forming background to Madame's letters.

1672–8 Louis XIV's Dutch war.
France's enemies eventually include the United Provinces of the Netherlands, the Emperor, various German Diets and Spain. The Palatinate remains neutral.

1678 Peace of Nijmegen ends Dutch war.

1679 Installation of French Reunion Chambers.

1681 French occupy Strasbourg.

1683–99 Turkish wars. Various German Princes fight for the Emperor.

1685 Revocation of the Edict of Nantes.
Charles II of England dies. James II succeeds.
Charles, Elector Palatine, dies. Louis XIV claims Liselotte's Palatine inheritance.

1686 League of Augsburg formed against Louis XIV. Signatories include Emperor, various German Princes, Spain.

1688 James II flees to France. William III is called to England.
French troops devastate the Palatinate.

1688–97 War of the League of Augsburg.

1689 Heidelberg Castle destroyed by Melac.
William (–1702) and Mary (–1694) joint rulers of England.
England and Holland enter League of Augsburg.
James II lands in Ireland in an unsuccessful attempt to regain the English throne.

1690 James II, defeated at the Battle of the Boyne, returns to France.

1697 Peace of Ryswick ends war of the League of Augsburg. France recognizes William III and the English protestant Succession.

1700 Charles II of Spain dies, after appointing the Duc d'Anjou as heir to Spain.

1701–14 War of the Spanish succession. Louis XIV fights for his grandson the Duc d'Anjou, now Philip V of Spain. The Emperor Leopold I, allied to Holland and England, supports his son the Archduke Charles.

1701 James II dies at St Germain. Louis XIV recognizes the Old Pretender as James III in contravention of the agreement of Ryswick.
English Act of Settlement assures Protestant succession through the House of Hanover.

1702 Death of William III of England. Queen Anne succeeds.

1705	Archduke Charles recognized as King of Spain by several Spanish provinces.
	Emperor Leopold I dies. His elder son Joseph I succeeds.
1711	Emperor Joseph I dies. The Archduke Charles, in Madrid as Charles III of Spain, returns to Vienna to become Emperor Charles VI.
1712	Peace Congress of Utrecht.
1713–14	Peace treaties of Utrecht and Rastadt.
1714	The Electress Sophie dies.
	Queen Anne dies.
	George Louis of Hanover becomes George I of England.
1715	Louis XIV dies. His great-grandson, aged 5, succeeds as Louis XV.
	The Duc d'Orléans becomes Regent of France.
	Jacobite rising in Scotland.
1716	John Law founds Paris Bank.
1717	Formation of Triple Alliance between France, England and Holland against Alberoni's attempts to re-establish Spain as a first-class power.
1718	Alberoni attacks Sardinia.
	Quadruple alliance between Emperor, England, France and Holland against Spain.
1719	War between France and Spain.
	Fall of Alberoni.
	Law founds Mississippi Company.
1720	Peace between Quadruple alliance and Spain.
	Law becomes Comptroller General of France.
	Mississippi bubble bursts. Law leaves France.
1722	Coronation of Louis XV.

INDEX

Carllutz. *See* Degenfeld, Raugrave Charles Louis von

'Carlos III' of Spain. *See* Charles VI, Archduke of Austria

Caroline, Princess of Wales (1683–1737) (Caroline of Ansbach), daughter of the Markgrave of Brandenburg-Ansbach, married Prince George Augustus of Hanover (later George II of England); Princess of Wales 1714–27, Queen of George II 1727–37; Liselotte's pen-friend: writes at great length to Liselotte, 183; delivered of a dead son, 186; birth of a son, and altercation over choice of godfather, 191; death of her last-born, 192; and the inoculation of her daughters against smallpox, 240–1; other references, 71, 98, 121, 178, 179, 185n., 187, 213, 214

Caroline, Princess, daughter of the above, 240–1

Carthusians, 119, 120

Cellamare, Antonio del Giudice, Prince de (1657–1733), Spanish ambassador in Paris, 202, 203, 204

Celle, plague in, 181

Chaillot, 196

Chamillart, Michel I de (1652–1721), Louis XIV's minister of war, 136

Charges. See Appointments, buying and selling of

Charles II, King of Spain (1661–1700), 89, 93; for his wives *see* Maria Anna of Pfalz Neuberg; Marie Louise d'Orléans

'Charles III' of Spain. *See* Charles VI, Archduke of Austria

Charles V (1500–58), King of Spain and Holy Roman Emperor, 226

Charles VI (1685–1740), Archduke of Austria, and Holy Roman Emperor from 1711, recognized as Carlos III of Spain by certain Spanish provinces, 114, 148

Charles XII, King of Sweden (1682–1718), 110

Charles (1651–85), Elector Palatine from 1680, Liselotte's only legitimate

brother: death, 44–5; other reference, 159

Charles Louis, Elector Palatine (1617–80), son of Frederick V of Pfalz-Simmern and Elizabeth Stuart the 'Winter Queen', father of Liselotte, 35, 92, 160, 211, 222, 223, 238, 244

Charles de St Albin, Abbé (d. 1764), son of Philippe II d'Orléans and La Florence, 184 *and n.*

Charlotte, Electress (1627–86), daughter of William V Landgrave of Hesse-Cassel, married Charles Louis the Elector in 1650, mother of Liselotte, 45

Charolais, Comte de, 243

Charolais, Mlle de. *See* Maine, (Anne) Louise Bénédicte de Bourbon-Condé, Duchesse du

Chartres, Ducs de. *See* Orléans, Louis, Duc de Chartres et d'; Orléans, Philippe II, Duc de Chartres et d'

Chartres, Mlle de, youngest daughter of Philippe II d'Orléans, 183 *and n.,* 242; for other Mlles de Chartres *see* Lorraine, Duchesse de; Orléans, Louise Adelaide d'

Châteauthiers, Anne-Madeleine de (1661–1741), one of Liselotte's *dames d'honneur*, 198, 221, 225

Chausseraye, Marie Thérèse le Petit de Vernot de, maid of honour in Liselotte's household, 101n., 224

Chelles, convent of, 166n.; 221; Abbess of (*see* Valois, Charlotte Aglaë d'Orléans, Mlle de)

Chevalier, the. *See* Lorraine, Philippe de Lorraine-Armagnac, called the Chevalier de

Chevreuse, Jeanne Marie Colbert, Duchesse de (1652–1731), daughter of Louis XIV's minister Colbert, married to Charles Honoré d'Albert de Luynes, 27

Chirac, Pierre (1650–1732), physician to the Regent, and from 1731 to Louis XV, 217

R